Geometry and Art

GEOMETRY AND ART

in the Modern Middle East

edited by
Roxane Zand

SKIRA

Art Director
Marcello Francone

Design
Luigi Fiore

Editorial Coordination
Emma Cavazzini

Editing
Valeria Perenze

Layout
Giorgia Dalla Pietà

First published in Italy in 2019 by
Skira editore S.p.A.
Palazzo Casati Stampa
via Torino 61
20123 Milano
Italy
www.skira.net

Printed and bound in Italy. First edition

ISBN: 978-88-572-4016-9

Distributed in USA, Canada, Central
& South America by ARTBOOK |
D.A.P. 75, Broad Street Suite 630,
New York, NY 10004, USA.
Distributed elsewhere in the world
by Thames and Hudson Ltd., 181A
High Holborn, London WC1V 7QX,
United Kingdom.

Dedicated to the memory
of beloved friend Sherine Jafar

The idea for this book took form over the past two years during frequent visits to art fairs and exhibitions where we observed an increasing reference to geometry as central concern in the works of artists from Islamic cultures. This core preoccupation struck us as different from the use of geometry by artists in the West. Though there is no formal discourse around the subject and much more has been written about calligraphy as the leitmotif of the Middle Eastern visual canon, more artists than ever are delving into geometry for expressive purposes.

Since it is impossible to include every artist in this category, we decided to select a limited number – in this case twenty-four – and provide above all a platform for the artists themselves to express and share their manifestos and images of their works, as different and varied as this may appear, and with minimal intervention on our part. Any selection process is inevitably a subjective one. However, the aim here was to be as representative as possible within the confines of our resources – including the range of media, types of works, and geography. We selected artists who focus on geometry as the main, not incidental concern of their practice. The primary mission of the book has been to spark discussion on the topic and invite further in-depth investigations that would lead to a more considered understanding of geometry as contemporary artistic practice, and as source of inspiration in shaping visual arts from Islamic cultures.

In this journey I have been indebted to my distinguished co-author Dr. Sussan Babaie, without whose scholarship this book would not have been possible. I would also like to thank Skira, our publishers, in particular Massimiliano Pagani, as well as Iraj Bagherzadeh of IB Tauris, our tireless research assistant Cyrus Naji, and my colleague Ashkan Baghestani. A special thanks to Anna Somers Cocks and Morad Montazami for their comments, and Philip Hook and Edward Gibbs at Sotheby's who encouraged the project. My thanks also to Rose Issa, and the Barjeel Foundation for their help with images.

Roxane Zand

Contents

Geometry in a New Perspective

Roxane Zand

One of the most rewarding aspects of working in the arts is to witness the flourishing of artistic discourse in any given canon, none more arguably dynamic at present than in the current Middle East. Equally rewarding has been the ability to participate in, and initiate discussion or debate around a new theme. This volume is intended to generate just that: an invitation to explore the rapidly growing (yet long-established) manifestation of the geometric mode in Middle Eastern art by looking at a diverse cross-section of practicing regional artists. Geometry as a genre is strongly rooted and boldly represented in our geography due to its Islamic origins, yet is not confined to it, as this journey uncovered for us. Along the way it became impossible to ignore the rich engagement of the Western artistic canon with geometry at certain points of its trajectory. While it is not in our scope of discussion to explore both in depth, a further reward of this book has been to make art historical connections, draw larger inferences, and suggest possibilities which will hopefully provoke even more questions: for example, how do artists engaged with geometry envision their own work as part of a wider dialectic? In the context of the dominant Western artistic canon, can it be said that we have a school of Middle Eastern Geometrists? Are the artists featured in this book engaged in a form of religious art, or are they part of the global contemporary art world, even as they are forming a visual language and identity of their own?

Geometry as the study of spatial order through the measure and relationships of forms has, throughout the ages and across geographies, provided infinite possibilities for artists, architects, craftsmen and designers. The mathematical laws and principles developed in ancient India, Greece, and Egypt permeated the early development of aesthetics and the later use of linear perspective underpinning much of Western art – from the analysis of symmetry, to mathematical recursion and logical paradox, from the *camera lucida* to contemporary use of fractals. Parallel to the West, in Islamic tradition geometry was arguably even more important since its principles permeated every construct and pattern, at times seeming to imbue these with a symbolic, cosmological and philosophical significance well beyond the visual aspect. Its intricate design schemes are based on the grid system that create patterns using inter-woven sequences, links, and units in infinitely repetitious, proportional relationships, and with a complexity that has inspired much analysis of the contemplative and sacred dimensions of Islamic art. Opinion is divided as to how much symbolism and significance can be read into these patterns. Many scholars feel that there is little evidence to support the idea that the artists who created the artefacts, or the beholder himself was to embrace any hidden symbolism beyond the sheer beauty of the patterns and the Oneness of Allah or God. Indeed, early Islamic artists/craftsmen remain largely anonymous, merely executing the templates and instructions of the master-artist in building or creating surface patterns, and although the 'salutory' or 'purificatory' effects of the contemplation of geometry on the human mind has been highlighted by sources as ancient as the tenth-century Ikhwan al Safa, and as recently as Hans Belting in 2011, there is little to support deliberately coded significances. That said, numerology, Sufism and mystical thought have been present in Islamic cultures since ancient times and it is hard to trace how these influences may or may not have infiltrated the visual language. Certainly the perceived aniconic nature of Islamic art would seem to invite deeper forms of expression embedded in these complex patterns – but the extent of it is challenging to determine.

Dürer, the fifteenth-century German artist, maintained in his *Underweysung* that "geometry is the right foundation of all art", and studied the use of regular polygons in both Islamic and Gothic decoration. While Islamic pattern was frequently based on 'geometric progression' (where every number in the set is equal to the square root of the numbers on either side of it), Dürer and his contemporaries perfected 'arithmetic progression' (where the difference between any number and its successor is constant). While the Greek mathematician Proclus declared the circle to be the most perfect of all figures, Baghdad, in the eighth century, came to be built as a perfect circle. Such connections can be incidentally or regularly spotted. Over time however, and with the rediscovery of linear perspective during the Renaissance, a significant distinction emerged between the place of geometry in European artistic practice, and that in Islamic tradition – namely, what Belting calls "represented geometry" as opposed to "representational geometry". In Europe, geometry was not depicted for its own sake, but instead used for depicting the world. It was above all a tool. In Islamic tradition, geometry was celebrated for itself and for its laws of harmony, beauty, richness and complexity – and thus the primary subject of artistry.

In modern times, the parallels of geometry in Western and Islamic cultures take on an even more interesting dimension. By the early twentieth century, even as Cubism was breaking the rules of geometry by playing havoc with visual expectations, other subsequent movements such as Constructivism, Suprematism and even the later Bauhaus and Schematic Compositionists continued to refer heavily to geometric depictions in their abstractions. Malevich and Lissitzky among others, or the De Stijl movement and the works of Mondrian, Van Doesburg or Rietveld exemplify this. The tessellations of Annie Albers' textile works in the 1930s, the light art of the Zero Movement, the compositions of François Morellet, or Viktor Vasarely's optical illusions make us realise to what extent these geometric experimentations – such as the visual play of Op Art and Kinetic Art – take osmotic inspiration from early mathematical and geometric information. Similarly, recent Middle Eastern artists have acknowledged the influence of these very artists alongside their own Islamic heritage. Ebtisam Abdulaziz for example, refers to the infinitely expandable possibilities of Op Art in her work, or the organised mathematical precepts of Systems Art which move her creativity. Pakistani artist Rana Begum who observes the ritual of repeated daily prayer, finds inspiration in the repetitions of Donald Judd or the meditative work of Agnes Martin. German-Egyptian artist Susan Hefuna draws from both her legacies; her 'architectural' drawings – though never using straight lines – are based on observations of fundamental geometries in city environments. In a different but equally articulate shorthand, Mehdi Moutashar co-opts his discovery of minimalism and geometric abstraction, as well as the inspiration from Matisse and Morellet into his art production. The work of American

Philip Taaffe, on the other hand, is fully rooted in the teachings of Islam, Sufism, and the glories of Byzantine patterns due to his extensive travels – re-defining the boundaries of how a Middle Eastern or 'Islamic' artist is identified. The Iranian architect Nargess Hashemi, referring to Beatriz Colomina's theory on female architects, manipulates units, scale and optics to produce plans which uncannily reference Bosch. A number of these 'geometrists' (such as Sayegh, Mater, and Al Homoud) reconfigure calligraphic elements to create novel geometric forms that conceivably speak to the Bauhaus approach. However many ways this cross-referencing fertilises the creativity of artists operating in the geometric space or using Islam-derived patterns and motifs, the result offers the world a rich and vibrant visual feast.

In the more contemporary setting of the art market, the question that has arisen is whether art focussed primarily on geometry and originating in surface pattern – an art seemingly 'separated' from concept – can move beyond certain confines, into the "lofty edifice" (to quote Nasser Rabat) of the contemporary art world. Can artists dotted around the globe in locations as wide apart as Southeast Asia, the United States, and the Middle East, be said to function in any sort of 'movement' or artistic discourse where a connected visual vocabulary is forged? Does the practice of these artists who share certain shared predilections add up to an independent identity as 'Geometrists', in the same way as that of pioneering deconstructionist calligraphists like Hossein Zenderoudi, Nja Mahdaoui, Ahmed Moustafa, Mohammad Ehsai, or others of the Hurufiyya or Saqqakhaneh movements? Could one argue that this same kind of de-construction – undoing the proportional laws stated by Ibn Muqla in the tenth century – is now also paralleled by a secularisation of Islamic pattern where rules are broken and boundaries pushed, in order to create novel effects, challenge perceptions, and engage with meaning and concept? These are some of the questions that moved and provoked us, and which we hope the reader will also ask, as they leaf through this volume, appreciating the enduring legacy of Islam-inspired geometric art as a testament to its resilience and pervasiveness.

Selected bibliography
Herman Weyl, *Symmetry*, Princeton University Press, Princeton, NJ 1952.
Ernst Gombrich, *Art and Illusion*, Phaidon, London 1960.
Dan Pedoe, *Geometry and the Visual Arts*, Dover Press, 1976.
Hans Belting, *Florence and Baghdad: Renaissance Art and Arab Science*, HUP, Cambridge, Mass. 2011.
Khaled Azzam, *Arts and Crafts of the Islamic Lands*, Thames & Hudson, London 2013.

The Spectacle of Geometry

Dr. Sussan Babaie

Geometry has long been recognised as one of the key aspects of design and artistic imagination in the arts and material cultures of the Islamic world. The use of geometry in pattern design was ubiquitous in many visual traditions, from Celtic to Native American arts, among others; it also permeated the arts of the Mediterranean and Greater Iran before the advent of Islam. The real breakthrough, however, was brought about by practitioners in the fields of science, art and aesthetics during the Islamic period. Their highly sophisticated thinking about and through geometry gave life to diverse patterns and complex formulae in the making of art objects of every medium and type, ranging from metalware and textiles to architectural surfaces, and across the vast expanse of the Islamic world.

Already in the ninth and tenth centuries, when Baghdad was the most vibrant centre of cultural production in the known world, the science of geometry had generated interlinked debates with aesthetic, philosophical, religious and practical dimensions.[1] The design of *muqarnas* in Islamic architecture is among the most visible of the intersections of geometry, form and function.[2] *Muqarnas* appears as a geometrically derived cellular structure resembling a honeycomb that is made of a number of concave elements of small niches (or squinches). It comes in a variety of materials, including stucco, stone, wood and glazed tilework. The units are designed in clusters to fill the void between the square geometry of a room and its vaulted crown in the form of a dome or an *iwan* (a semi-open vaulted porch). While *muqarnas* tends to be in a three-dimensional format, the other widely encountered geometric patterning is the *girih*, Persian for 'knot'. The *girih* design refers to a web-like interlace of geometric patterns, mainly of star and polygon shapes, carried out in two- and three-dimensional compositions in glazed and unglazed brick tiles, and in wood or stucco carving.[3]

Equally compelling are the innovative developments in Islamic ornamentation by using algorithms to create different brick patterns on building façades or weaving designs in textiles. These repeat geometric patterns are found in a variety of compositions, colour schemes and materials, in two- or three-dimensional contexts, across the Islamic world, with results that are often breathtaking in their complexity and intricacy.

Much of this immensely exciting repertory of motifs, patterns and materials has been studied as one of the 'characteristic' features of Islamic arts and categorised as ornament. Ornament, however, has had a rather chequered art historical past: 1) it is seen through the lens of European arts and thus essentialises Islamic arts, an approach that does not account for historical particularities of any given example; and 2) it is understood as decorative, enchanting but not necessarily as having the capacity to contain meaning. The two methods of approach to understanding ornament, of which geometry is a category, delight in the proliferation of ingenuity and variety of patterns, and by extension a generalised assumption of unity in diversity. Accordingly, all Islamic patterns are understood to emanate from the same urge to transform surfaces, whether as an aid for contemplation of the infinite variety and complexity of the created phenomenon, as manifestations in abstract designs of divinely-inspired ideas, or as spiritual representations of inner truths. To some degree, all these assumptions are valid. Yet, none relies on historical, geographical, or cultural criteria for analysis. There is, in other words, no limit to the ahistoricity of many of such interpretive suggestions for the way ornament and especially geometry may have functioned.

Some aspects of the application of geometry find firm footing in discussions about its enormous significance for the art of writing. Calligraphy or the art of beautiful writing is ennobling for the fact that the abstract shapes of letters were developed for the purposes of recording and transmitting the word of God, the Qur'an.[4] The rules of writing in the Arabic script, and their extension to Persian and other languages in the Islamic world, relied on the standardisation of geometric shapes, the dots and lines, to create visual harmony among the letters in a word and their compositions in a line. In the case of calligraphy, the aesthetics of geometry and the significance of the text reinforced the cultural significance of the science of geometry. Calligraphy, in other words, is itself dependant on geometry. As noted by Alpay Özdural, "The circle was used as a proportioning device in both the proportioned script and in geometric patterning in a cultural context deeply imbued with a mathematical conception of beauty as a harmony between parts and the whole … ."[5]

In his magisterial study of ornament, Oleg Grabar developed a theoretical device for the analyses of Islamic arts through the intermediaries of patterns.[6] In his schema, ornament encompasses calligraphy, alongside stylised and curvilinear vegetal patterns – often referred to as arabesque in European languages and *islimi* (Islamic) in Arabic and Persian – figural representations, architectural motifs, and above all, geometric patterns. The intricacy of designs, the charisma of articulated materials, and the visual excitement of the ornament in Islamic arts, Grabar argues, produce heightened surface sensuality that facilitates the viewer's direct access to the art object or building. His theory of ornament derives from Islamic arts but is also applicable to arts from other periods and places. Most importantly, his new interpretation helps decouple the phenomenon from the Eurocentric analyses where ornament is reduced to the frivolous and the ornamental. Instead, ornament, including geometric patterns, becomes the visual vehicle for meaning-making; ornament is, from his point of view, *the* meaning.

Geometry and the dazzling varieties of patterns and methods of execution become the intermediary level of encounter with meaning. The fact that geometry and geometric patterns derive from proportional designs, are mathematically anchored, and are dependent on a well-balanced synthesis of appropriate parts has been linked by scholars to emanationist philosophy and the Islamic notion of the unitary nature of God and His utter transcendence.[7] Thus, as Carol Bier has suggested in the case of medieval Iranian architecture – but also developed by others for the Arab lands – the proliferation of geometric patterns as ornament points to a link between the practitioners – artists and craftsmen – and the discourses around Islamic philosophy, mathematics and science.[8] In her approach, geometry, patterns and their mathematical properties suggest potential meanings beyond simple decoration and posit geometry as visual commentary.

Scholarly debates around the meaning of geometry remain unresolved, in large part because there is little security in generalising about a single theory or a cluster of meanings for the entire history of Islam and across its vast geography. But while geometry might carry different meanings in different Islamic cultures at different times, the path between proportion and symmetry in visual representations – a geometric pattern – on the one hand, and the notion of beauty to be quantitatively embodied, on the other, do provide us with some tools of analysis toward an aesthetic intuition in the arts inspired by Islam.

As much of the evidence of geometric patterns – on buildings from Iran to Spain and in carved and inlaid woodwork from Egypt to India – might indicate, the principles governing human response seem to be predicated on the degree of excitement the design solicits: how stunning and impressive the pattern is; how breathtaking the crafting is; how vital the textures and surfaces are. Such sensory experiences as perceived by the viewer may have analogues in the prevailing conceptions of spirituality or sensuality appropriate to the time and place of the work of art.

In part, the visual deployment of geometry may be understood as an outcome of a search for an aesthetic language that would convey the Quranic view of creation. As the teachings of Islam spread, the idea that all creation emanates from the supreme divine source, God or Allah in Arabic, inspired the creative minds of scientists, including astronomers and mathematicians, to invest a great deal of close study of nature and to discover the traces of that divine energy in the underlying structure of nature. Artists, poets, and craftsmen partook in this rejuvenated spirit of enquiry by exploring geometric patterns of great complexity. These visual motifs were not so much enslaved to the strict science of geometry but injected creative liberties in order to make extraordinarily varied and visually engaging repeat patterns to enliven surfaces of objects and buildings. Some scholars attribute this fixation on geometry in Islamic arts, and on epigraphy, to the aniconic tendencies in Islam. In fact, the arts of the Islamic world demonstrate a variety of artistic choices made in different parts of its vast spread, including lively traditions of figural representation. Thus, neither the ubiquity of geometric patterns nor that of epigraphic decoration in the arts of Islam are necessarily due to an injunction against figural images. Rather, they should be seen as creative choices of visual expression. Artists of the modern and contemporary era make these choices intentionally and are keenly aware of the historical rootedness of geometry and of pattern-making as a vector for creative expression of belief, as much as of observation of nature and of intangible truths.

This book brings a range of contemporary artistic practices together with the aim of viewing geometry through the lens of modernity or post-modernity. The artist statements speak to an extraordinary diversity of attitudes toward geometry and a recognition of the significance of geometry in Islam. From this point of view, the intention is not to totalise either Islam the religion, or Islamic as a qualifier. Instead, as the artist statements and their sample works demonstrate, our interest is in the differences: one might derive inspiration from the rhythm of daily prayer in the practice of Islam; or be inspired by the metaphysical potentialities Islamic practices of Sufism offer; or be moved by the paths of science from medieval to modern. In all instances, and without imposing any interpretive analyses, the readers are invited to explore the particularities of each artist's work and their articulation of the different facets of geometry. Ideals and ideas in these works remain as varied and complex as those we try to unearth from the visual and material cultures of the histories of the Islamic world.

[1] An excellent consideration of the debates, both of early Islamic history and of modern scholarship, is found in Terry Allen, *Islamic Art and the Argument from Academic Geometry*, Solipsist Press, Occidental, California 2004; http://www.sonic.net/~tallen/palmtree/academicgeometry.htm#ftn.necip. Accessed 18/11/2018.
[2] *Muqarnas* has been studied extensively in both general terms of its form, function and meaning and in a more scholarly context of specific instances of its utility as a signifier of a political agenda. For a survey of the former and a study of the latter points, see Yasser Tabbaa, 'The Muqarnas Dome: Its Origin and Meaning', *Muqarnas* v. 3 (1985): 61–74.
[3] Gülru Necipoğlu, *The Topkapı Scroll – Geometry and Ornament in Islamic Architecture: Topkapı Palace Museum Library MS H. 1956*, Santa Monica, California 1995.
[4] Annemarie Schimmel, with Barbara Rivolta, 'Islamic Calligraphy,' *The Metropolitan Museum of Art Bulletin*, v. 50, no. 1 (Summer 1992).
[5] Alpay Özdural, 'On Interlocking Similar or Corresponding Figures and Ornamental Patterns of Cubic Equations,' *Muqarnas*, v. 13 (1996): 191–211, 188–189.
[6] Oleg Grabar, *The Mediation of Ornament*, Princeton 1992.
[7] A summary of the arguments on the link between aesthetics and Islamic philosophy is found in Allen, *Islamic Art and the Argument from Academic Geometry*.
[8] Carol Bier, 'Art and Mithāl: Reading Geometry as Visual Commentary', *Iranian Studies* 41, no. 4 (2008): 491–509.

Ebtisam Abdulaziz
Anila Quayyum Agha
Zeinab Al Hashemi
Lulwah Al Homoud
Rashid Al Khalifa
Ahmad Angawi
Dana Awartani
Rana Begum
Kamal Boullata
Monir Shahroudy Farman Farmaian
Nargess Hashemi
Susan Hefuna
Sahand Hessamiyan
Mohamed Abdul Latif Kanoo
Ahmed Mater
Mehdi Moutashar
Mouteea Murad
Naqsh Collective
Nima Nabavi
Timo Nasseri
Mahmoud Sabri
Samir Sayegh
Philip Taaffe
Gebran Tarazi

Ebtisam Abdulaziz

I rely on abstraction and experimentation in producing geometric paintings, and autobiographical drawings in which I connect human nature, with all its flaws and shortcomings, with what we are conscious of inside. I emphasise the possibility of subconscious creativity and innovation. Most of my pieces are intimately connected to the human being, whichever surrounding environment, and the issues that might affect it. It is like an autobiography of the human mind and all the issues and messages it accumulates. My works resemble the shapes of the optical illusion movement or Op Art. The elements of my work are geometric artistic expressions that have visual illusions, infinitely expandable or shrinkable. These shapes cannot seem to move or change except through operations that occur in the visual system itself.
My ultimate objective here is not just to please the mind, but to also express its desire to explore the imagination and infinite dimensions beyond the limits of the visual.
Some of my other geometrical work relates to my degree in mathematics; it belongs to the style of Systems Art, which is based on precise and organised mathematical elements. These elements are organised in such a way that the viewer can only enjoy the nuances within, if they understand them. An example is *Re-Mapping the Arab World.* This artwork is a type of abstract art characterised by the use of very simple standardised forms, usually geometric in character, either in a single concentrated image or repeated in a system arranged according to a clearly visible principle of organisation.
In Systems Art, the concept of process-related systems and systems theory, which are involved in the work, take precedence over traditional aesthetic, material and object-related concerns. The strategy of the work is closely related to systems, creating map drawings for Middle Eastern countries including Iran, by following this system. Each Letter (from A to Z) has a different Number, (a=1, b=2,… z=26), so the Letter A is different from the letter B. Two letters will make one point (a, b)=(1, 2)=(X, Y). Two points will make a line and so on. Any mistakes in this type of art cannot be admitted since the diagram will break and not be sustained. Each line is as important as every other line. All of the lines have become one thing: they create the shape of each country. This is systemic, geometric art, and the mode by which I've chosen to create the new Middle East Art Map.

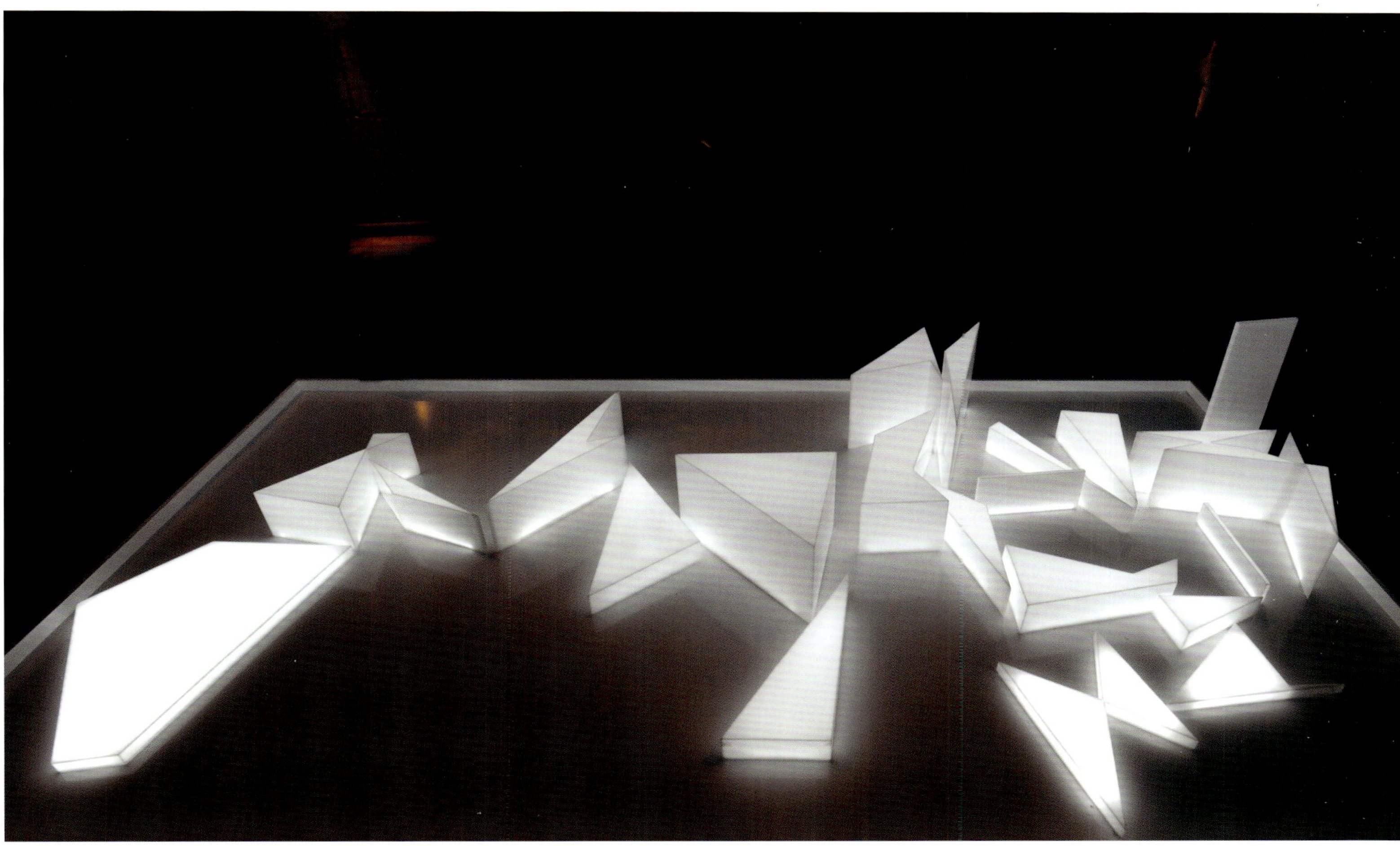

Re-Mapping the Arab World, 2010
White acrylic shape, LED light, aluminium sheet,
white wooden base, 200 x 400 x 34 cm

Untitled, 2016
Acrylic on canvas, 91 x 122 cm

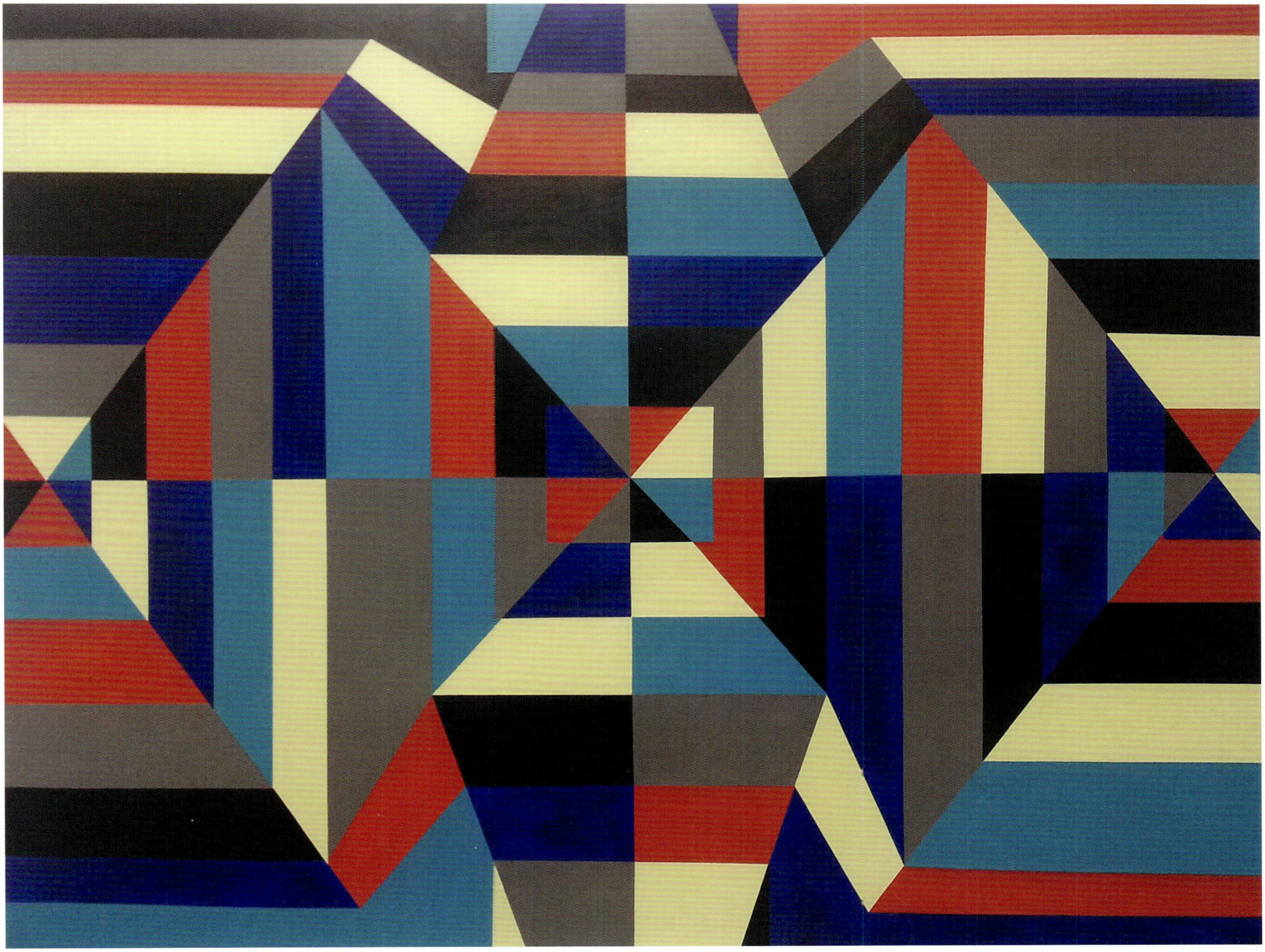

Untitled, 2016
Acrylic on canvas, 91 x 122 cm

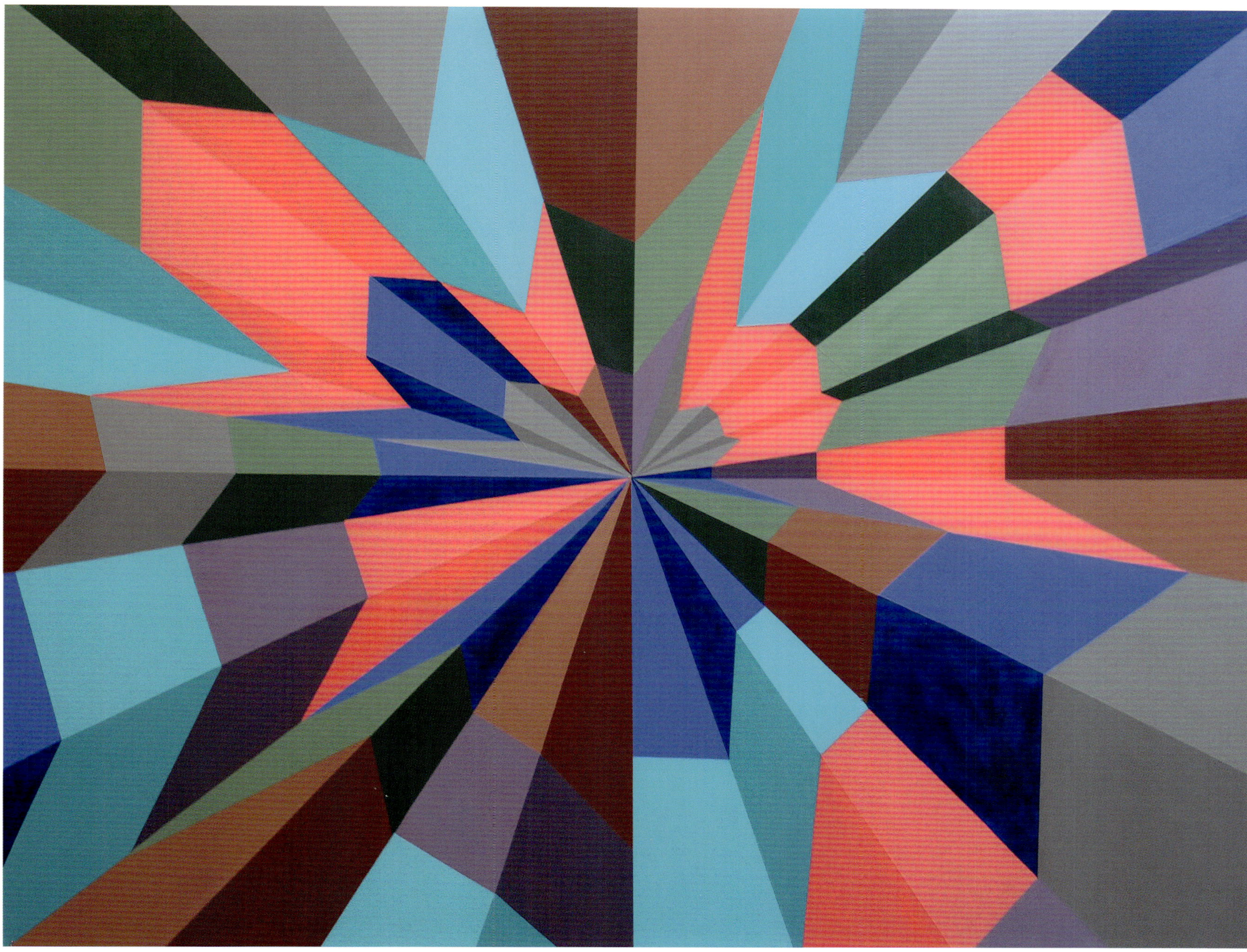

Anila Quayyum Agha

My fascination with contrasting cultures, spiritual/religious rituals, and art and architecture adds layers to my artwork. My personal history and memories of growing up in Pakistan as a woman are a part of my narrative. I want to continue the examination of exclusionary politics, shifting identities within cultures, and public and private spaces. We live in divisive times with a surfeit of social and political issues resulting from multiple wars, mass exodus of refugees/immigrants, and racial, gender and economic misunderstandings. Through my artistic practice my intent is to touch upon the topical issues of our times and bring people together, to create dialogue and influence a broader audience. My work is an ever-expanding, all-encompassing meditation on the nature of boundaries, of categorisation, of alienation. I make work to transcend the seemingly impenetrable borders of race, religion, gender, and culture that so often prevent the true intersections and exchanges in our current world order.
In South Asia and the Middle-East, public and private, gender demarcated architectural spaces are often constructed with elaborately carved marble, plaster and wooden screens and tiles. Calligraphy and stylised floral and geometric patterns are hallmarks of Islamic Art and Architecture and known for a contemplative focus, providing the public with an understanding of the underlying order of both the cosmos and the natural world through symmetries found in nature. I have chosen to integrate such elements into both my drawings and installations to add conceptual and metaphorical weight and meaning.
In exploring the interpretation of geometric design in my work, I show the interplay of nature and artifice. The layered investigations into geometrical patterning in Islamic sacred spaces and the results depicting contrasts like certitude and fluidity allow for more complex work, by introducing size, scale, pattern, repetition, form and structure.
The geometric motifs within my patterns are familiar to Islamic audiences around the world. Appropriation of Islamic motifs allows me to elevate the ordinary which, when explored, reveals the complexities of symbiosis between cultures and civilisations and the amorphous borders in between. Within my work I invite the viewer to confront the contradictory nature of all intersections, while simultaneously exploring boundaries.
In my work I use light and pattern, along with the palpability of reflection, to question the assumptions of geometric design as a form of the pure and transcendent and thus opposite to representational art. The shadows cast in all directions by the light spilling through the sculpture's cutout surfaces work magically, creating dynamic and intricate designs with the accompanying distortions that transform the interiors in tandem with the movement of the audience in the space. With these freshly designed patterns, reminiscent of lace inspired by Islamic motifs, I create an inclusive space, welcoming and feminine. The sculptures, lit with a single light source, create varied shadows and generate successive interpretations, all the while relying on the purity and inner symmetry of geometric design. My work also provokes an investigation into questions of authenticity, which are central to the post-colonial condition. The intertwining of light and shadow, through the original and derivative, are at the core of the various renditions of the pattern; they mirror the post-colonial quest for originality and purity. In a contextual milieu where difference and divergence dominate most conversations about the intersection of civilisation, my work explores the presence of harmonies that do not ignore the shadows, ambiguities and dark spaces, but rather explore this in novel and unexpected ways.

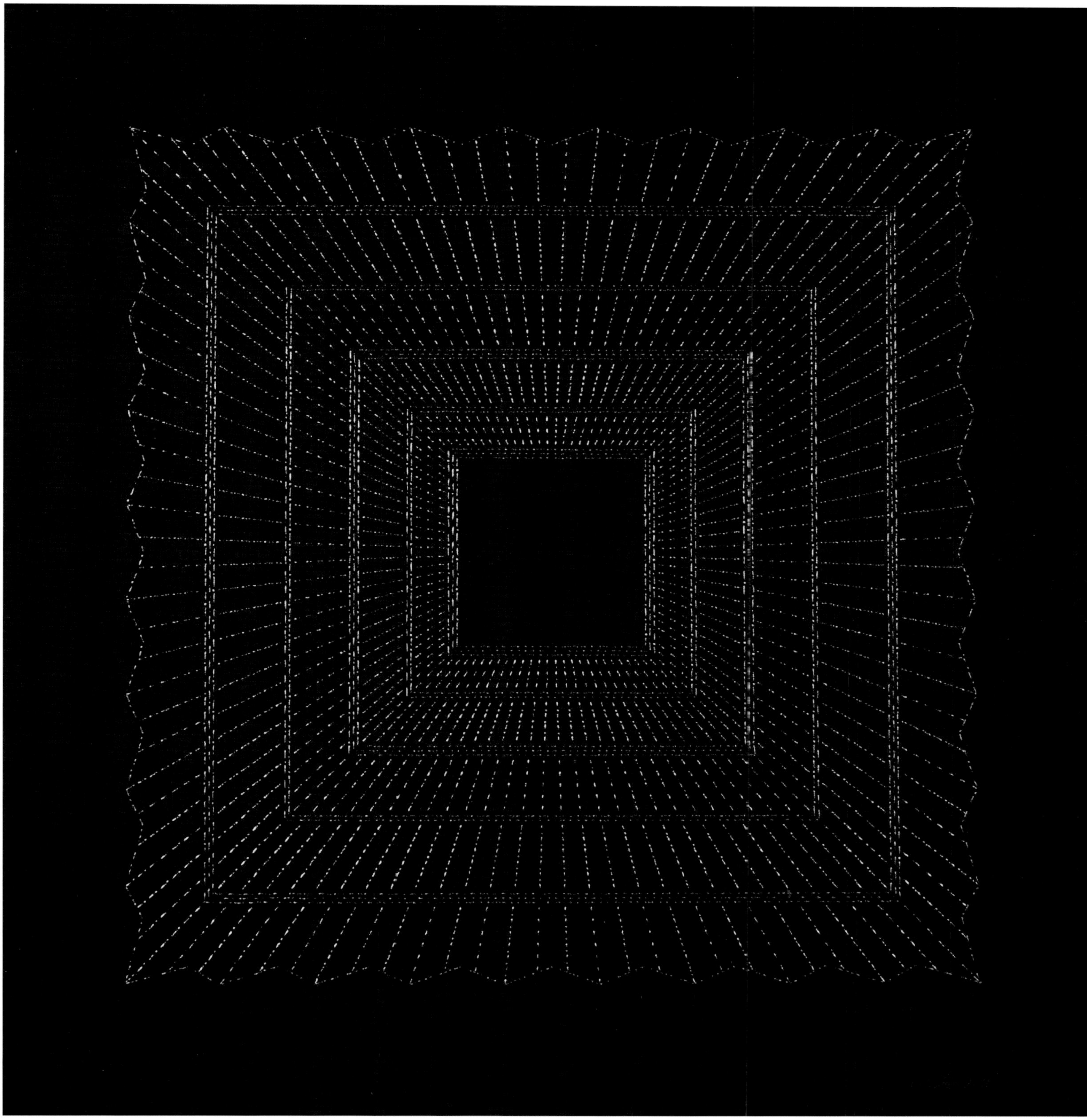

Kaaba-Copper, 2016
Mixed media on paper (black and copper beads and embroidery on black paper), 74 x 74 cm

All The Flowers Are For Me –
Red Art, 2016
152 cm cube, laser-cut, lacquered
steel, light bulb
Cincinnati Art Museum
Photo Anila Quayyum Agha

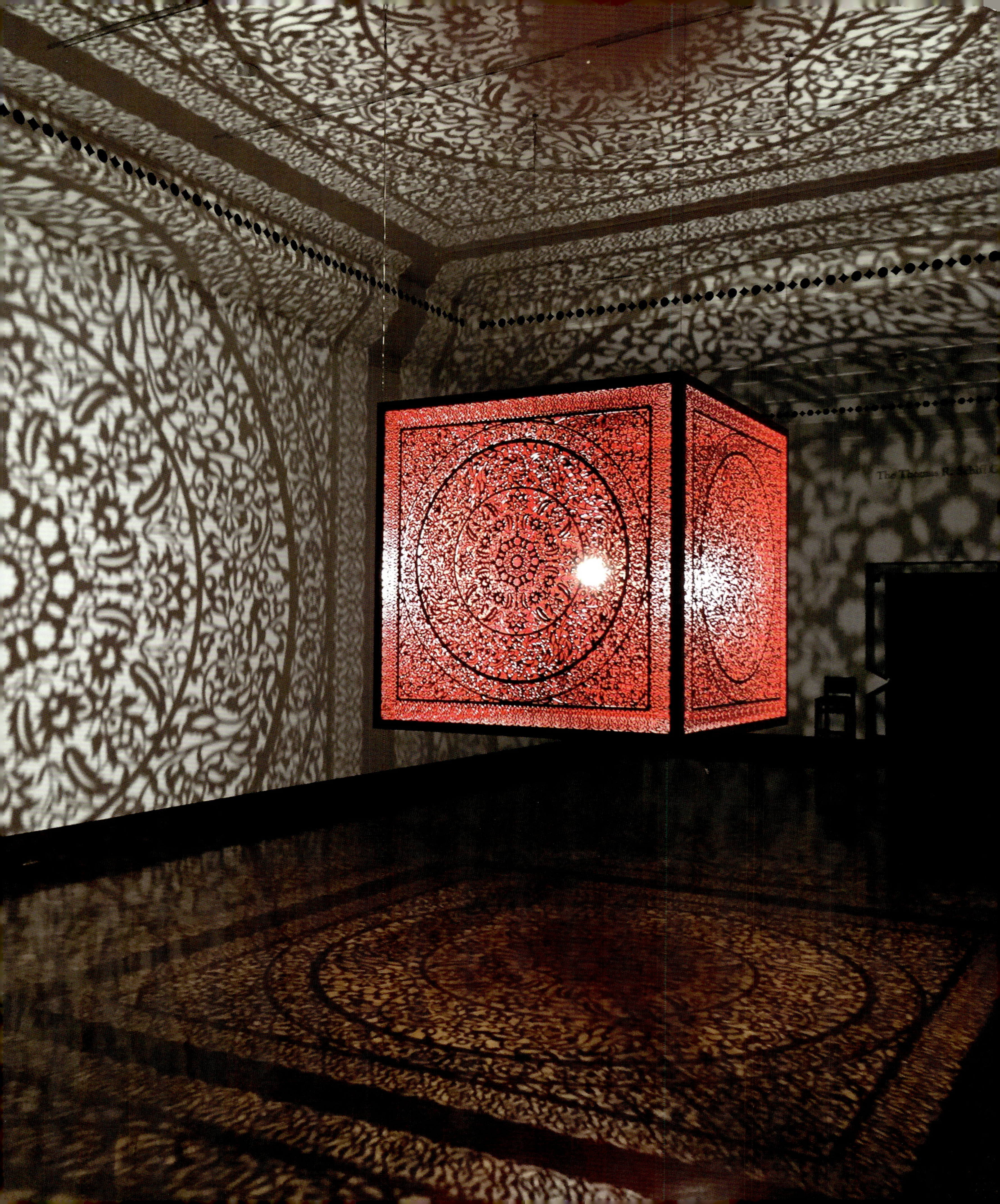

The Greys in Between
Site-specific installation at MOCA Jacksonville, 2018
Overall size of sculpture: 46 cm
Octahedron size: 25.4 cm; tetrahedron size: 12.7 cm, plus a 7.6 cm space between the two. The work was installed in a 89 x 50.8 cm space with the three inner walls painted a dark charcoal grey

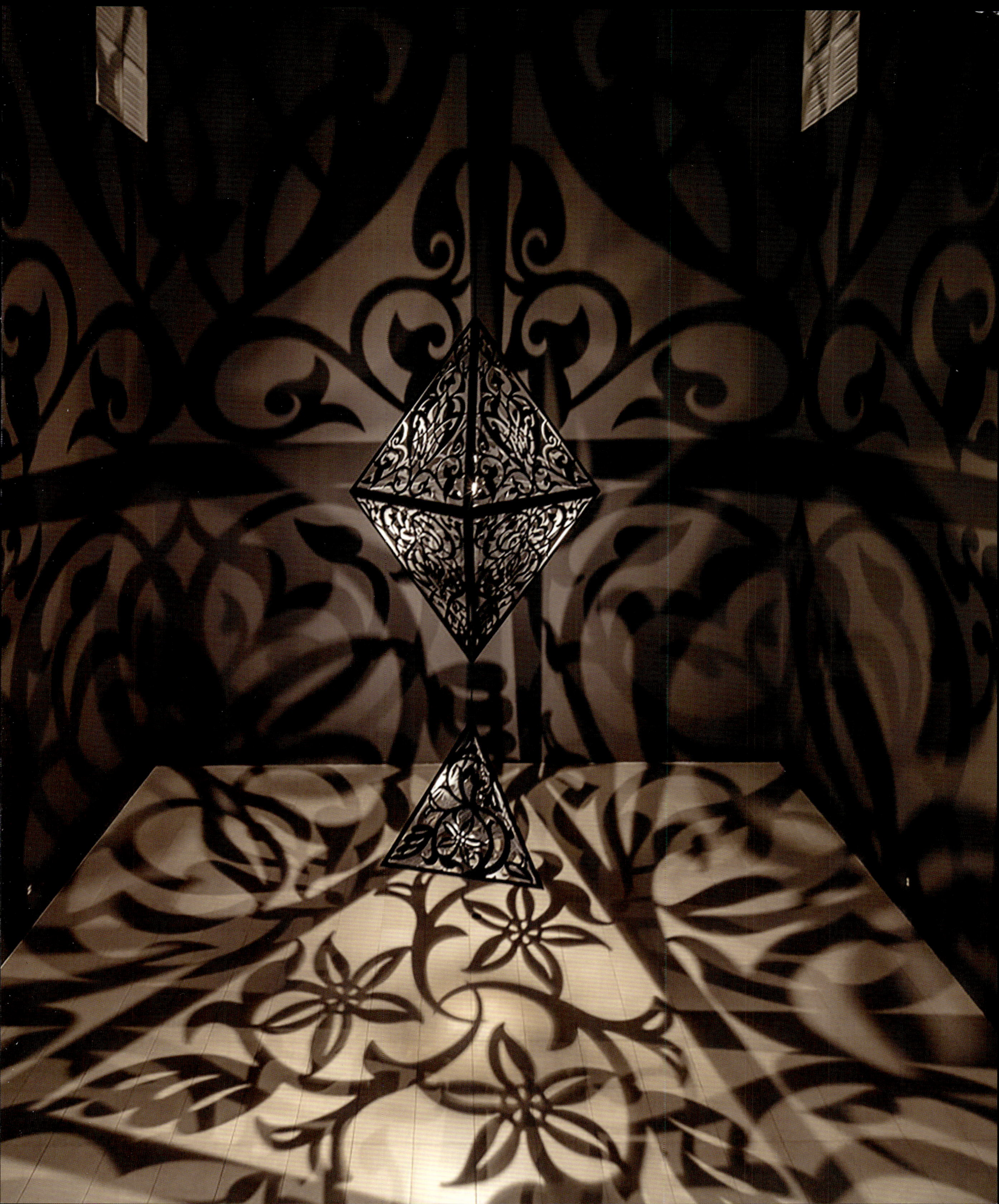

Zeinab Al Hashemi

The influence of geometry in my work

From Fibonacci's sequence to the golden ratio in nature to the sacred geometry in architecture, to Mandelbrot set, all the way to Islamic geometric patterns and Leonardo Da Vinci's use of sacred geometry, geometry exists all around us, starting with sound vibrations that cause a flow of repeated patterns the naked-eye cannot capture.

I have always been interested in building installations in the geometric sense. As an artist I am inspired by both what the eye captures and how it perceives it, as truth. I change perceptions at both the macro and micro levels, through how the geometry and the architecture of nature are translated into my work. The ability to look beyond the current state of things and push the boundaries to a different realm seems to attract the viewer's curiosity; to some it is an alien vision while to others it is familiar, but they can relate to it on many levels. The mystery of geometry in science, physics, and arts has invited people to keep seeking. For me, repetition brings me into a meditative state, through simple calculations and codes applied in the right way to achieve perfect and harmonious forms.

Working closely with artisans and makers, my attention was drawn to the idea of allowing the body to create rhythm and reiteration.

By using natural and simple elements to create practical and functional tools utilised in the past mostly for survival purposes, attention to aestethics was somehow always present. This inspired me to dig deeper into the history and tradition of our crafts, where everything is connected in a concrete, tangible form. This research has led me to hidden mysteries and codes that are both artistically inspirational and speak to the senses.

On a personal level, I've always liked multiples of 3, putting things in sets of 3, or the repetition and results of 3, 6, and 9. I notice the number 33, or 333 in different places – streets, buildings, hotel rooms, any random place.

It started out as a game, but later became co-opted into my work. I wanted to understand more about these numbers, and came to realise that these are very powerful numbers in nature – just observe the golden ratio, or the pyramids in Giza. In the words of Nikola Tesla, "If you knew the magnificence of the numbers three, six and nine, you would have the key to the universe". According to him 9 is the unity, the universe itself, its vibration and energy.

Geometry cannot be limited and reduced to one type in space and time. Since the beginning of time, man has used it to create knowledge, form and life. If we can simplify this and apply it somehow in all aspects of our life, many things will take on a new meaning. For me, it provides the core of my artistic practice.

Metamorphic is made of eight layers of metal mesh and stained glass, evoking the colours of the land and water.

Hexalite is intended to challenge audiences to interact with reflections and explore connections. In numerology the repetition of the number 3 symbolises spiritual creation, and represents harmony and balance here.

Metal-Morphosis utilises the same underlying pattern as the 16-pointed star to symbolise the evolution of geometry in Islamic art.

The sculpture is made out of four metal meshes rotated four times, transforming them from a functional state to a decorative state.

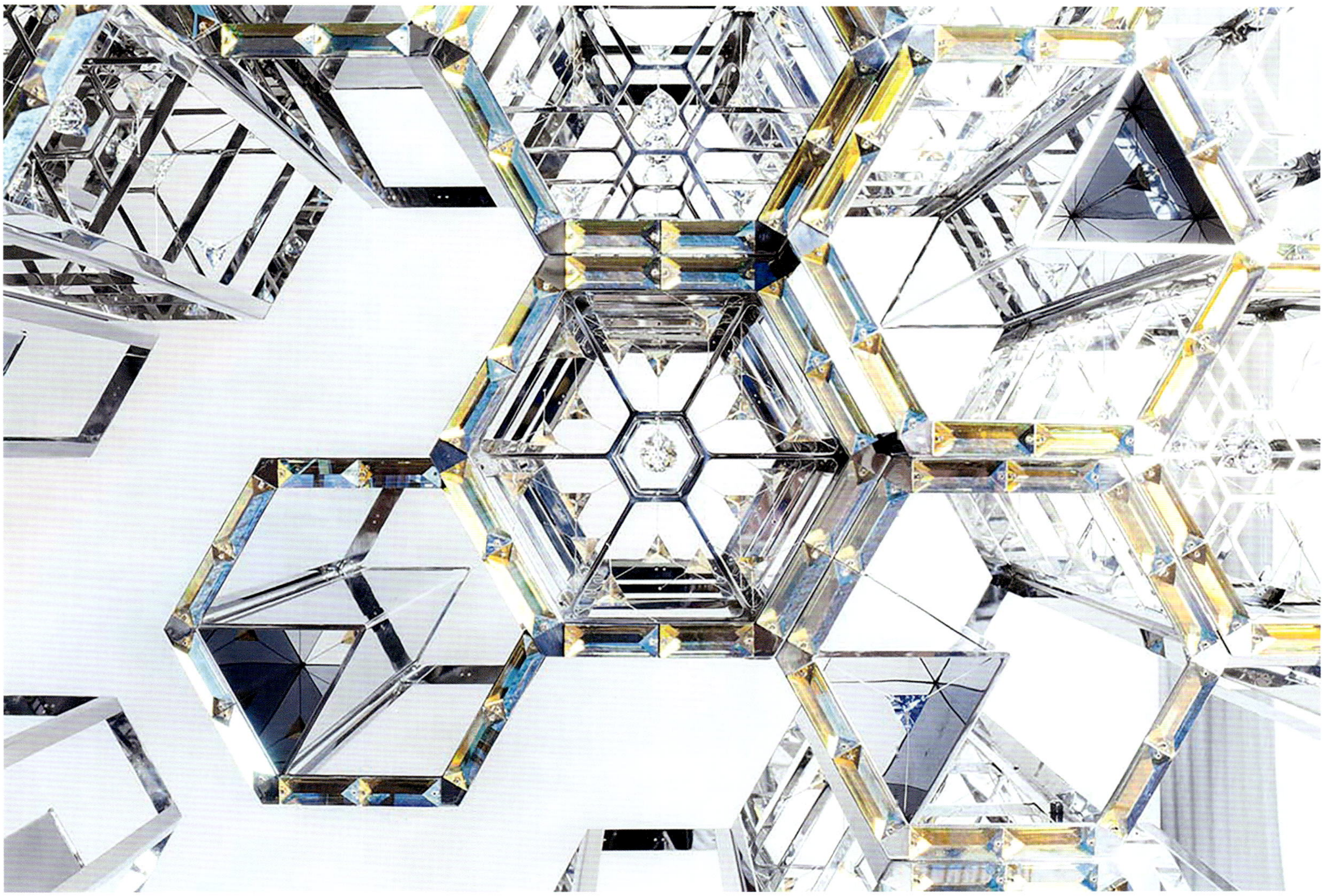

Hexalite, 2016
1,145 Swarovski crystals and
33 hexagonal mirrored-steel structure
Dubai Design Week 2016

Metal-Morphosis, 2017–2018
Metal mesh and mirror
Sharjah Islamic Arts Festival,
2017–2018

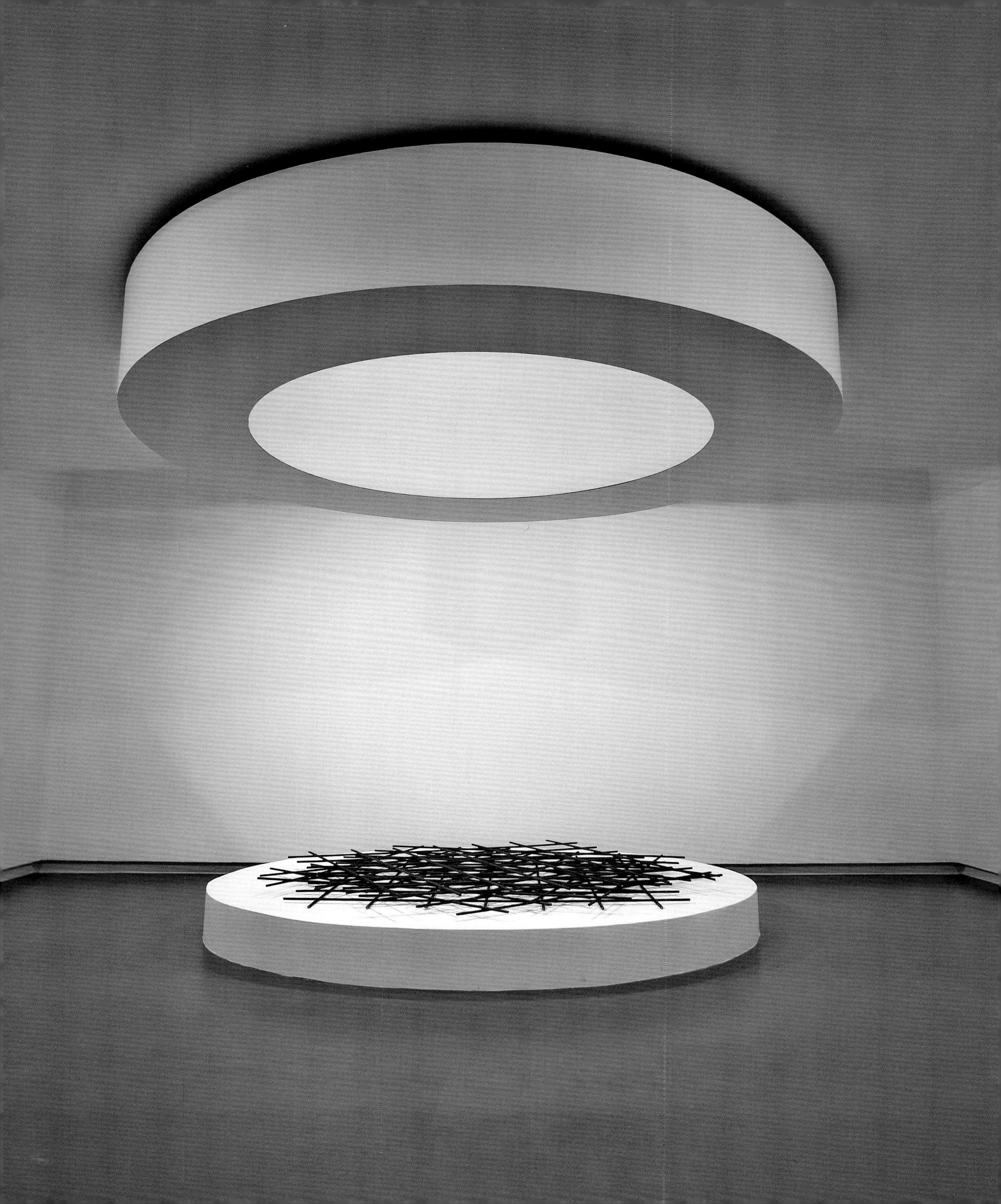

Metamorphic, 2017
Suspended structure, stained glass,
welded metal mesh
Part of the opening exhibition at the
Louvre Abu Dhabi

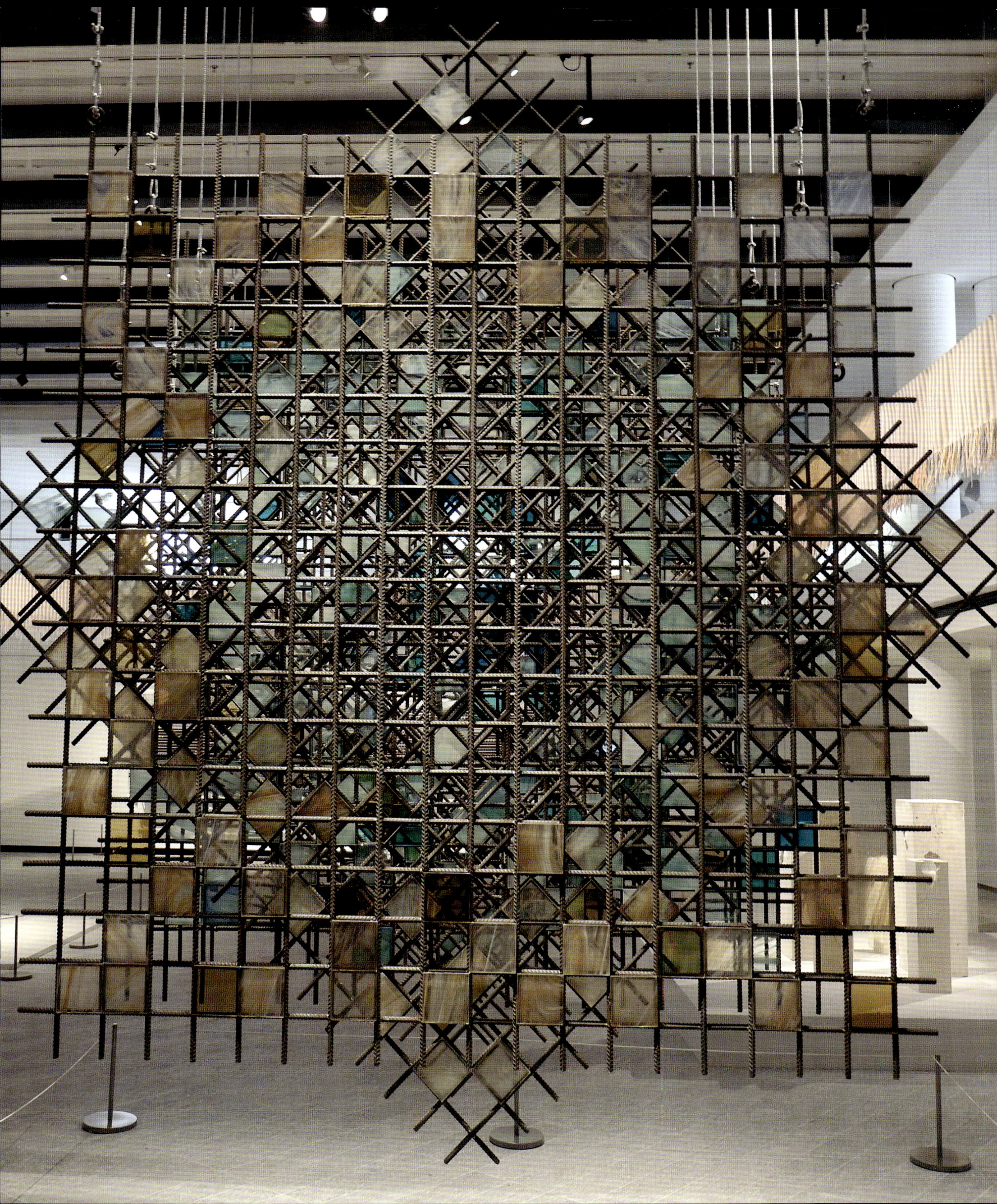

Lulwah Al Homoud

Geometry as a liberating form of expression
Geometry is also defined as the branch of mathematics concerned with the relationship among higher dimensional analogues, it is this ethos of geometry that my art is concerned with. It allows the artist to experiment with a higher level of spatial awareness, using lines and shapes to create endless perspectives, define new relationships while allowing the spaces in between to inspire an inner dialogue.
Ostensibly, my inspiration comes from researching Islamic geometric patterns, the designs of which are based on accumulated knowledge from different cultures and sciences from around the Islamic world. These intricate compositions, which are based on the repetition of basic shapes, do not comply completely with strict geometric rules, instead they bring a unique sense of freedom seen and experienced in the way the patterns repeat and evolve. This level of abstraction fascinated me and I find it worthwhile spending my lifetime's work, creating art in this manner.
This abstract language liberates the individual from the limitations of current time and space and the feelings and experiences that come between them. This abstract visual language is the eternal one concerned with balance, harmony and eternity. Engaged with the concealed laws of existence, I understood the concept of repetition without monotony and growth without a boundary, with complementary contrasts and relativities.
I have not repeated or reproduced the geometric designs done centuries ago by Muslim artists but instead I have used a complex mathematical equation using a combination of the written Arabic language, one of the biggest inspirations in my art.
As Arabic writing implies, geometric rules and principles begin with a dot and progress to lines and curves, creating infinite ideas and meanings. I have created a new ratio for the Arabic letters based on the Vedic Square, a 9 x 9 grid to create new codes for each letter. By constructing layers of shapes and lines, a visual ambiguity occurs, changing perspectives while simultaneously creating movements from a still composition.
Building upon the ethos of geometry, that of a relationship among higher dimensional analogues, my art is concerned by this as well as the rhetoric between substance, essence and fate. It raises a question about what is abstract; what is solid; what is common and what is particular. This discourse moves back and forth between the humanities and the sciences, constantly shedding and reconstructing subtle layers.
Arguably, what is most incongruous in this discourse is what is most convergent within it: communication. Using a pure language, this work locks together geometry, faith and beauty, pushing the boundaries of what we know, how we know it and how it is perceived.
For me, geometry is a liberating expression, it denies our ego and looks at who we are as part of a whole in harmony with the rest of creation.

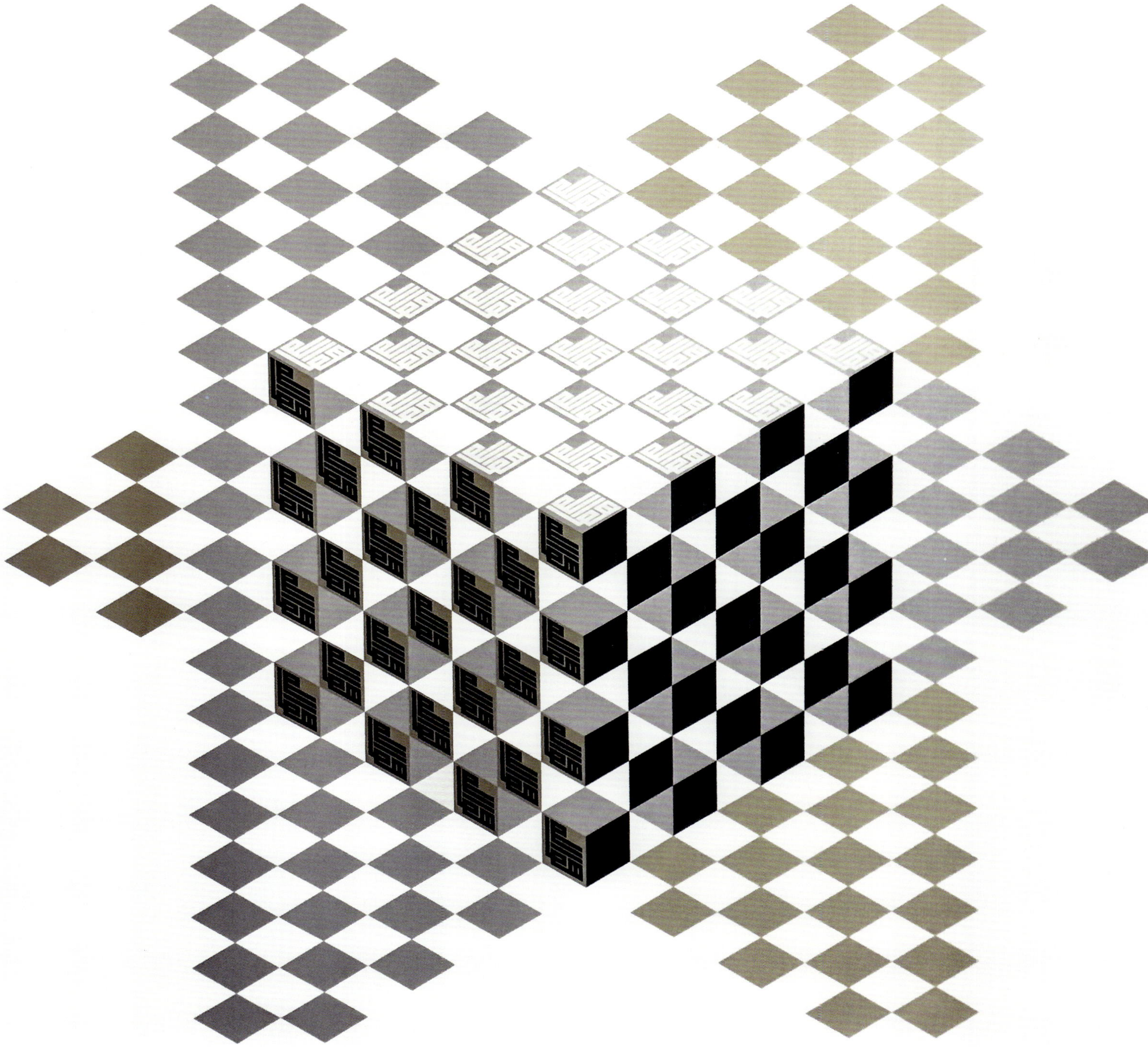

Cube within triangles, 2016
Silkscreen on archival paper, 152 x 170 cm

Rumi 3, 2018
Mixed media on handmade paper, 112 x 82 cm

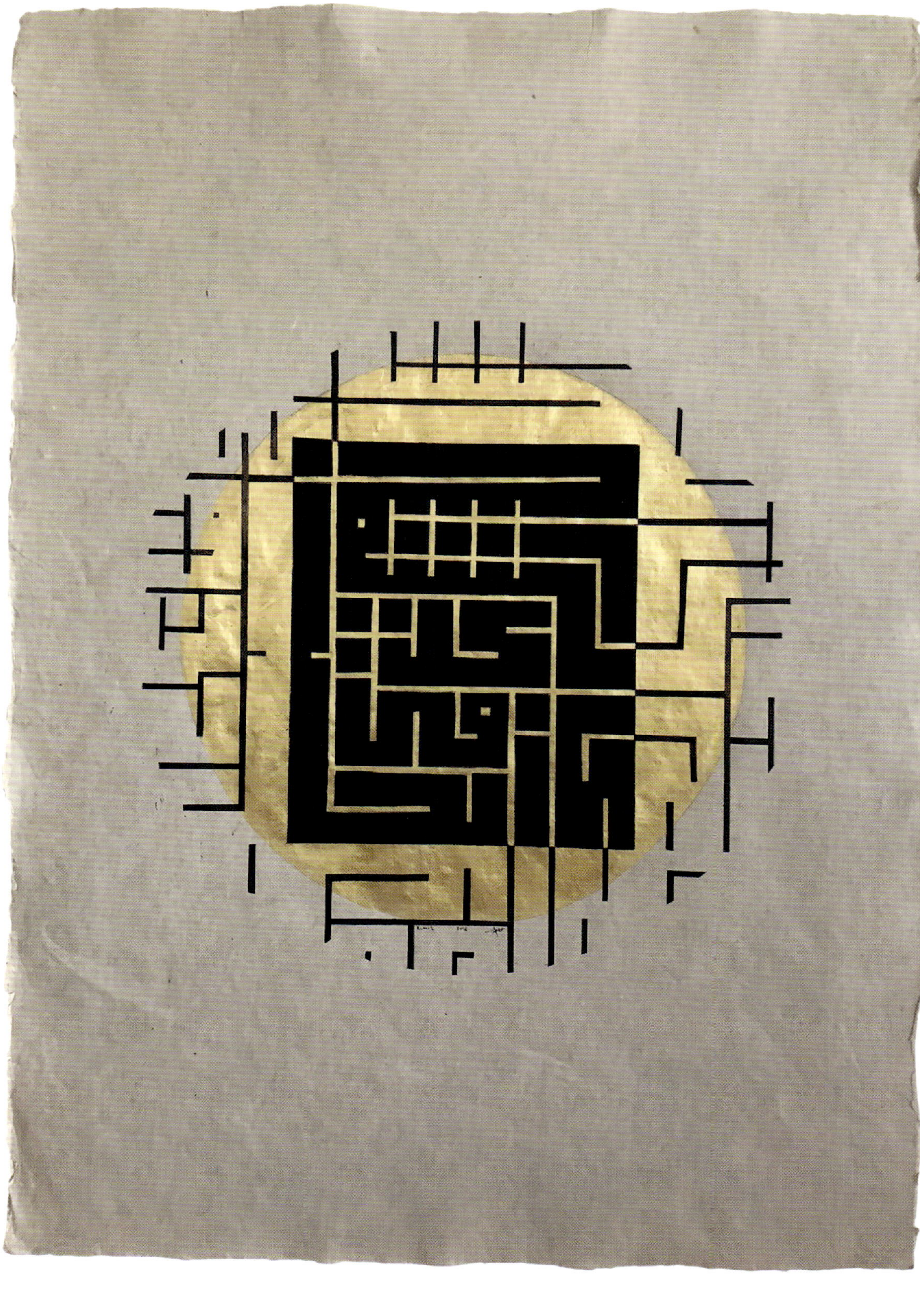

Al Ghafour, 2017
Mixed media on archival paper, 100 x 100 cm

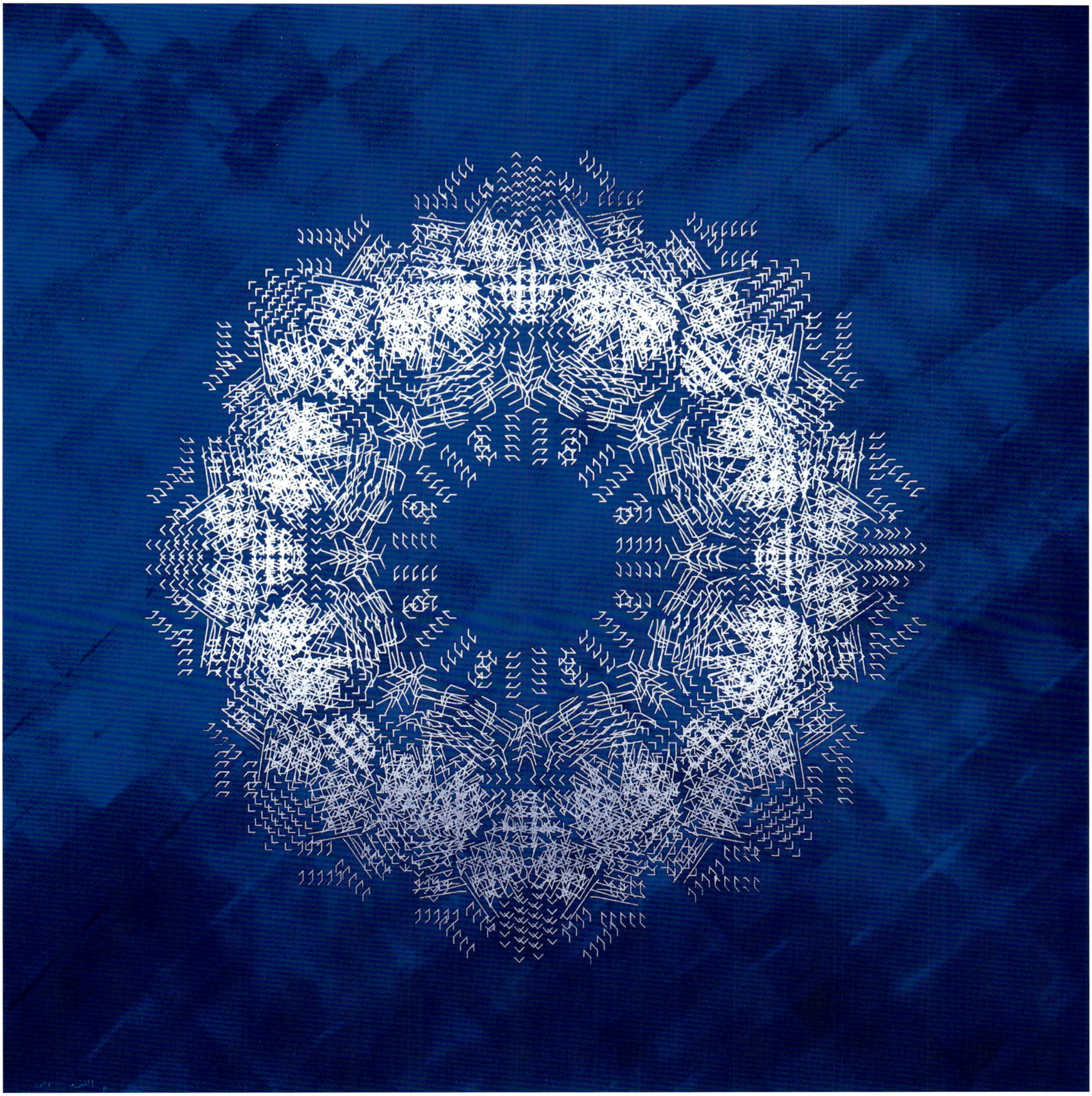

Rashid Al Khalifa

Geometry within Rashid Khalifa's work
The foundation stones of my work are colour and form. Rich colours embody my early work, which shows my love of French Impressionism. Colour is the principal focus at this stage, layer upon layer of sumptuous oil envelop the surface contained within the context of a traditional landscape. I wished to lose myself in the colour field, and in the late 1980s, I was drawn to abstraction – colour is contained in a shape, body, vase, flower – these shapes flow across the surface of the work.
Form takes two paths in my work, firstly figurative and secondly architectural – not in the physical form but the theoretical. It is within this sphere of understanding that I assess the geometric form. Initially stripping back the form so that the colour is the embodiment of the artwork, I sought to develop this concept by making the surface of the artwork enter the viewers' space. The square convex form of the early *Convex* works from the late 1990s show my desire to strip away the figurative nature of my training and to centre on form and colour. In the early part of 2000 I moved from a convex canvas surface to metal – showcasing the form of the surface – and the strong geometric surface intercut by a circle became the basis for my works. Still concentrating on colour, it is now poured on a surface behind the open circle. These two geometric forms contain the visualisation of the artwork. The viewer is enveloped by colour lost within the circle, in some cases the interconnecting forms are on the surface only, but still they are emblazoned by colour.
In my latest works there is a new understanding of form, looking at the Arabic screen as an influencer, I stripped the idea back, focussing on the illusive geometric shapes formed by the shadows held within the artwork. The mesh is brutally honest, colliding with bright colour it becomes alive. In these latest works, I have started to include shadows as a medium; the mesh allows for these shadows to flow across the floor creating a multitude of geometric patterns. Influenced by the British Constructivist Movement, I have used light and dark to explore abstract shapes in three dimensions. The importance of orderly and geometric composition, simplicity and lack of decoration in art is fundamental to this new work. Geometric abstraction connected art and architecture, creating a common interest with British sculptors breaking the boundaries of type and location.

Hybrids from *Penumbra Series*, 2018
(detail)
Matte enamel on aluminium,
150 x 150 cm

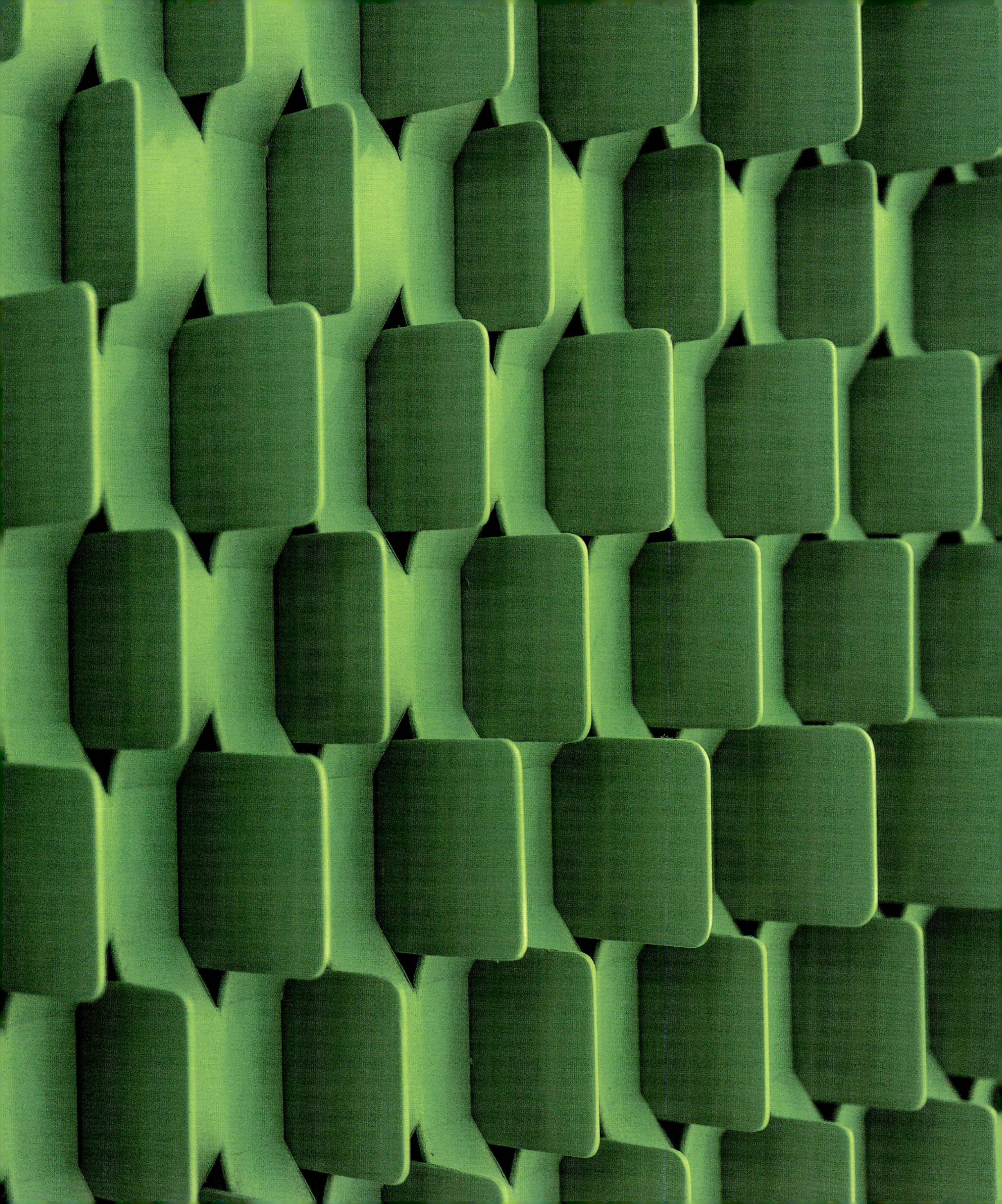

Mobile columns from
Penumbra Series, 2018
Dimensions variable

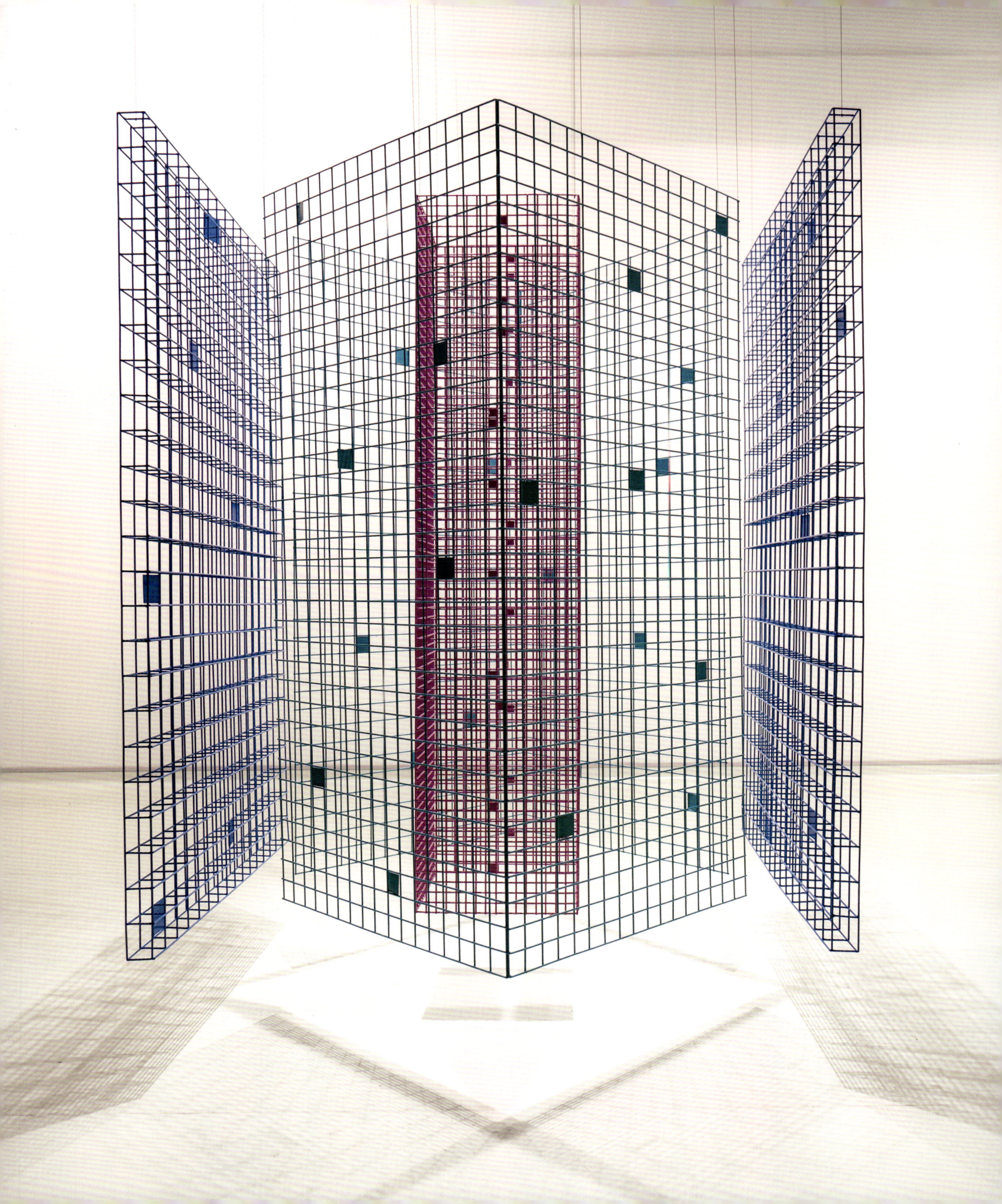

Grid maze from *Penumbra Series*, 2018
12 x 3 m

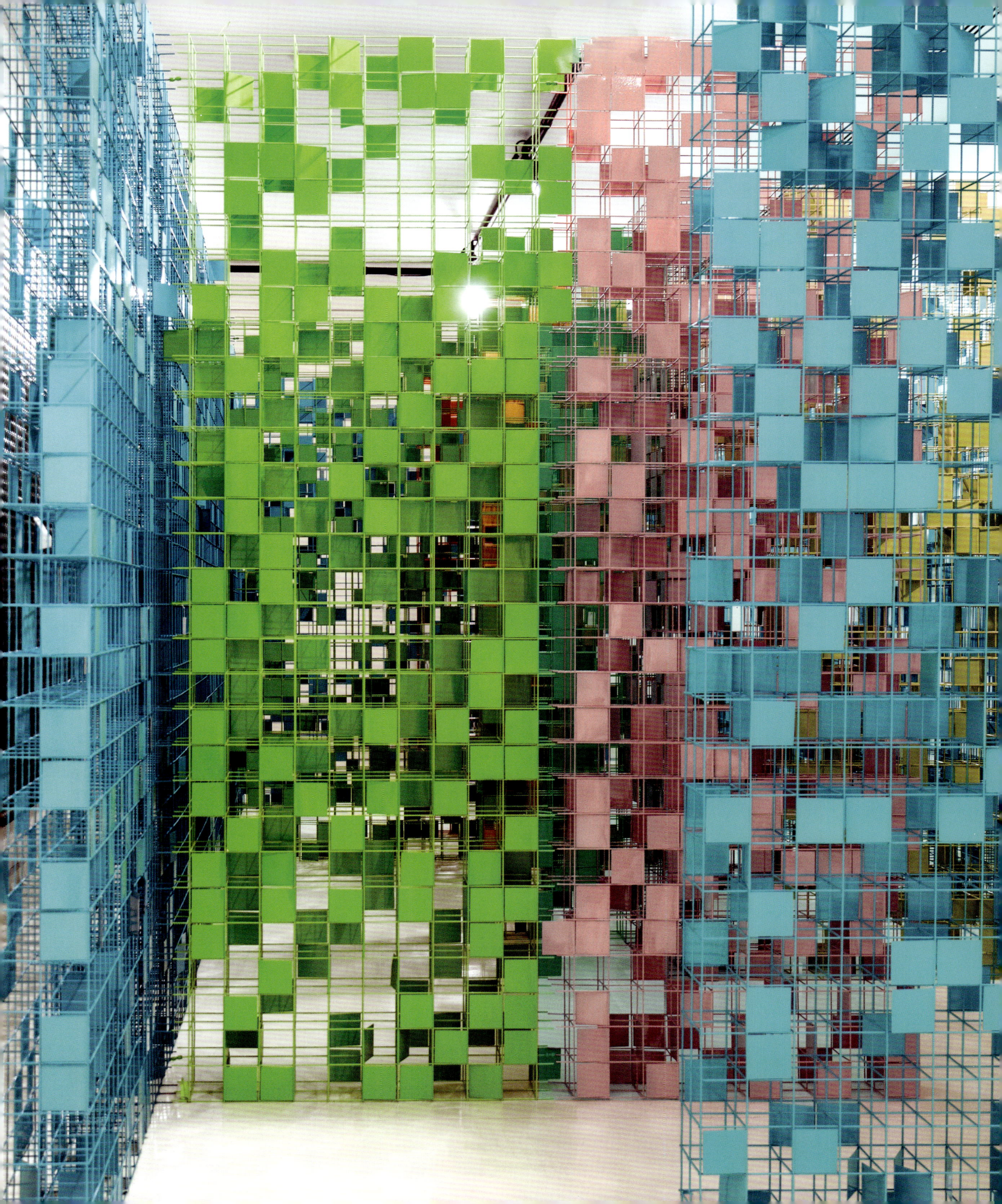

Ahmad Angawi

"Verily, all things have We created in proportion and measure"
The Qur'an [54:49], sūrat al-qamar (The Moon)

Each snowflake that has fallen and still falls into this world is unique and different, one from the other, yet all fall into the same geometrical six fold pattern. Geometry is a universal language that exists in creation. It is the law of physics and visual mathematics that exists in us and all around us. Through it I have been able to understand the idea of unity and diversity as well as diversity within unity. Growing up in a vastly multicultural community, I have learnt from a young age to appreciate the diversity of my hometown region, Hijaz, where for hundreds of years migrants from all over the globe settled and merged their cultures to create a truly cosmopolitan place, centred around Makkah. The region, to this day, inhales many cultures and exhales its own. The aftermath of this is witnessed in its unique Arabic accent and cuisine, and visually through its architecture and geometry. It is exactly this that remained a constant inspiration for my work as both a young artist and designer, and what has given birth to my fascination with geometry. I give emphasis to the process of making: investigating the pattern or, as I like to call it, "the pattern of making a pattern". There are often many paths and steps in making a geometrical pattern. I have found through teaching that it has been easier for my students to grasp the idea of manifesting a geometric pattern by steps, or seeing in layers similar to the way I have shown in my artwork. Seeing the beauty in each step, the process, as well as the beauty in the end result.
The law of geometry applies to all aspects of creation, from the macro level of the creation of the universe, to the micro-like composition of our genetics (DNA). Patterns exist in the universe just as they do in our bodies. That is why we feel comfortable and relate to geometrical patterns around us regardless of our cultures.
The idea of practicing traditional arts is that you are linking the body, mind and soul into making a beautiful object. The repetition of 'making' elevates the body by becoming skilful with your hands and in turn more in tune with your senses to produce work. Your mind is elevated by continuously developing tools and ways to improve and enhance your art, and thus your soul is in constant *dhikr* (meditation) in making and producing an object that is close to the heart.
"Know, Oh brother… that the study of geometry of the senses (*al-hindasa al hissiyya*) leads to proficiency in all the practical arts, while the study of intelligible geometry (*al-hindasa al-'aqliyya*) leads to proficiency in the intellectual arts, because this science is one of the gates that leads to knowledge of the essence of the soul, which is the height of all knowledge, the elements of wisdom, and the origin of all intellectual and practical arts."
Ikhwan al Safa

Mangour Progression, 2016
White ink on tempered glass and wood base, 5 panels, 270 x 90 cm

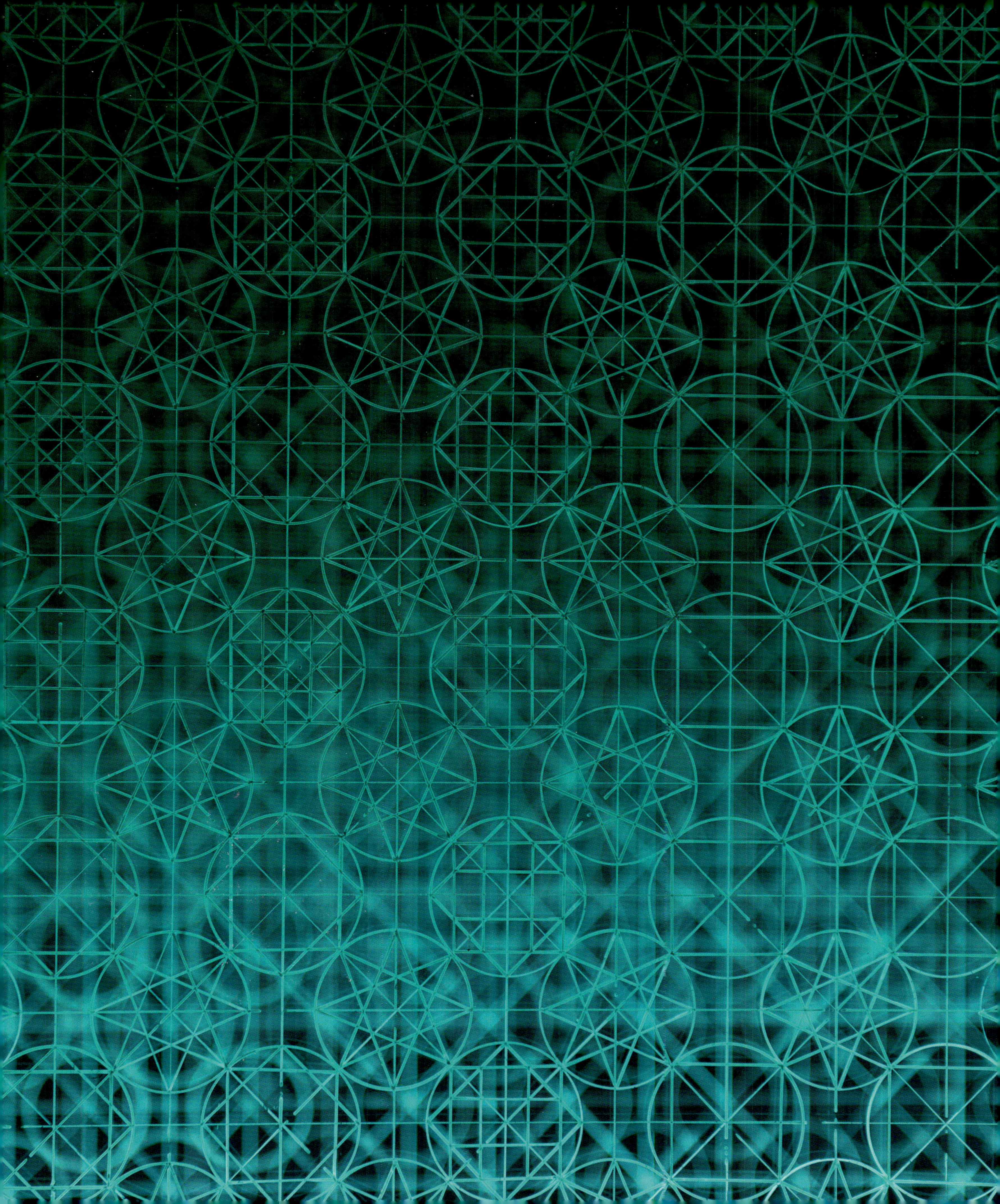

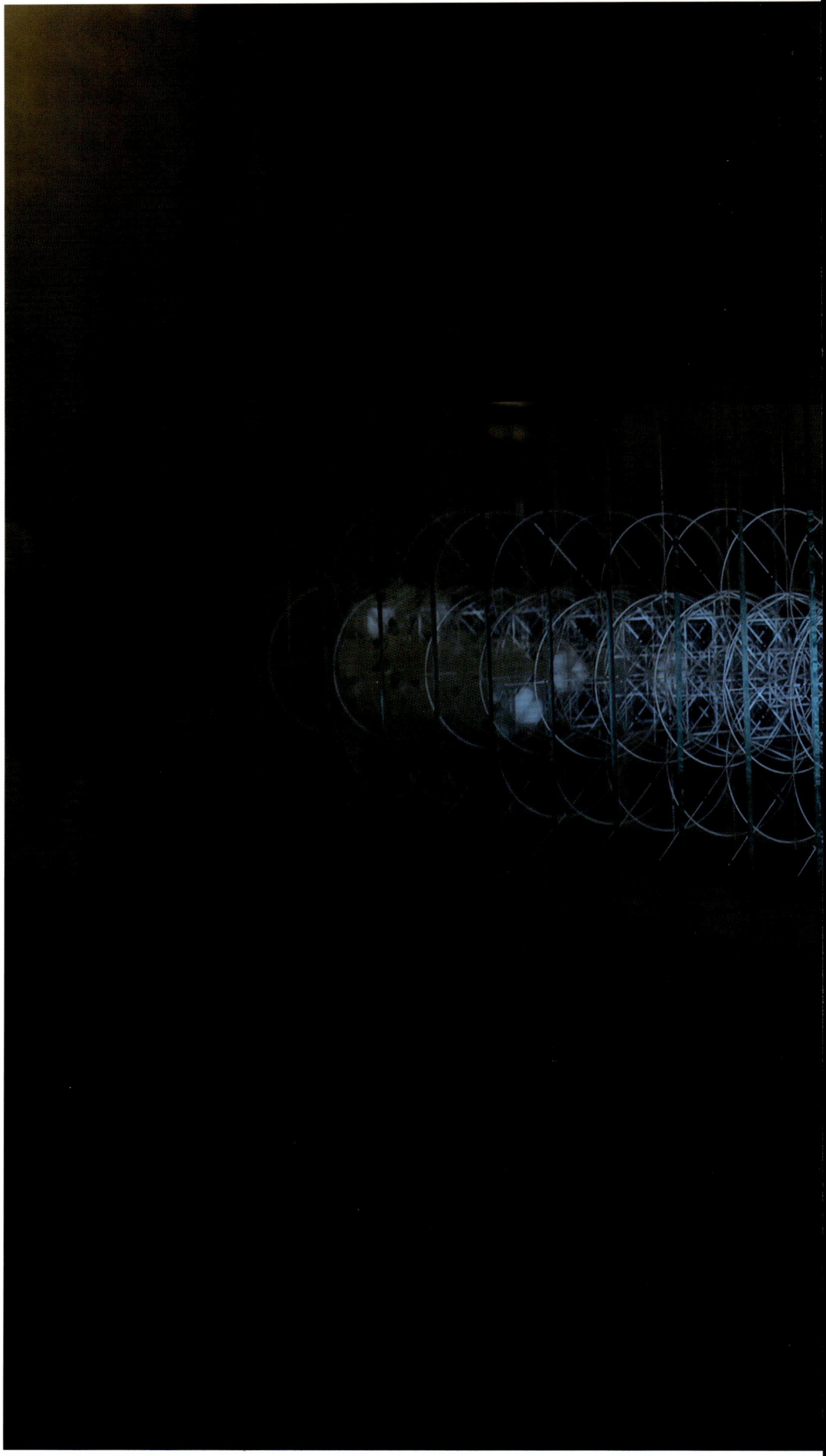

Geometry Unfold, 2016
White ink on glass, 20 pieces
Design Biennale, Somerset House, 2018

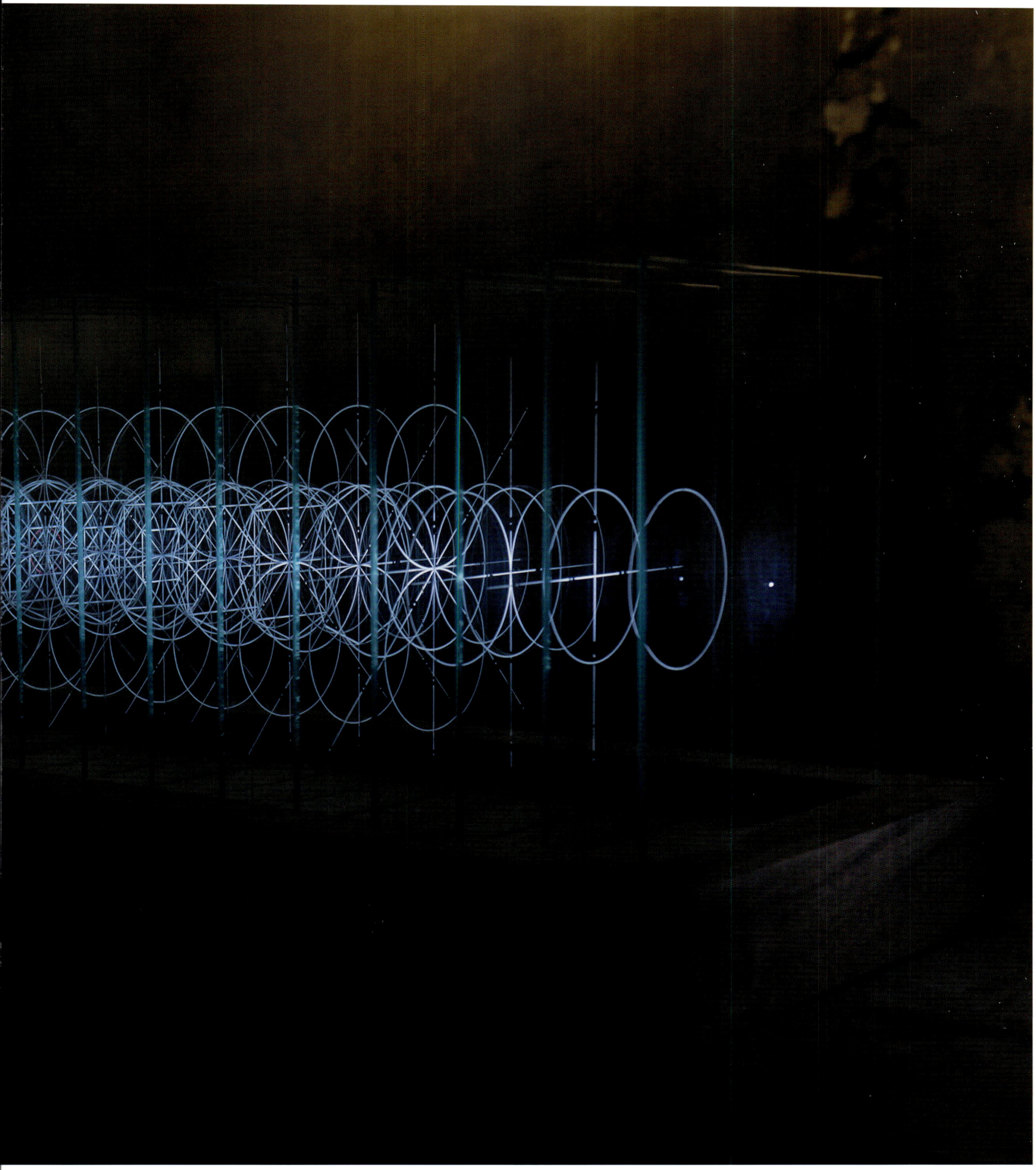

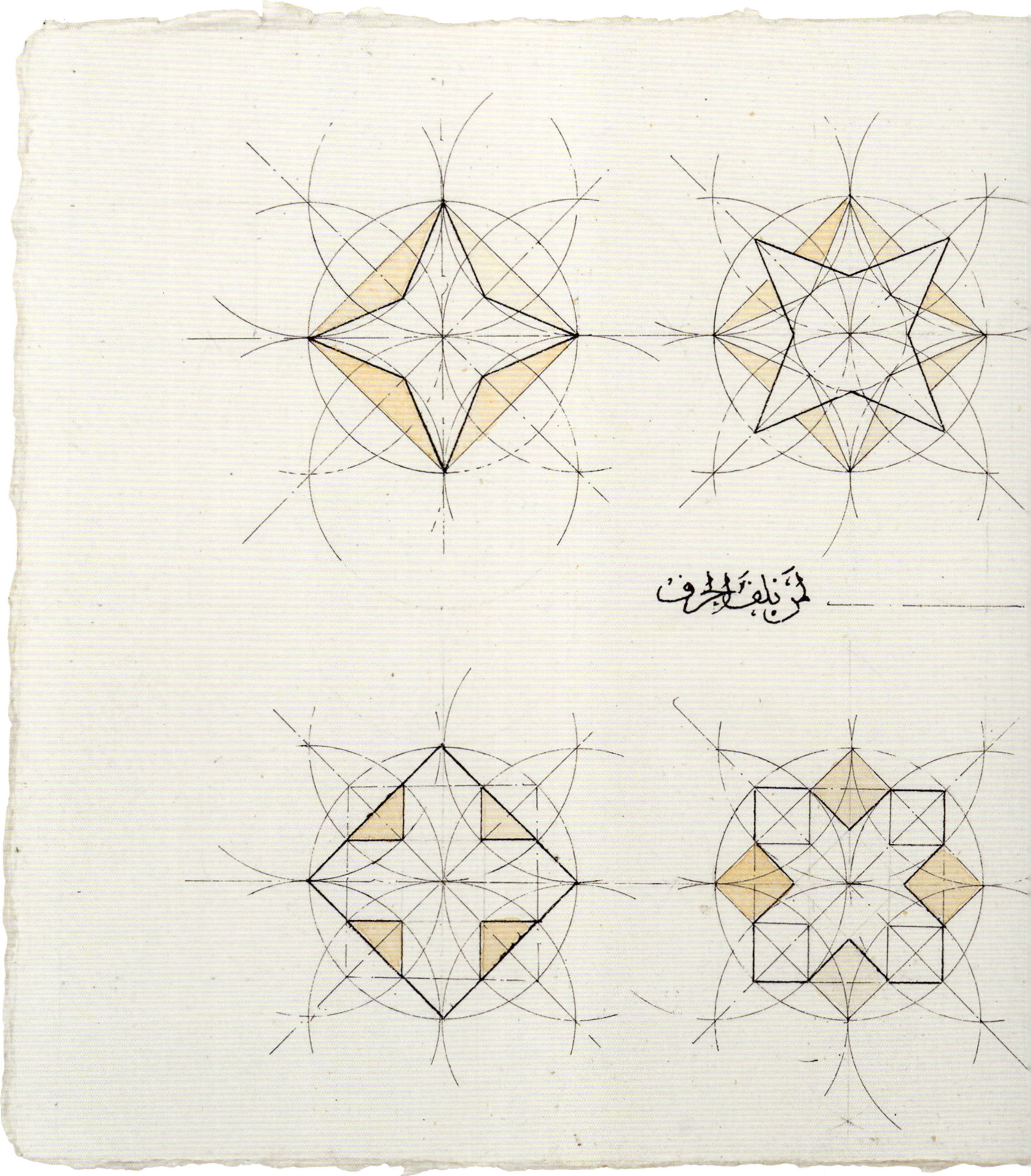

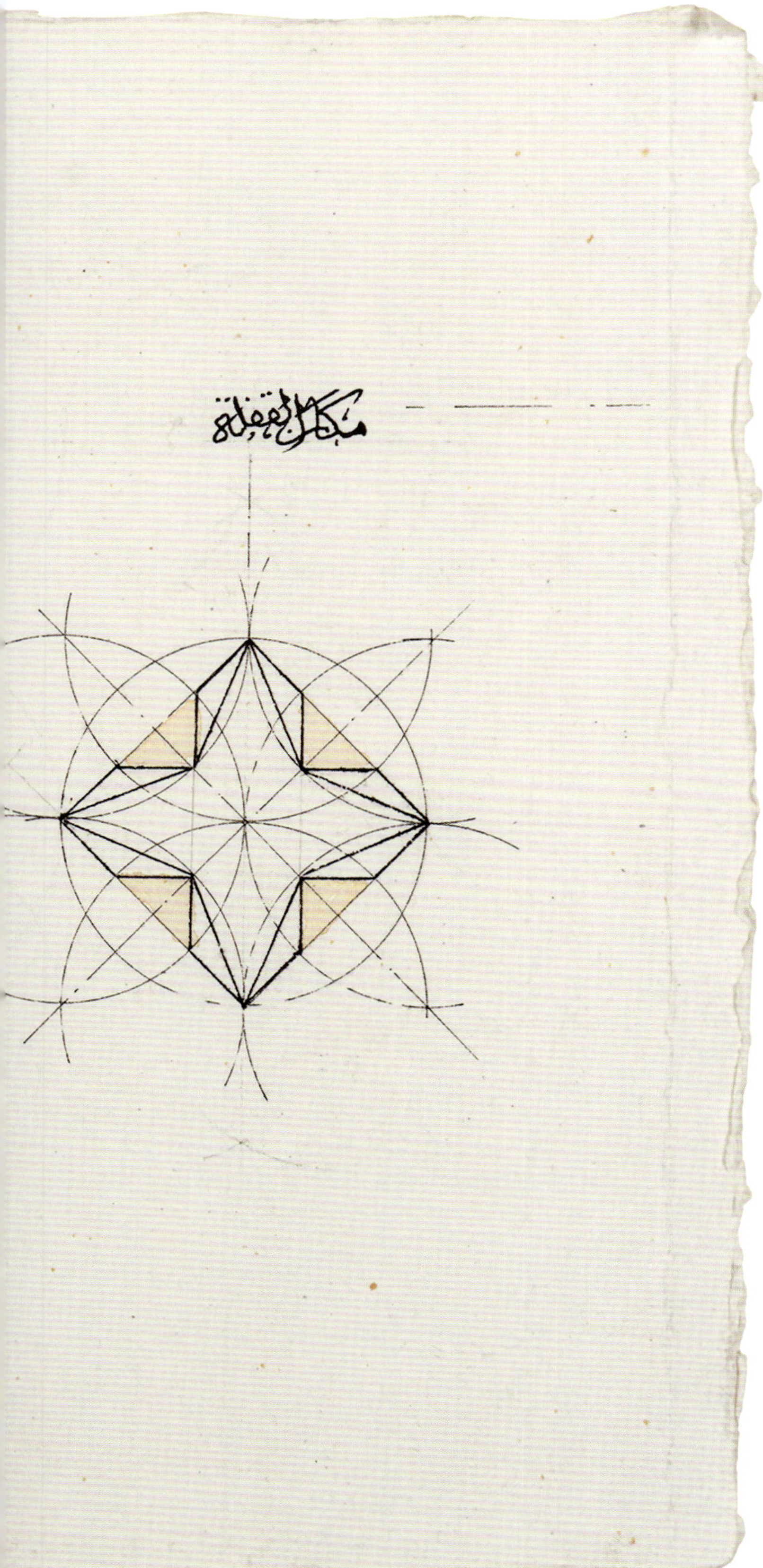

Letters of Mangour, series 2, 2016
Ink on handmade paper, 63 x 80 cm

Dana Awartani

The understanding and relationship that I and my work have with geometry transcend the dictionary definition of 'earth measurement'. In the Islamic tradition it has come to refer to the central law that corresponds to the essential rhythm of the universe, it is the source of harmony, balance, beauty, proportion and reflects the true essence of all phenomena manifested in nature, and it is this knowledge found within geometry that has captivated me for many years. I not only see geometry as an unfolding of number into space but rather as a timeless language of aesthetics which, through its mathematical and visually democratic origin, represents a universal language of beauty and harmony; in essence, geometry is the perfect reflection of the heavenly archetypes. The practice of geometry requires an immense amount of rigour and discipline which can be seen as a form of meditation, prayer or *zikhr* (remembrance), best articulated by Rumi: "Let the beauty we love be what we do, there are hundreds of ways to kneel and kiss the ground". In a world that often appears chaotic, the practice of sacred geometry and the study of its philosophical and spiritual dimensions enable me to build towards order and beauty, and experience a sense of one-ness that goes far beyond 'modern mentality'. It enables myself as the practitioner, to connect to the essential source and regain a sense of true humanness and identity while also unveiling the unity of creation. As the eminent scholar and philosopher Syed Hossein Nasr mentions: "Plato said 'Beauty is the splendour of Truth'… Traditional art provided this beauty on the external, formal level, which itself acts as a support for the attainment of inner beauty. This art also speaks, often in silent language, of the truth whose attainment constitutes the very raison d'etre of human life."

While practicing geometry I am also constantly aware that it is never divorced from meaning and is a multi-layered aesthetic that possesses a *zahir* and a *batin* or an 'inner' and an 'outer' meaning. The *zahir* is the sensible form that emphasises the quantitative aspect which is most readily comprehensible, and the *batin* is the essential or qualitative aspect which all things possess, and, as an artist, I attempt to deconstruct and translate its capacity to invest interpretation and meaning. Even though the art of geometry flourished under the Islamic enlightenment period, it cannot be attributed to one culture, as the study of geometry is built on practices and knowledge from ancient civilisations, including those of China, India, Africa and Greece. It's an art form that transcends borders, language and authorship; it belongs to everyone and yet to no one. It's an artistic discipline which hails from a diverse range of religious and cultural contexts while sharing a common origin in mathematical and geometrical principles, and it is this universality that I strive to translate in an ever growing hostile and polarised world.

Orientalism, 2014
PVC tape, 250 x 200 x 230 cm

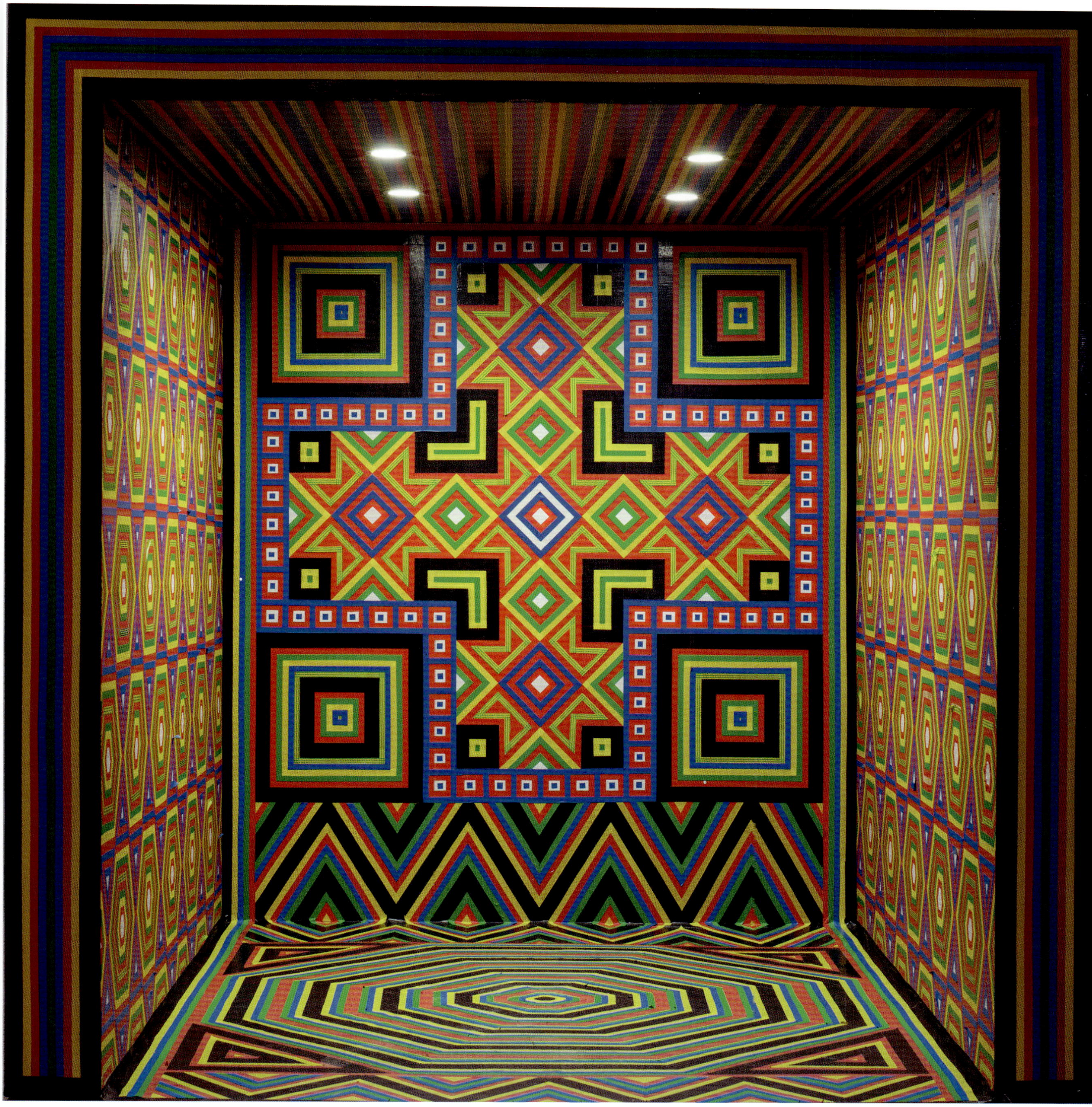

Installation shot of *The Platonic Solid Duals Series* at the Marrakech Biennale, 2016
Wood, copper and glass, dimensions variable

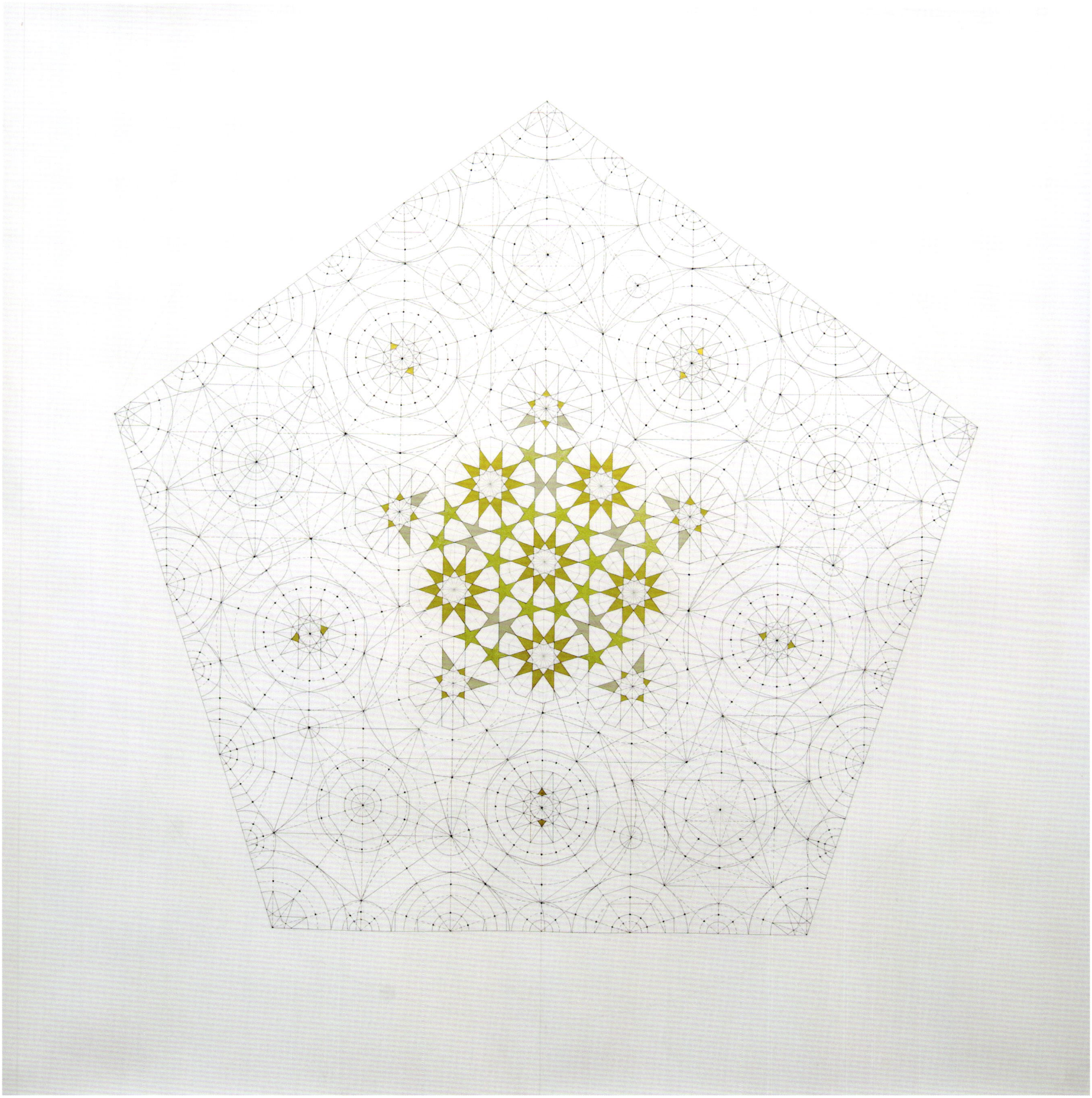

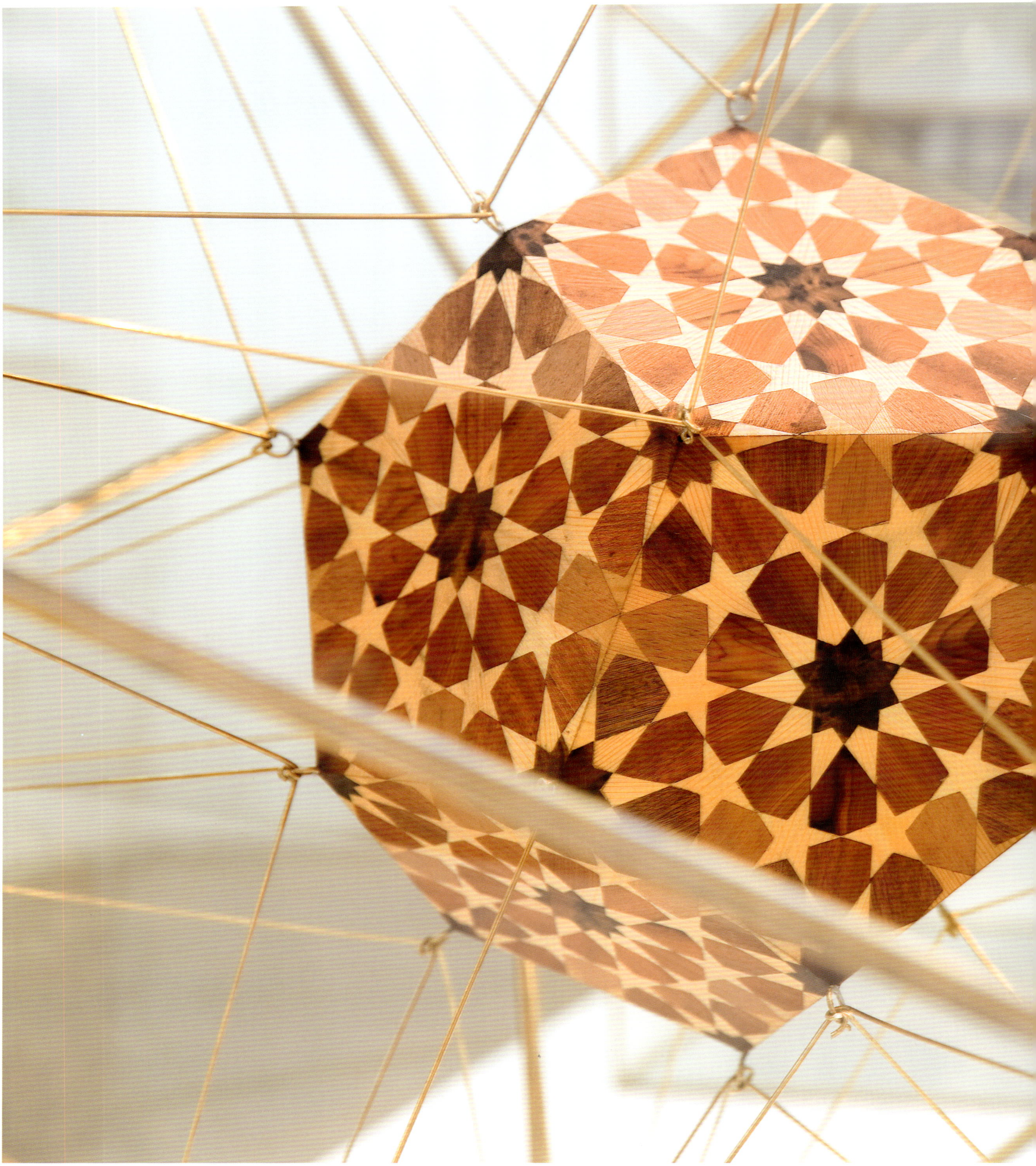

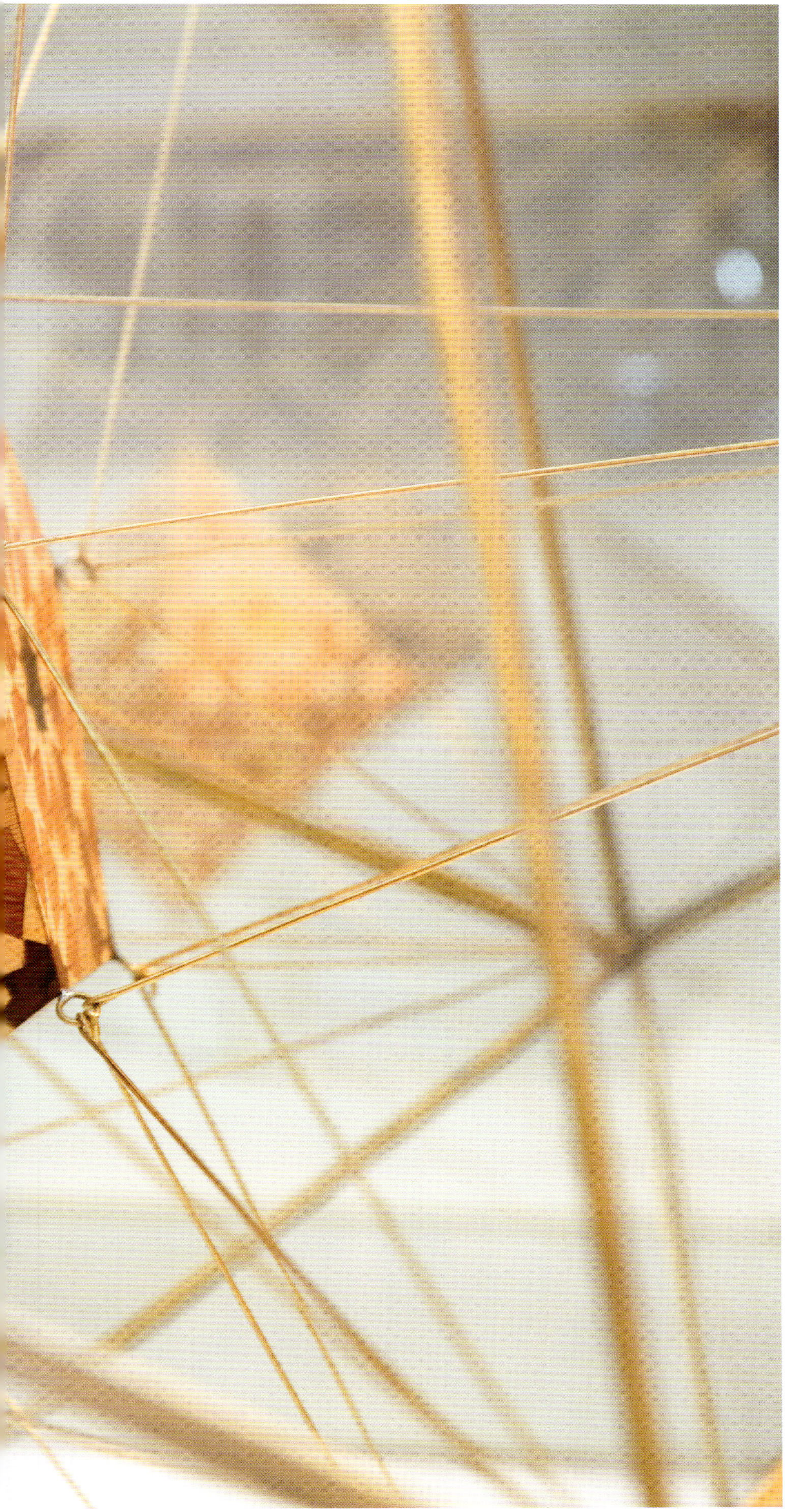

Detail of *Dodecahedron within an Icosahedron* from *The Platonic Solid Duals Series*, 2016
Wood, copper and glass,
121 x 100.2 x 100.2 cm

Rana Begum

The intricate geometric patterns of traditional Islamic art and architecture provided the background to my childhood. Later in life, I have come to draw inspiration from buildings such as Louis Kahn's monumental National Assembly Building in Dhaka. However, more than these physical manifestations of geometrical form, it has been my Muslim upbringing, that has contributed centrally to my work.

Reading the Qur'an and praying five times a day instilled in me a rhythm and repetition which I see reflected throughout my art in the decisive repetition of geometric forms. However, I have also used asymmetry and controlled misalignments to create unexpected juxtapositions and contrast. For example, extruded-aluminium box sections and mesh grids create regular and random patterns and intricate overlays; this repetition and rhythm lends a distinct meditative quality to my work.

Earlier in my career, I was interested in the artistic possibility of pure geometry and mathematical principle. However, this enthusiasm waned, and was replaced by a desire to create more instinctual work. Inspired by artists including Agnes Martin, Donald Judd and Sol LeWitt, I abandoned the mathematic principles that I found too constraining; they didn't leave ample room for fortuitous accidents. Nevertheless, basic geometric shapes continue today to facilitate my exploration into the universal elements of colour, light and form.

Living in a city, every day I am immersed in a matrix of geometry, light and colour. The urban environment is a great visual stimulus and source of inspiration to me, feeding the vivid colours and shapes of my work. I see light, structure and colour everywhere and often it is in the most quotidian objects that I find inspiration and motivation for my next piece of work – how the morning light casts shadows on metal shutters or vivid neon signs clamouring for attention. The modular nature of built structures and the defined angles of the city grid have had a marked influence on my work, combining a sense of order with elements of the transient and ephemeral.

My work doesn't follow any specific formula for the use of geometry. Rather, it responds to the material at hand with each work informing the next – line drawings give rise to wire sculpture, folded paper to folded metal. I like to work with industrial materials which are naturally geometric in shape and, rather than twisting and distorting them into organic forms, I allow the original geometric structure of the material to dictate the outcome. I try to create an experience for the viewer that is both sensorial and temporal, using a diverse range of influences and logical processes to produce a multifaceted experience.

No. 647 L Mesh, 2015
Paint on stainless steel,
213 x 136 x 0.5 cm

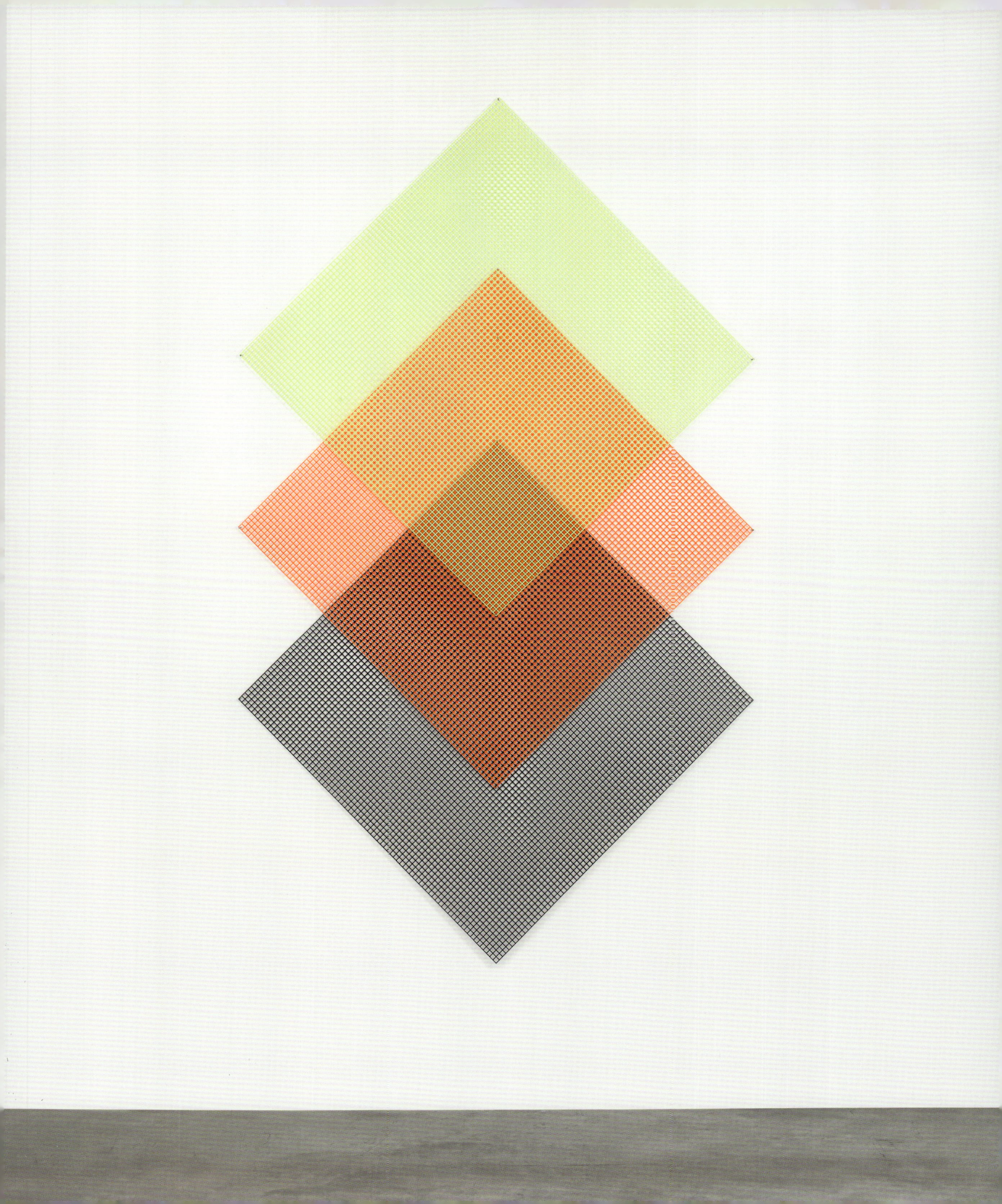

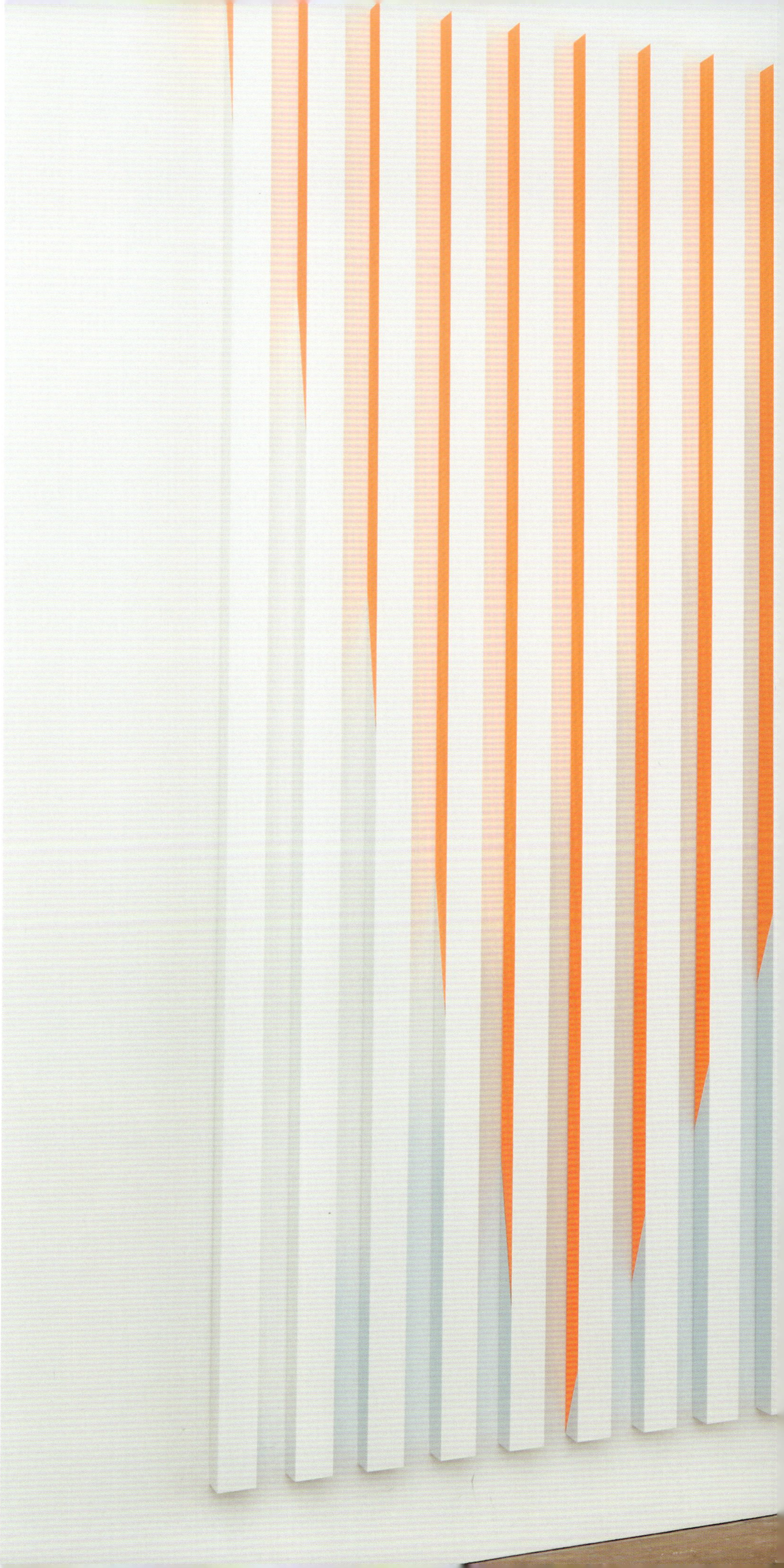

No. 794, 2018
30 sections, paint on powder-coated aluminium, 200 x 295 x 5 cm

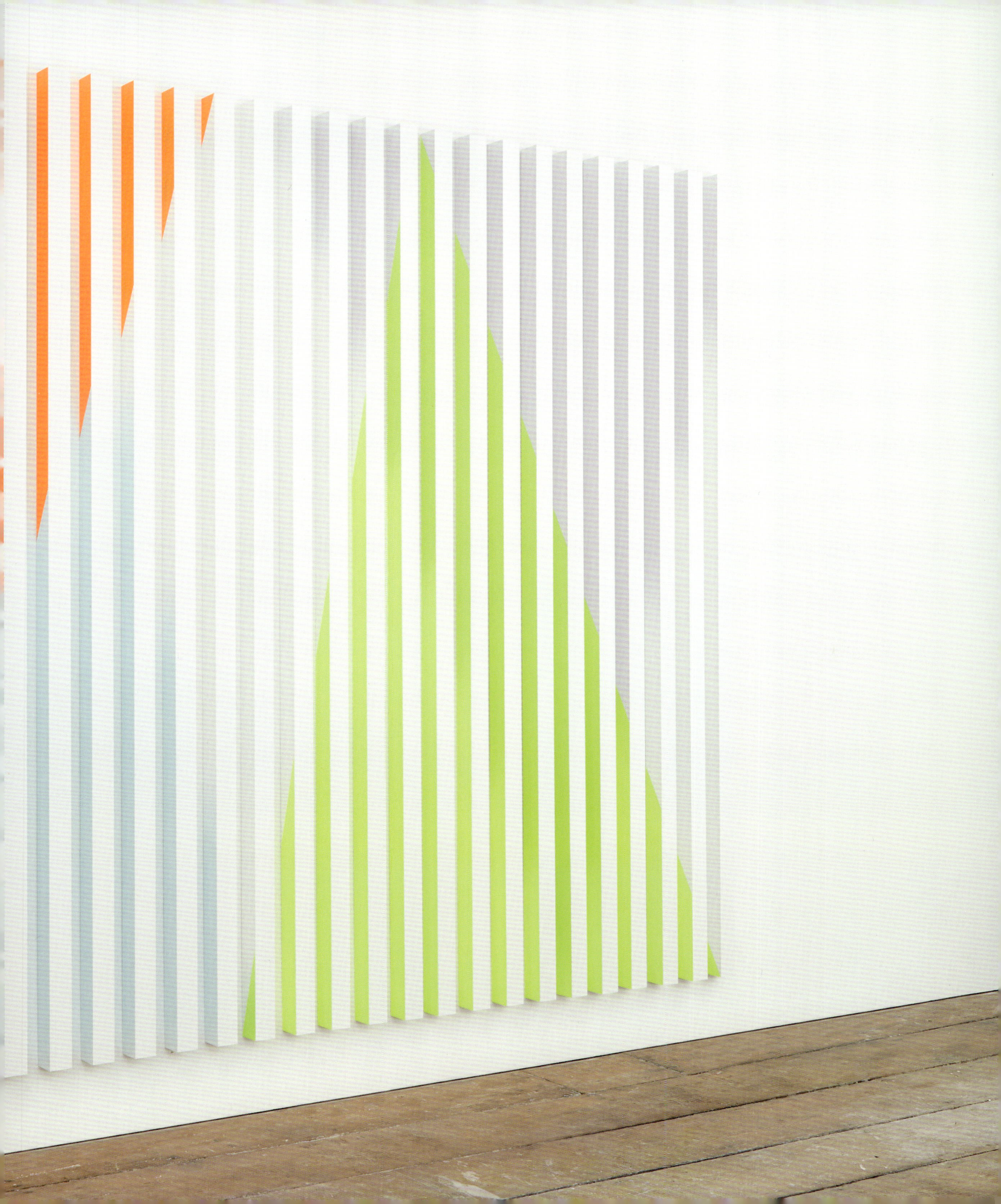

No. 680 Painting, 2016
54 panels, acrylic paint on MDF,
200 x 258 x 4 cm

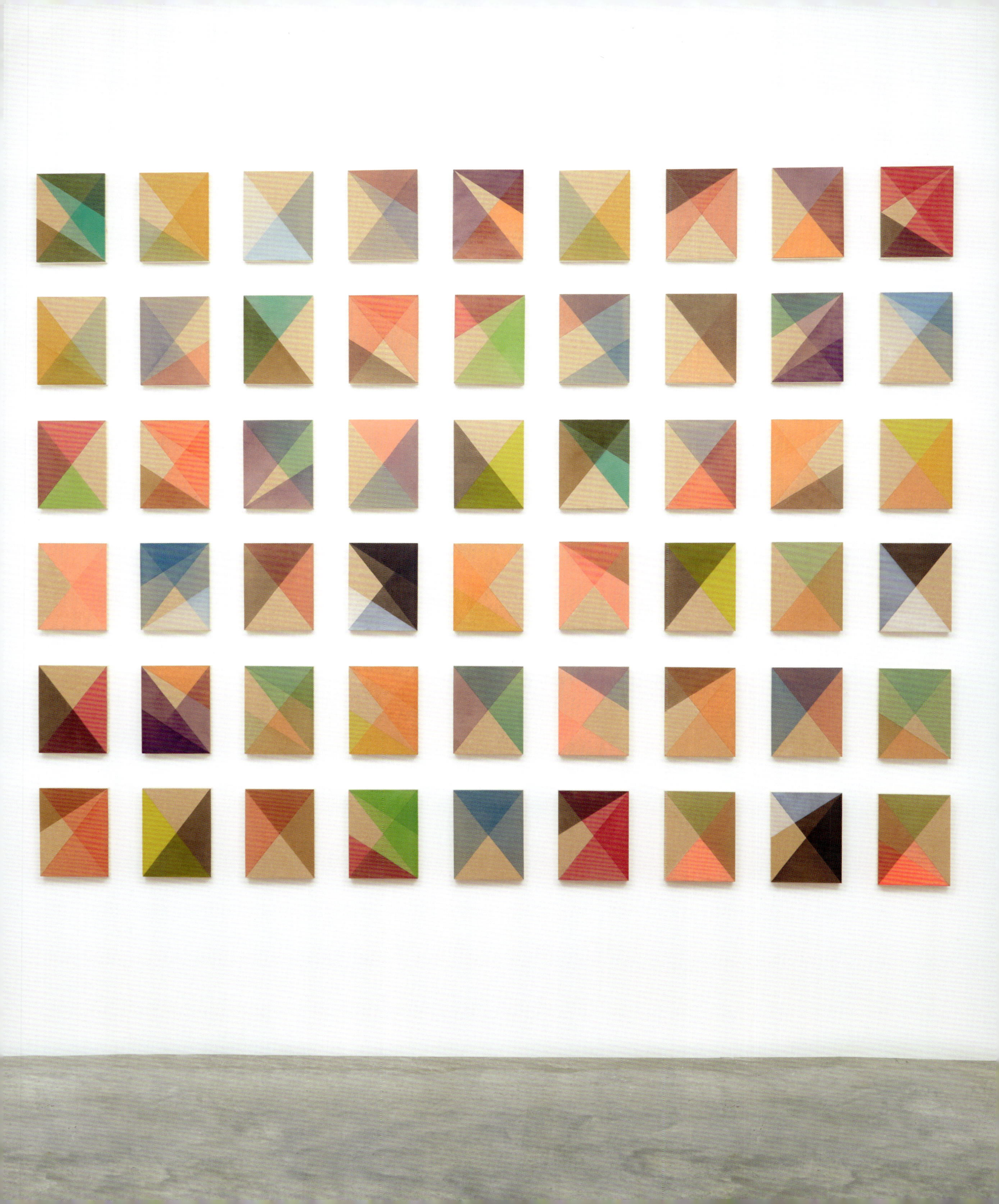

Kamal Boullata

Explorations of the square

During the early 1990s, I left the United States, where I had been residing for the previous twenty-five years, for Morocco and Spain, where I wanted to pursue research in Islamic art. After years of working on the exploration of the square, the eight-pointed star generated by two squares intersecting at 45 degrees intrigued me. The octagonal star not only seemed to be at the centre of every arabesque I examined, but its configuration, depending on the proportional subdivision of its module, formed the master grid of endless patterns. From the tiniest ornamental detail adorning a personal object to the most complex structures found in a monument, it was the same octagonal constellation, its derivatives, or its double or triple rotation within the circle that formed the underlying grid of the most complex arabesques. What was the secret principle of this master grid? How was it capable of generating all these enigmatic complexities of pure abstraction, which continue to create unspeakable pleasure for the eye and mind?

I was soon to learn that since antiquity, the square and the circle had been fraught with symbolical and philosophical connotations. The earth was often symbolised by the square for its four axes of spatial orientation, whereas the form of the circle represented the heavenly sphere. The rotation of the square within the circle was often referred to as the squaring of the circle. In it, the perimeter of the square is virtually equal to the circle's circumference. The geometric exercise sought to infer that the dimensions of the finite can express those of the infinite. It was through my research in Islamic art that I was finally able to retrace my earliest contact with image making. By 'looking hard' at the octagonal star made up of the intersection of two squares within the circle, I remembered Byzantine icons, whose motifs embodied the meeting between earthly and heavenly bodies. This meeting of the square and the circle was represented in the geometric shape of the *mandorla* surrounding the figure of Christ in the icons depicting the Transfiguration, Christ Pantocrator, or Christ on the Celestial Throne. In each of those themes the *mandorla* unfailingly took the shape of two superposed quadrangles within a circular form.

Once I saw the link between a central motif in the icons of my childhood and the octagonal star from which radiated those mesmerising arabesques evolved in Islamic art, I realised why all three monuments I could see from our roof in Jerusalem shared a common building plan. By circumscribing the intersection of two squares within a circle, the earliest ground plan of the Basilica of the Resurrection, the Church of the Ascension and the Dome of the Rock all sought to mark the divide between heaven and earth.

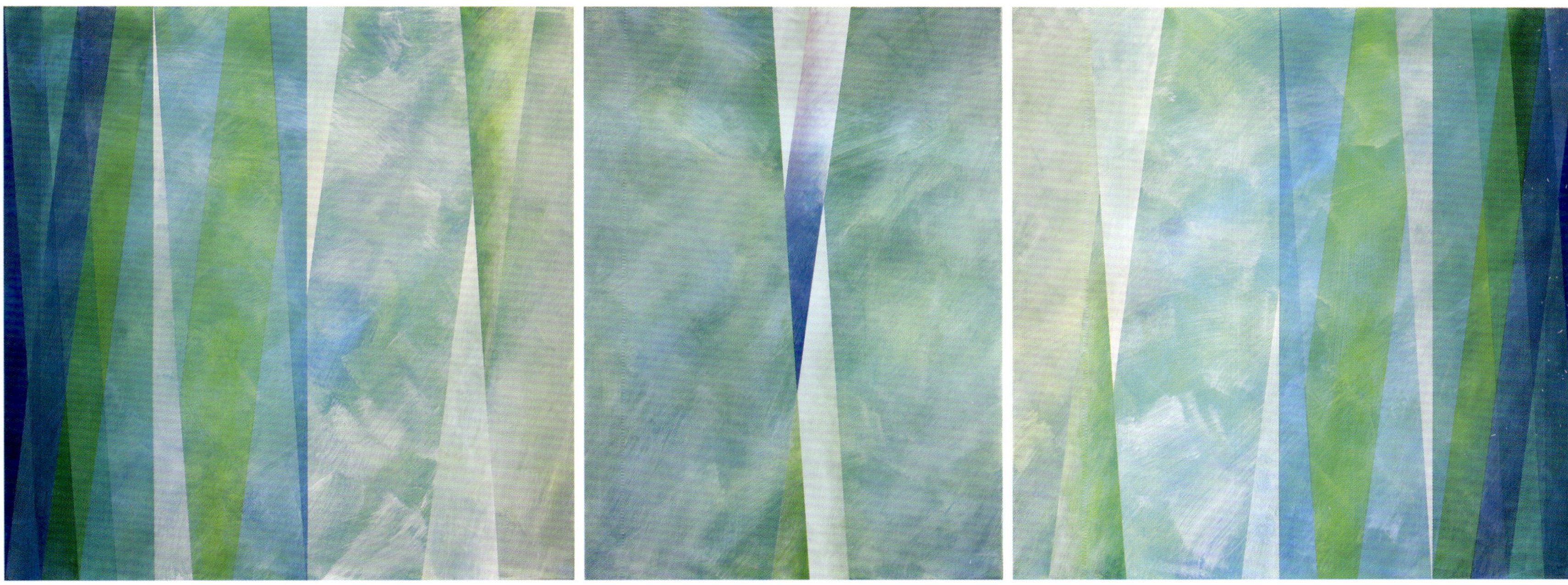

Nocturne, 2001
Triptych, acrylic on canvas,
130 x 390 cm
Collection of Ramzi and Saeda Dalloul
Arab Art Foundation, Beirut

Study 2, 1997
Acrylic on paper, 17 x 17 cm
Donation Claude and France Lemand
Museum of the Institut du Monde
Arabe, Paris

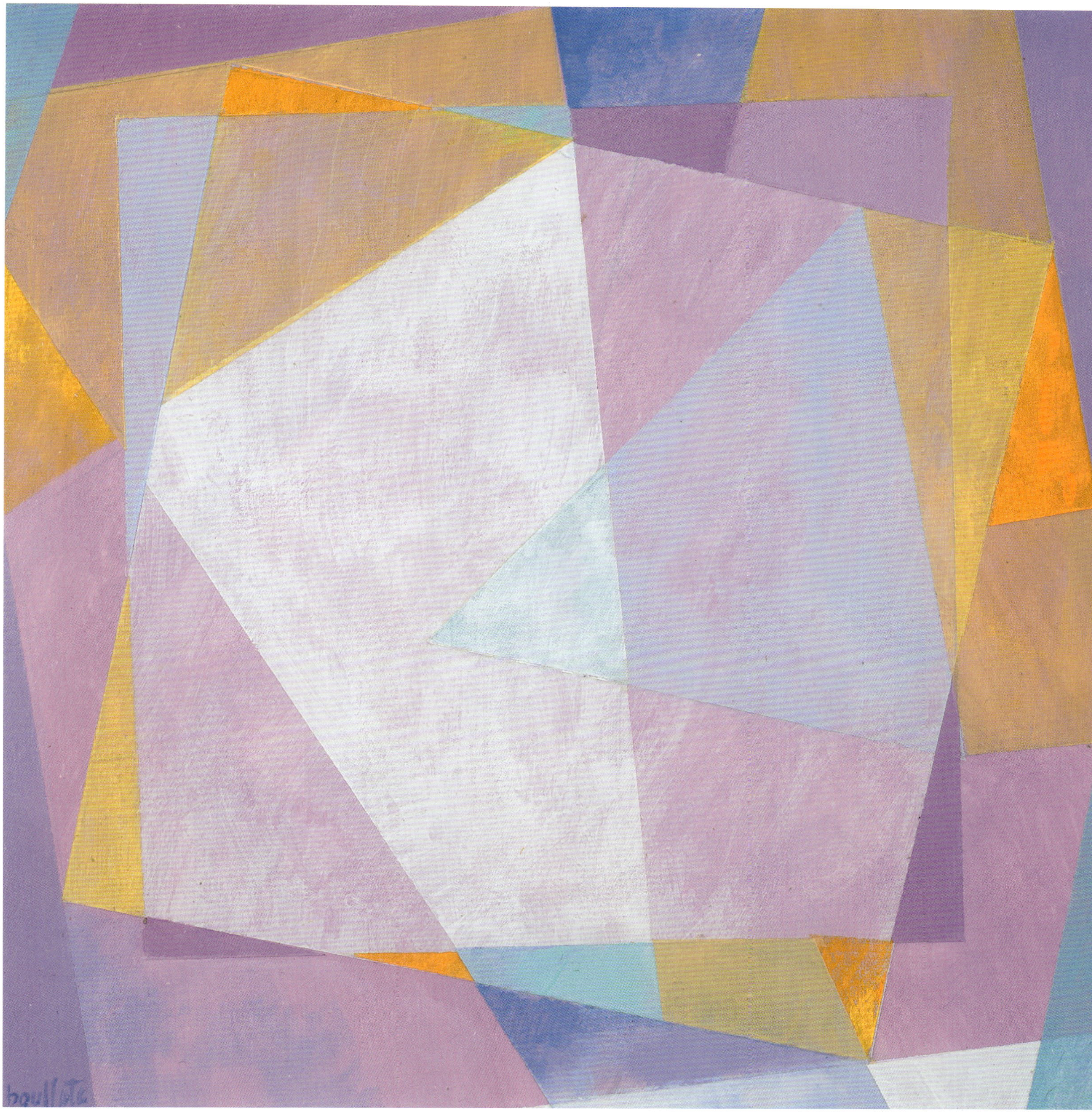

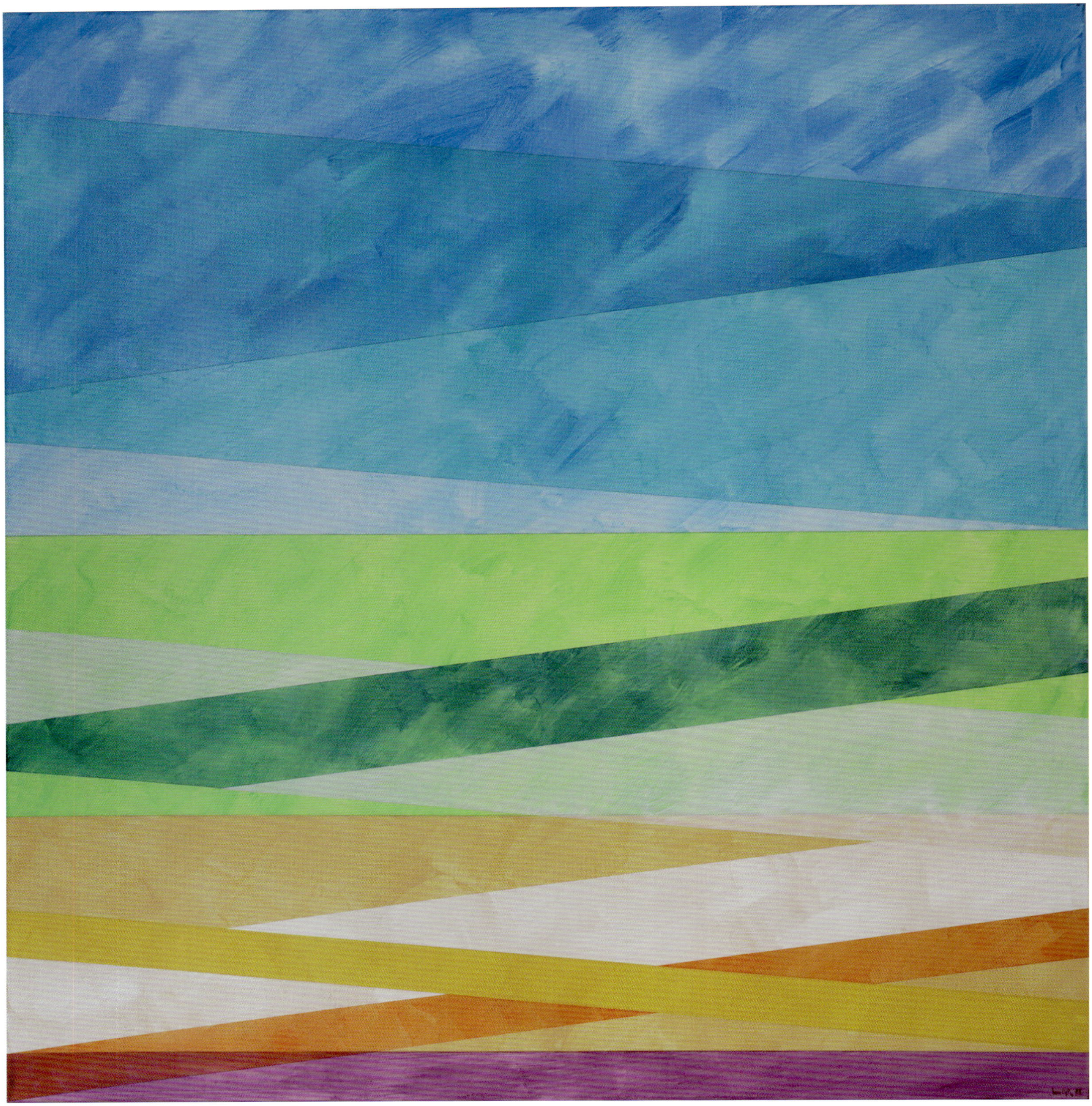

And There Was Light, N° 3, 2015
Acrylic on canvas, 100 x 100 cm

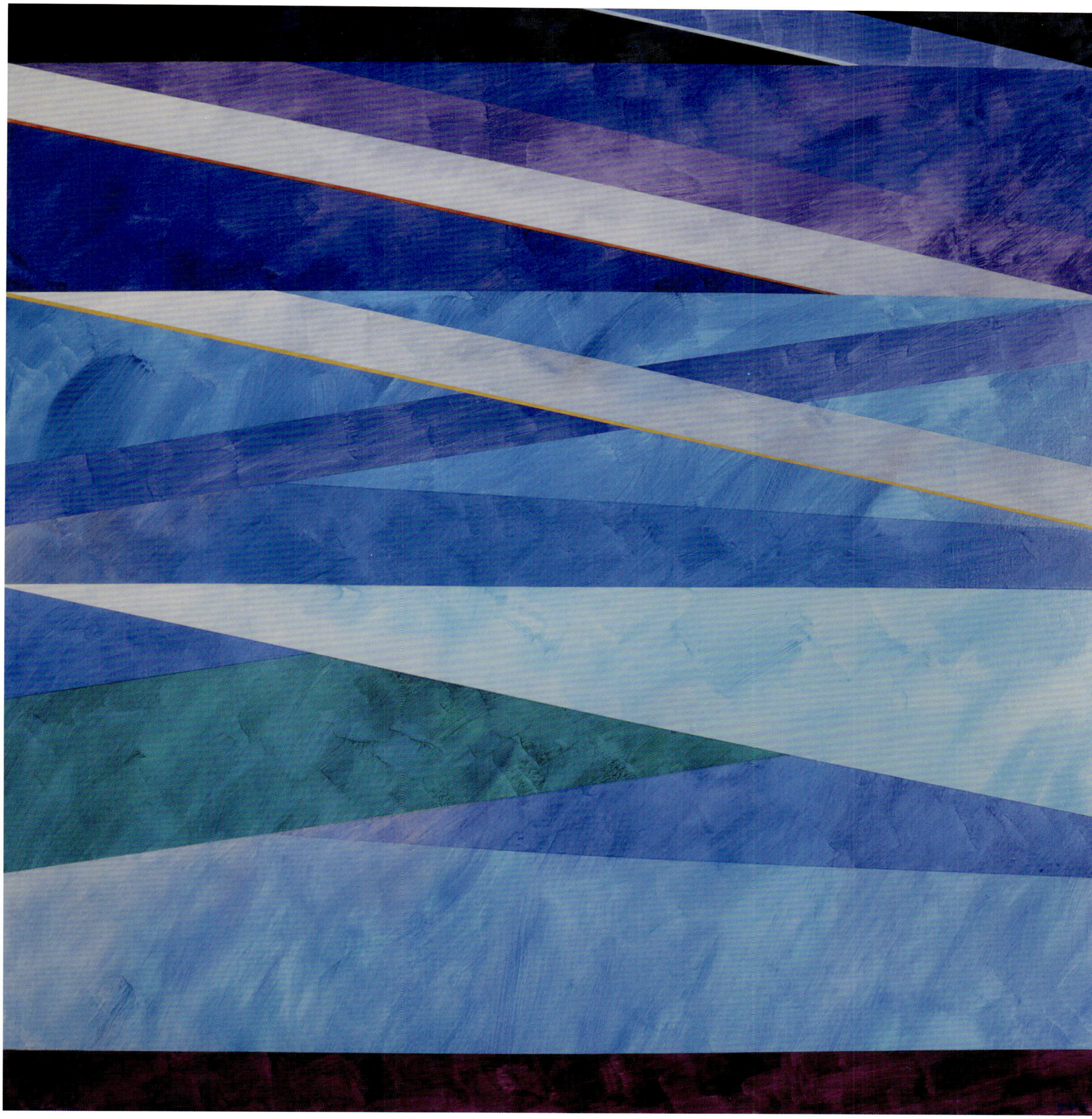

And There Was Light, N° 4, 2015
Acrylic on canvas, 100 x 100 cm

Monir Shahroudy Farman Farmaian

My art has always come from the feeling in my heart when viewing my surroundings. It began with counting nightingales and flowers on the wall as a little girl, progressed to tracing the memory of those birds and flowers onto paper and evolved into recognising the inherent geometry in nature and funneling it into more abstract expressionism. I am inspired by my country, Iran, by its history and art and architecture, and by my childhood. But I am influenced by everything I see every day and the experiences I have had in my life. It is this combination of memory, feeling and heart and what I see in front of me that provides the basis of all my artwork. And I see geometry everywhere. I see it in the symmetry of the gardens that surrounded me in Tehran and architecture in New York and the movements of a dancer. I see it in the shrines of broken mirrors and the stalls of the brightly coloured bazaar.
At the centre of this geometry, for me, is the hexagon. The mosques in Iran, with the flowers and the leaves, are based on hexagons. Islamic rugs are based on hexagons. The hexagon reflects the six directions – forward, backward, right, left, up, down – but it also reflects the six virtues of generosity, self-discipline, patience, determination, insight and compassion. It can connect everything and has the most potential for free form drawing as well as three-dimensional sculpture. Once I began experimenting with the hexagon in my geometric designs in the 1970s, it opened up a whole new relationship to the circle and related polygons. I began to see the triangle as a circle divided at three points, but also as the intelligent human being as in Islamic design. A square is a circle divided at four points, as well as the four directions North, South, East and West. The five sides of the pentagon are the five senses. All of these shapes have both the finite bounds of their definition and the infinite possibilities of meaning and interplay. For me, geometry is not an intellectual practice, it is an emotional one. I do not know the maths behind the shapes, but I know how they interact with each other and work together to create a single composition. There are endless possibilities when you see the geometry in nature and your environment.

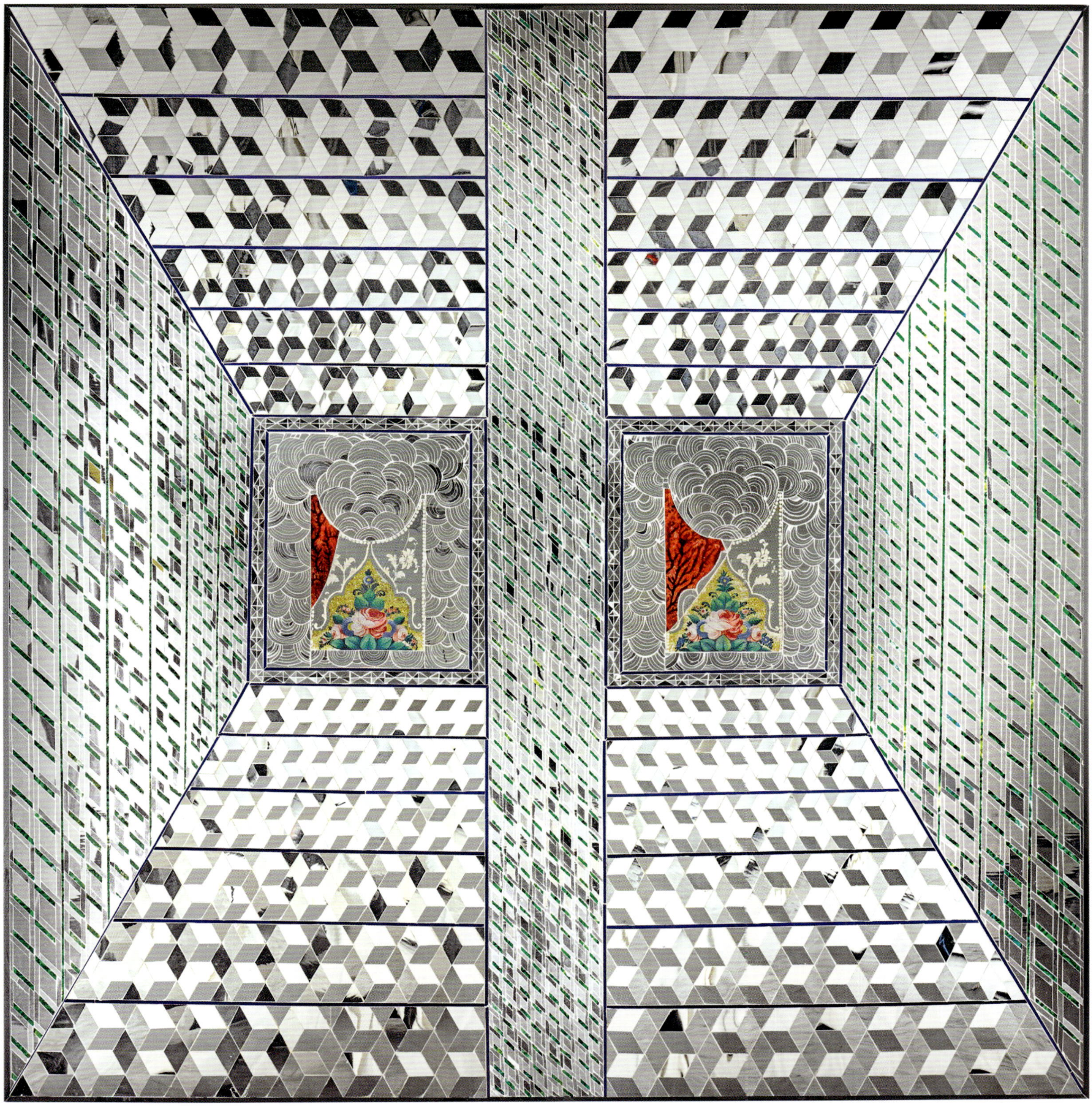

Recollections 1, 2008
Mirror mosaic, reverse-glass painting
and aluminium on plaster on board,
140 x 140 cm
Courtesy of Sotheby's

Geometry of Hope, 1975
Glass mirror work, 128 x 128 cm
Courtesy of Rose Issa

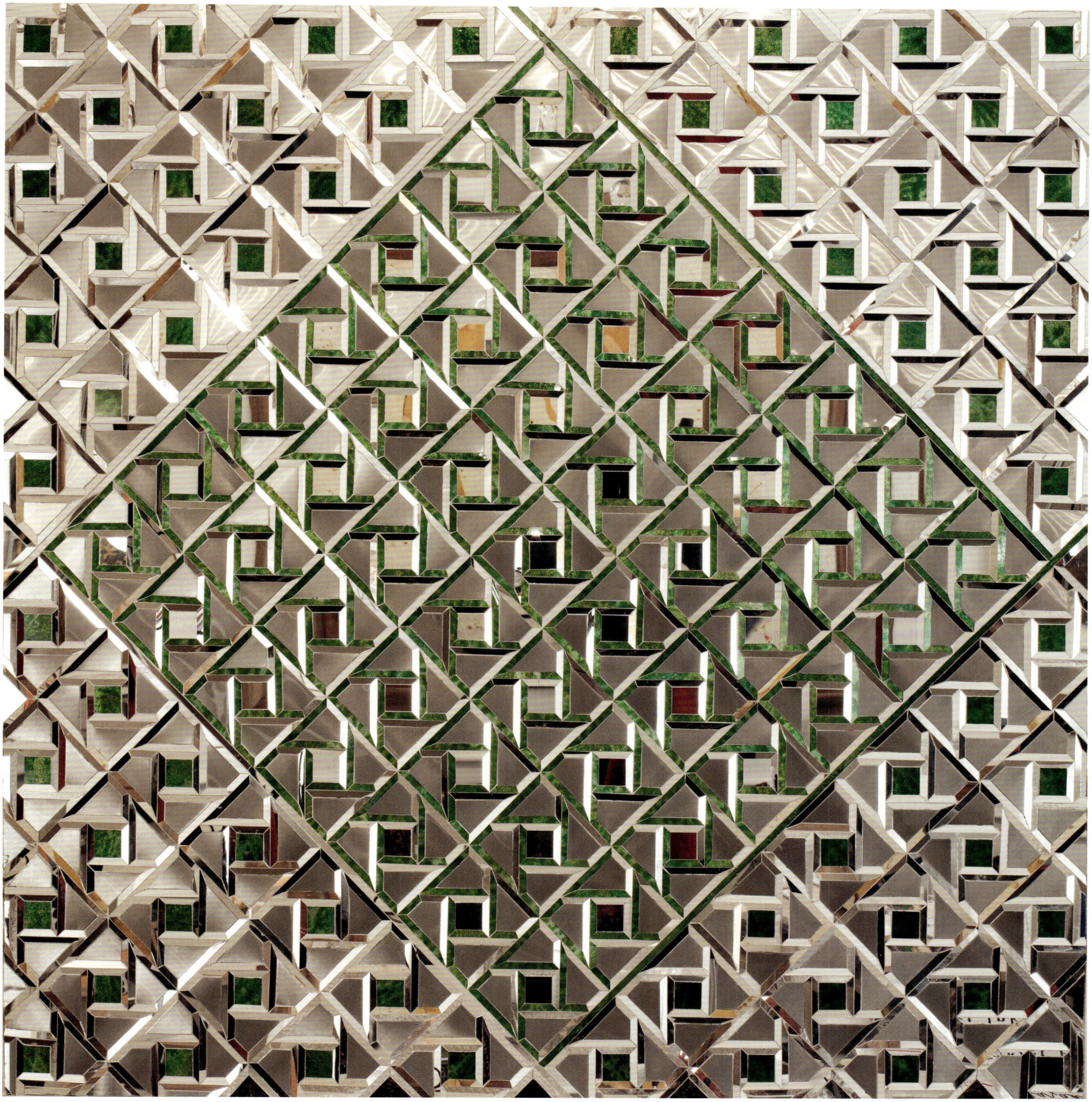

Third Family Hexagon, 2011
Reverse painted glass, mirrored glass,
and plastic, 122 x 20 x 12 cm

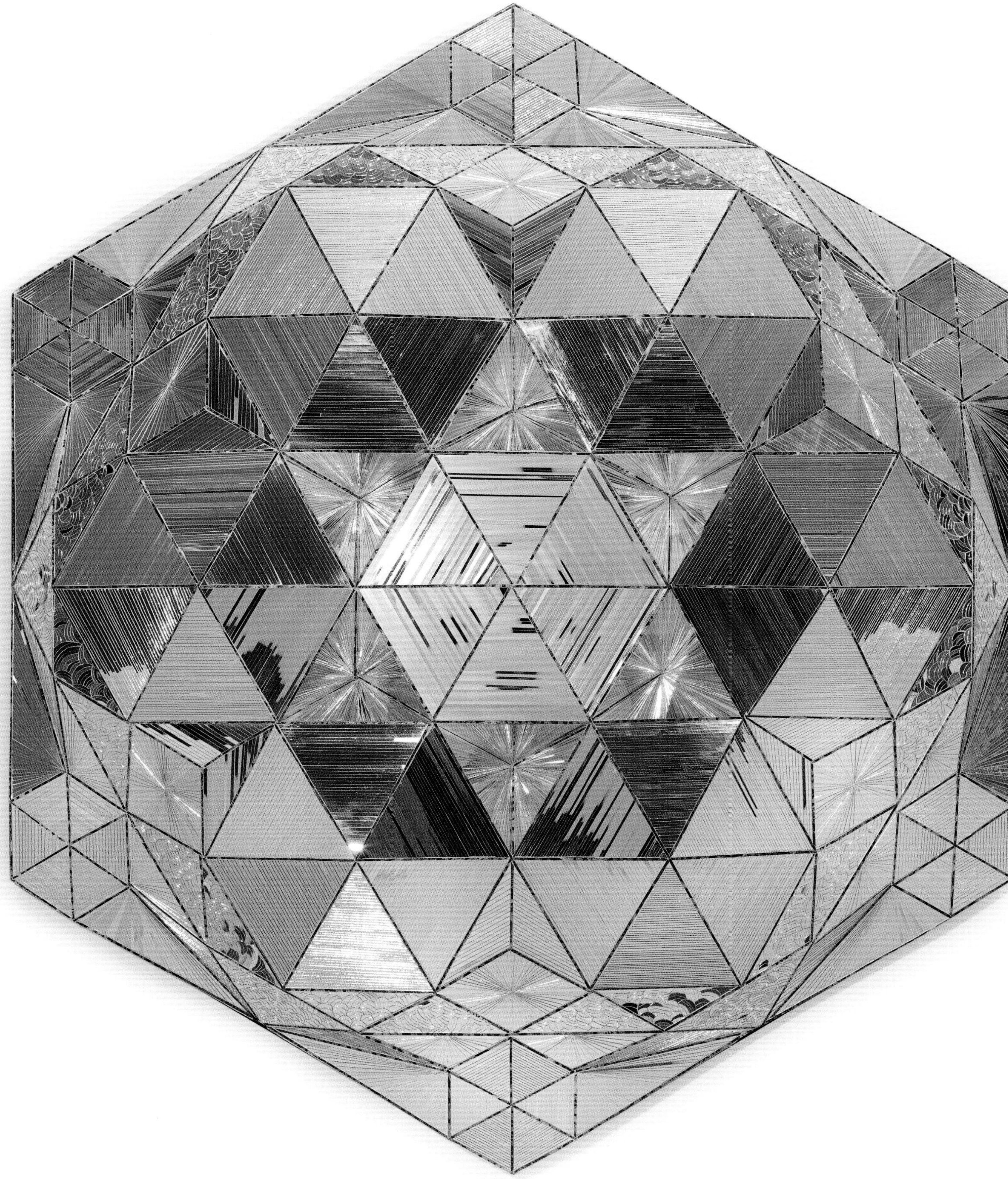

Nargess Hashemi

Futuristic geometrical urban spaces filled with soft colourful crochet interiors are the kind of utopian living spaces that I like to imagine. A square pixel, taken as a fold connected to other folds, can become a plane from which infinity as a whole could be unfolded. Holistic thoughts on how to build a more sustainable and functional future are wrapped in crocheted pieces and folded back into squares, diamonds, triangles and domes in geometric urban plans. They invite us to unfold them into a connected plane of imagination that shows us how we could live in a more integral, sustainable, community-oriented society.

In my practice, both the urban plans and the interiors contain something feminine; a universe that embraces and cares for us and yet has been kept marginal. As an artist, I have sought the courage to design a utopian version of our cities which currently tend to exclude our viewpoint and needs in the way they are designed. Alongside that, and much inspired by Beatriz Colomina's "women as the ghosts of architecture", documenting the marginalised role of female architects, I have divided the interior of these utopian homes by crochet curtains and walls that play with the idea of visibility and invisibility. Yet the idea of marginality encompasses much more and becomes the central point in understanding how, by mere design, we could make everyone an integral part of an equal society.

One of the main features of equitable spaces is their inclination towards a greener, more sustainable lifestyle: this means cities connected with cul-de-sacs that can reduce car pollution, powered by solar and renewable energies, filled with various green spaces and designed with a diversity of re-usable water features.

I also imagine services that merge culture and education into one interconnected experience, provide medical services and high tech transportation and other services unique to the needs of the community they are built for.

In the interplay of postmodern architecture and society, the convenience that has come with the architecture also comes with a soullessness and marginalisation of large groups of people, mostly due to being imported and not designed around people's needs. On the other hand, in the more marginal communities the less 'clean' outlook could lead to a less welcoming environment for others.

The idea here is to find a combination that can bring these two elements together, namely cities that are designed with architectural convenience around the needs of the communities they are built for.

In my maps every square represents an individual unit, if you enter any of these units, you will find an open space sectioned by large crochet pieces that allow you to have privacy without being fully separated from others, by pieces that hang like curtains from the ceiling, spread out of walls or rising from the floor. Delicate partitions separate two spaces without fully concealing them from one another. Crochet pieces are made from every day materials by a community of women.

More recently I have shifted from figurative to geometric paintings, yet elements of my work have stayed intriguingly similar. The everyday objects, such as the plastic table covers that were used as recycled textured layers in my work, have become the plastic water bottles I use as mould and filler in my crochet work. So although the style of work may have changed, my concerns remain very similar.

I want to boldly show the bigger picture of societies in which we could all live in a more respectful relationship with one another and with our planet.

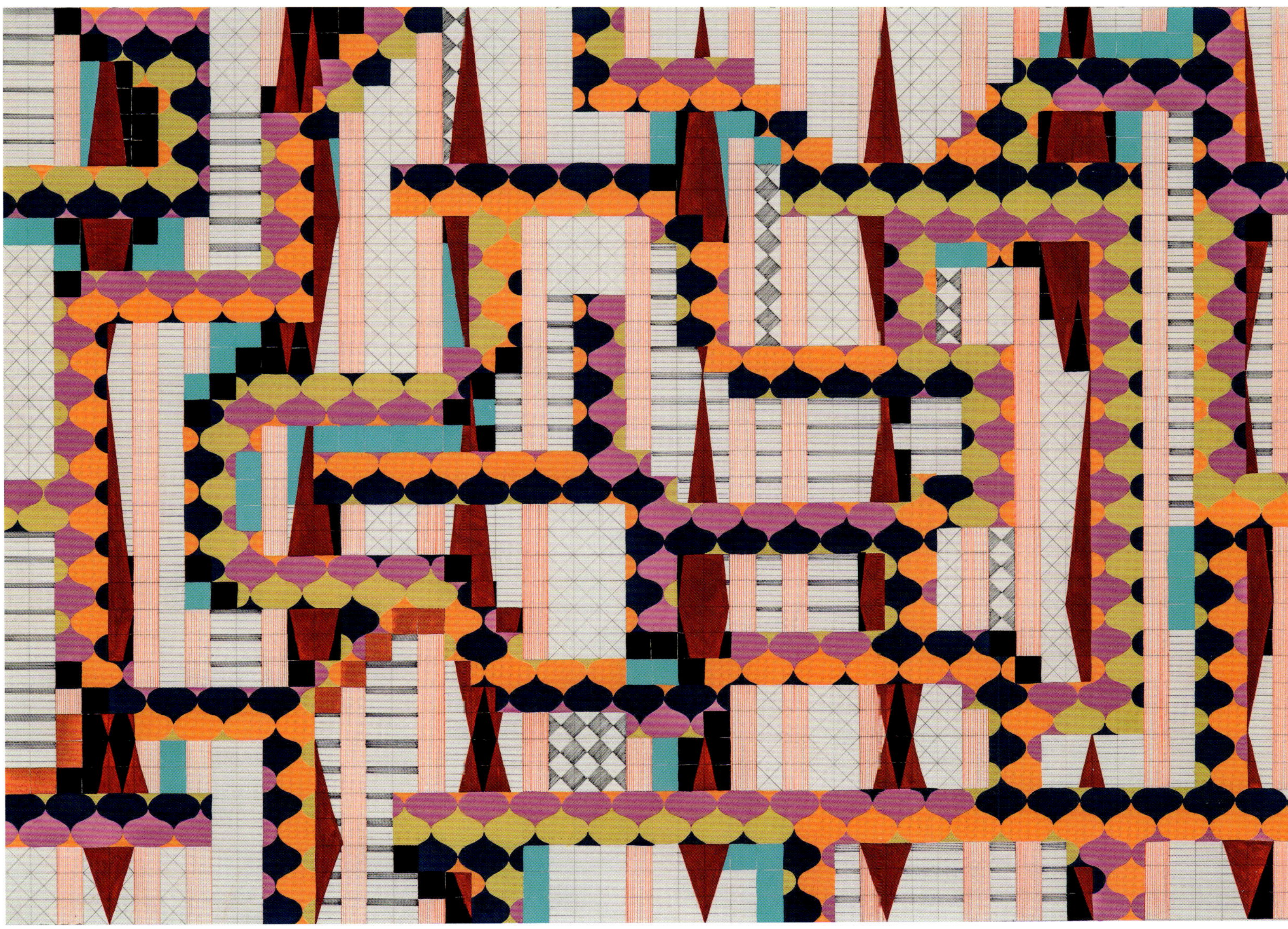

Satellite view from 500 m - complex for rehabilitation of immigrants, 2017
Pencil and gouache on cotton paper,
70 x 100 cm

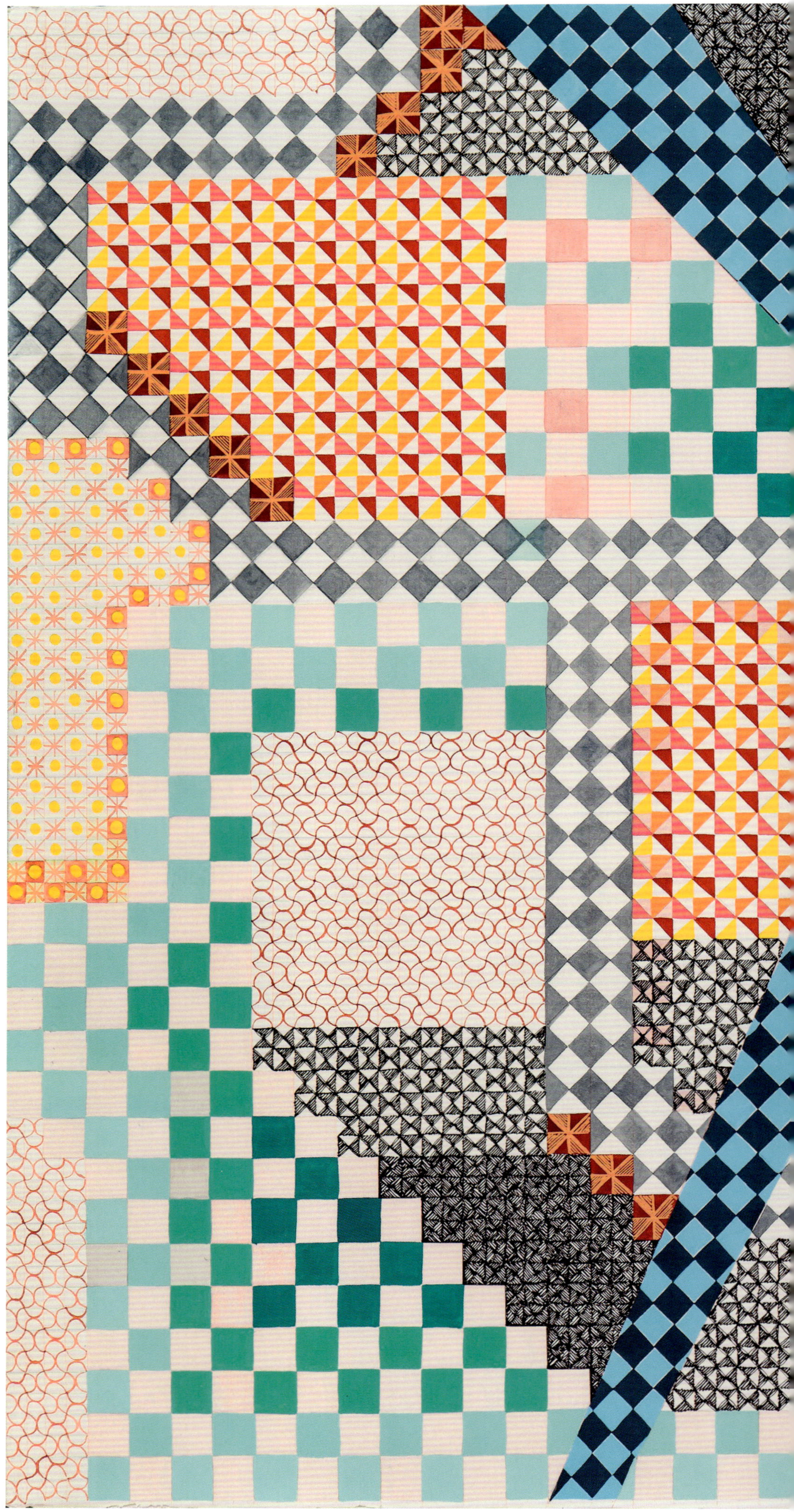

Satellite view from 500 m - cultural city for the less privileged, 2018
Pen, pencil and gouache on cotton paper, 70 x 100 cm

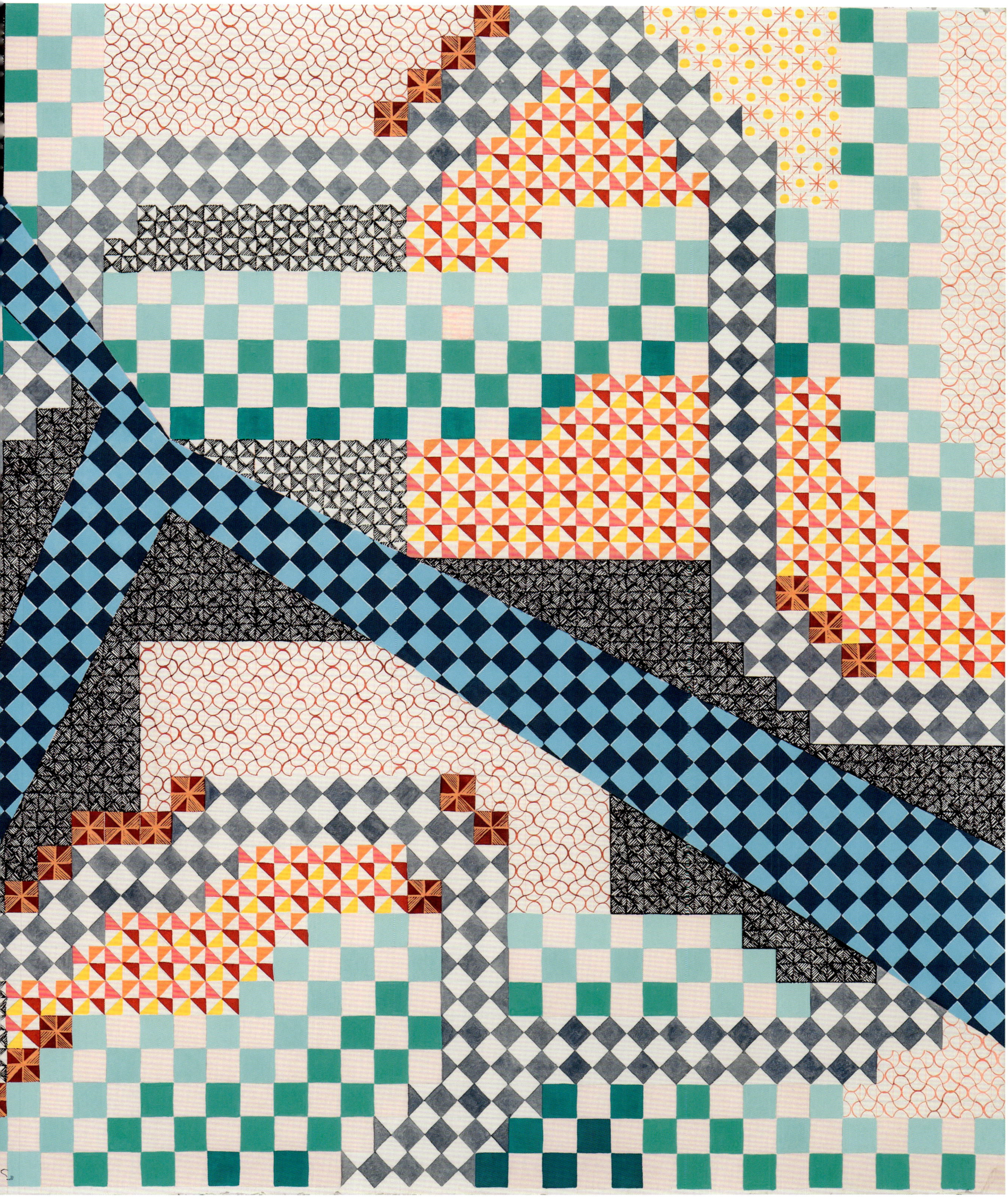

Satellite view from 500 m - housing complex for people and the research of handicraft, 2017
Pen, pencil, gouache on cotton paper, 100 x 70 cm

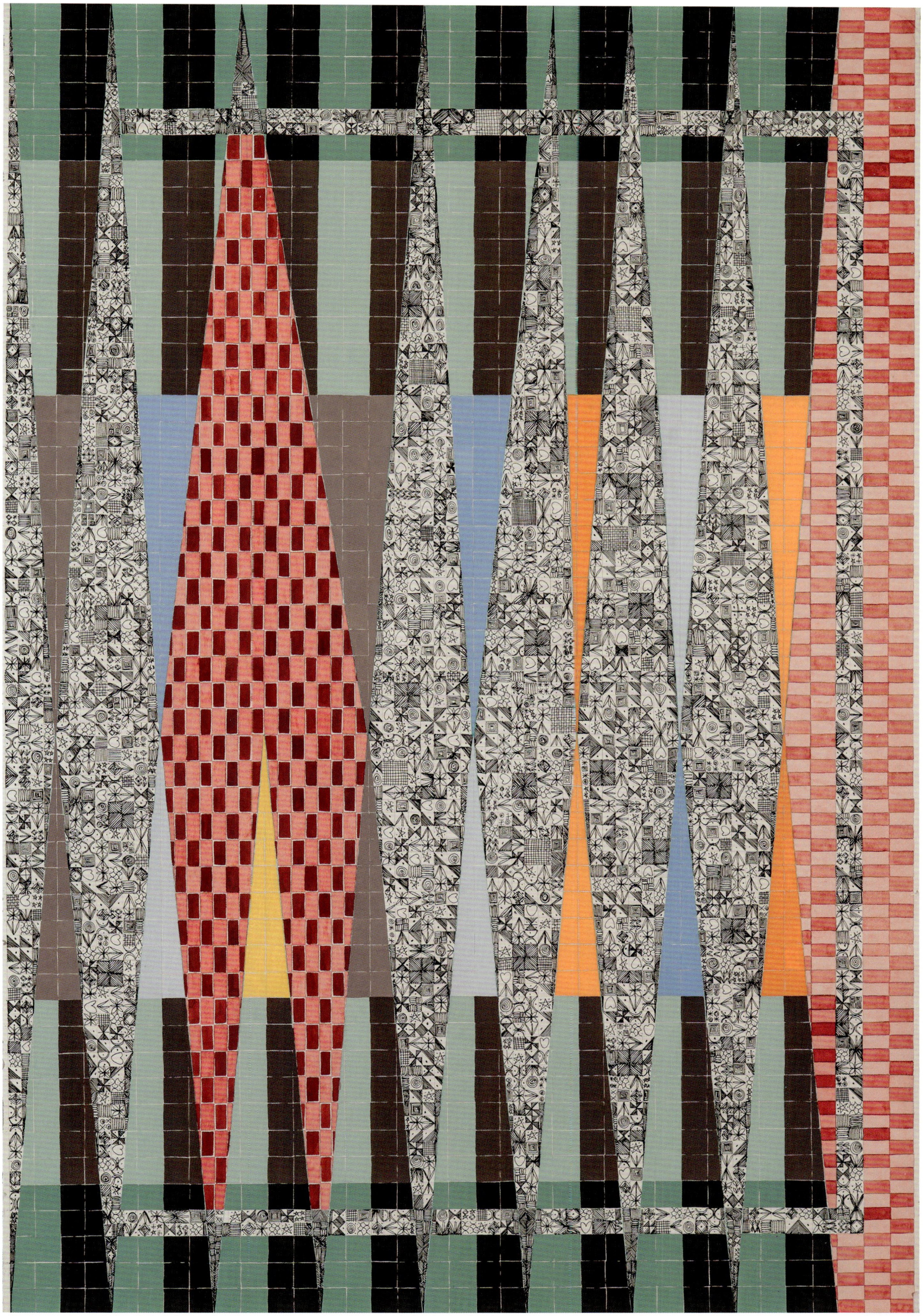

Susan Hefuna

There is no straight line in any of my works. As in nature each leaf of a tree is unique, each flower exists only once, our bodies and each cell are unique.
Structure is an important leitmotif in my work. I am connecting dots and lines using different media like drawing, installation, performance, photography, sculpture, and film to communicate with the world.
A cornerstone of my practice are multi-layered, sometimes geometric drawings with ink on tracing paper since 1992. These works on paper are documenting my walks through cities and observing spaces. Intersections of location and identity become visible in my *Buildings and Cityscapes* drawing series. The time of 'active doing nothing' and observing places for years before I actually start to draw or to shoot a Crossroads film is my essential working method. My intuition is guiding me where and when to document intersections all over the world since 2002 from windows or roofs, unveiling the order lying behind the appearance of the people crossing these specific spots.
My films are documenting a point in time and space, relevant both personally for myself and in general.
In an interview for *Flash Art* in 2010 I have said, "Show me what you draw and I tell you who you are. My drawings have no nationality, no gender. When I draw there is no time and space. It is its own universe."

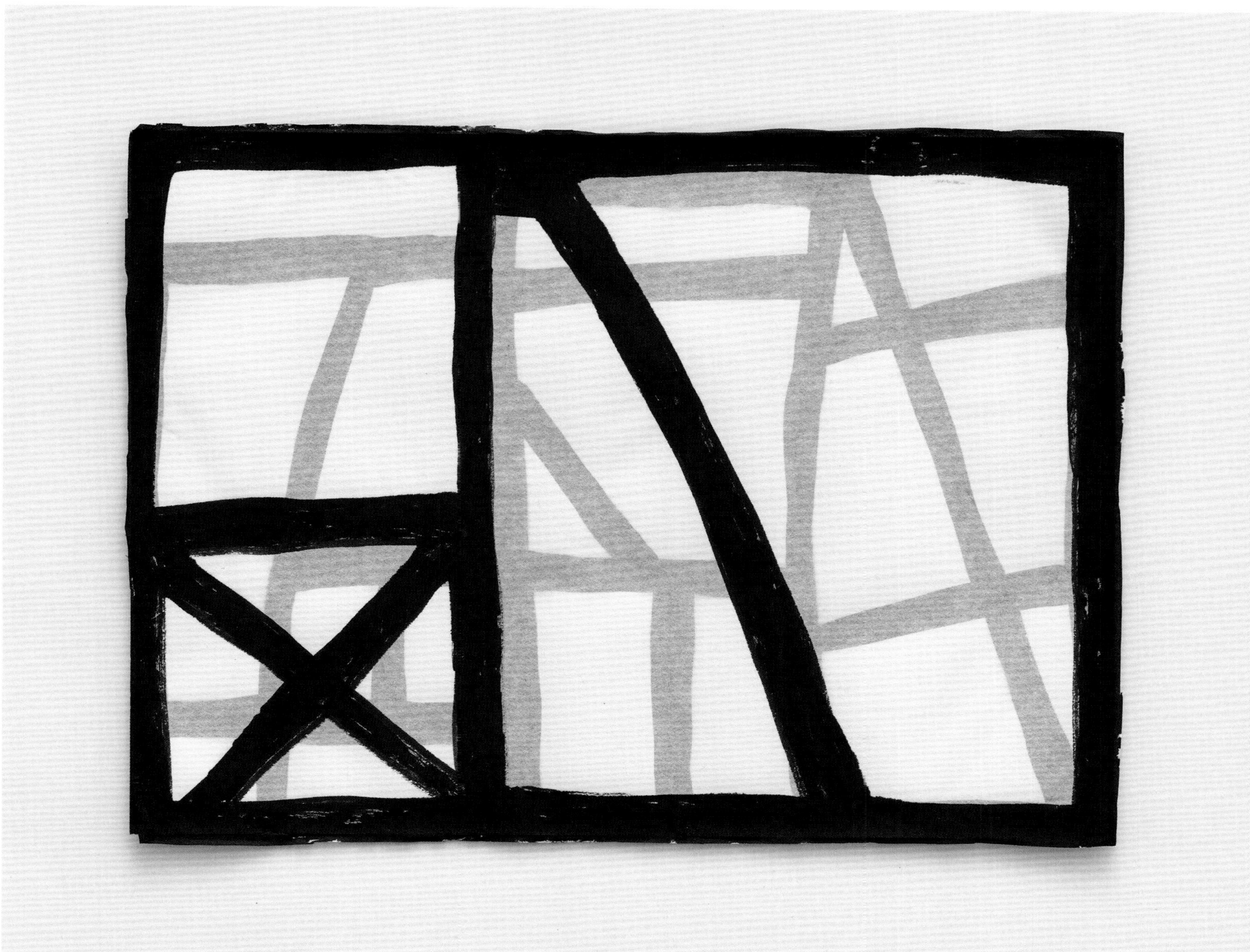

Cityscape Stein, 2018
Ink on rice paper, 29.7 × 42 cm

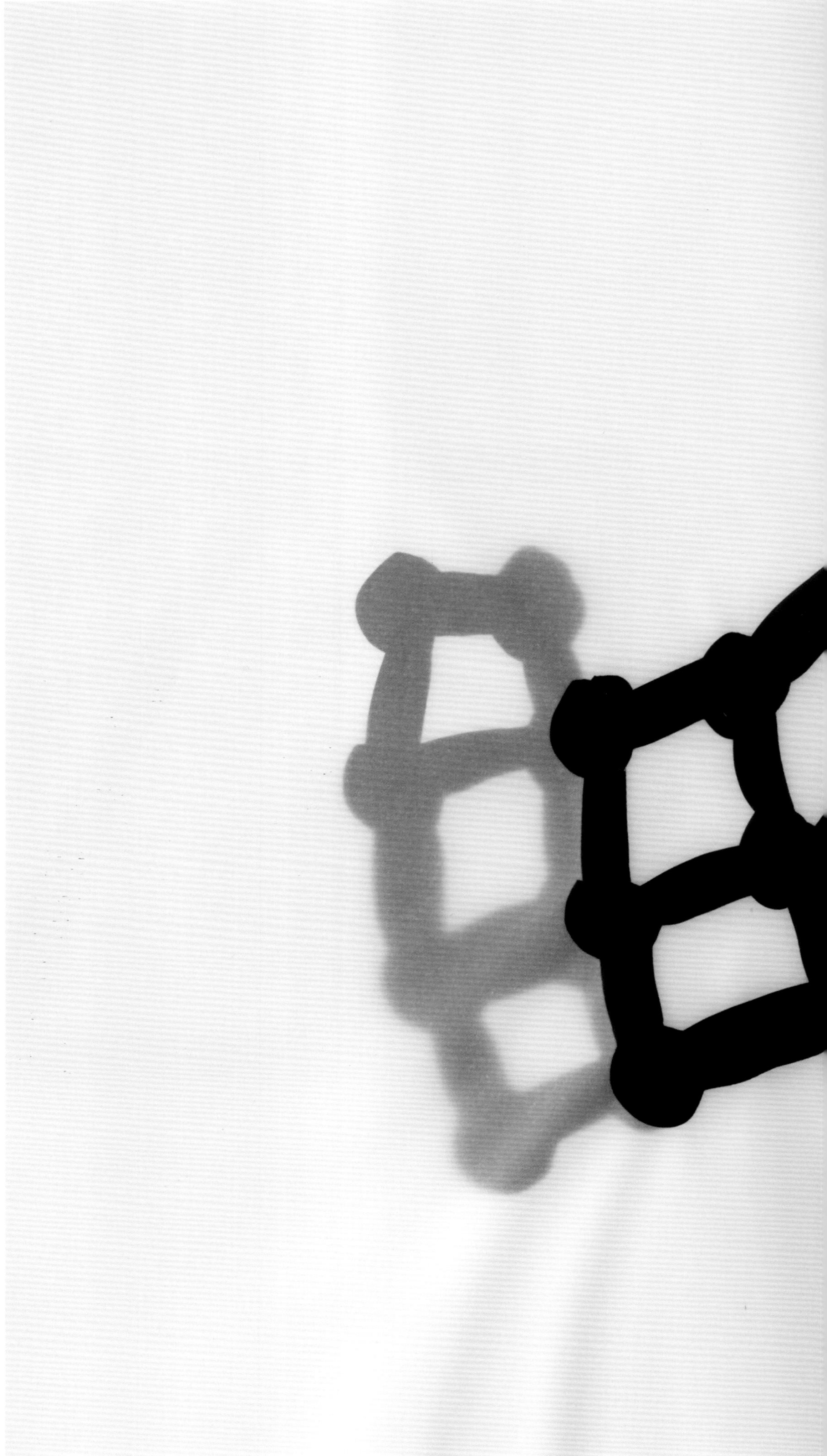

Intersection, 2017
Ink on tracing paper,
36 × 43 cm

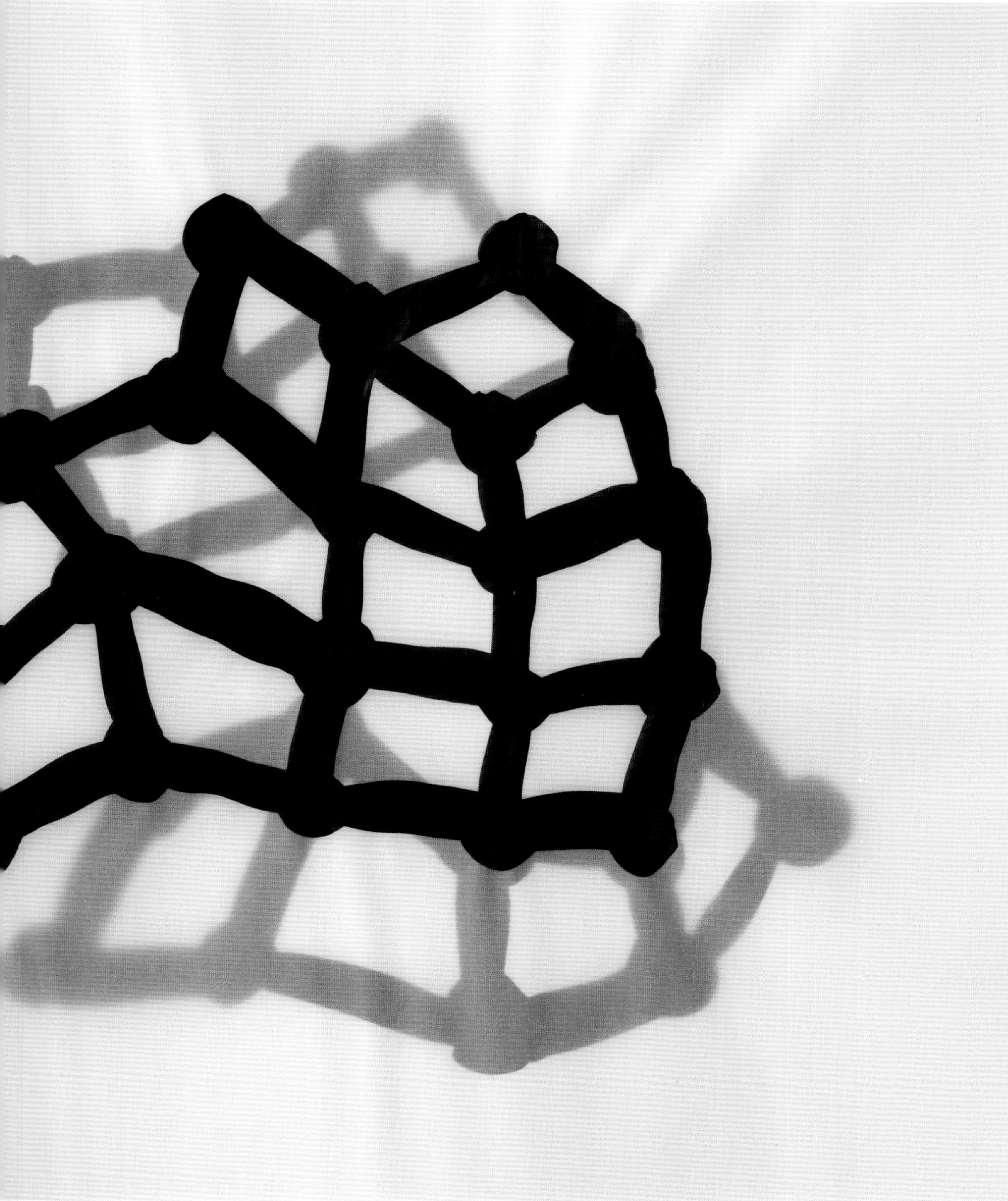

Gebilde, 2016
Casted aluminium,
72 × 148 × 32 cm
Unique

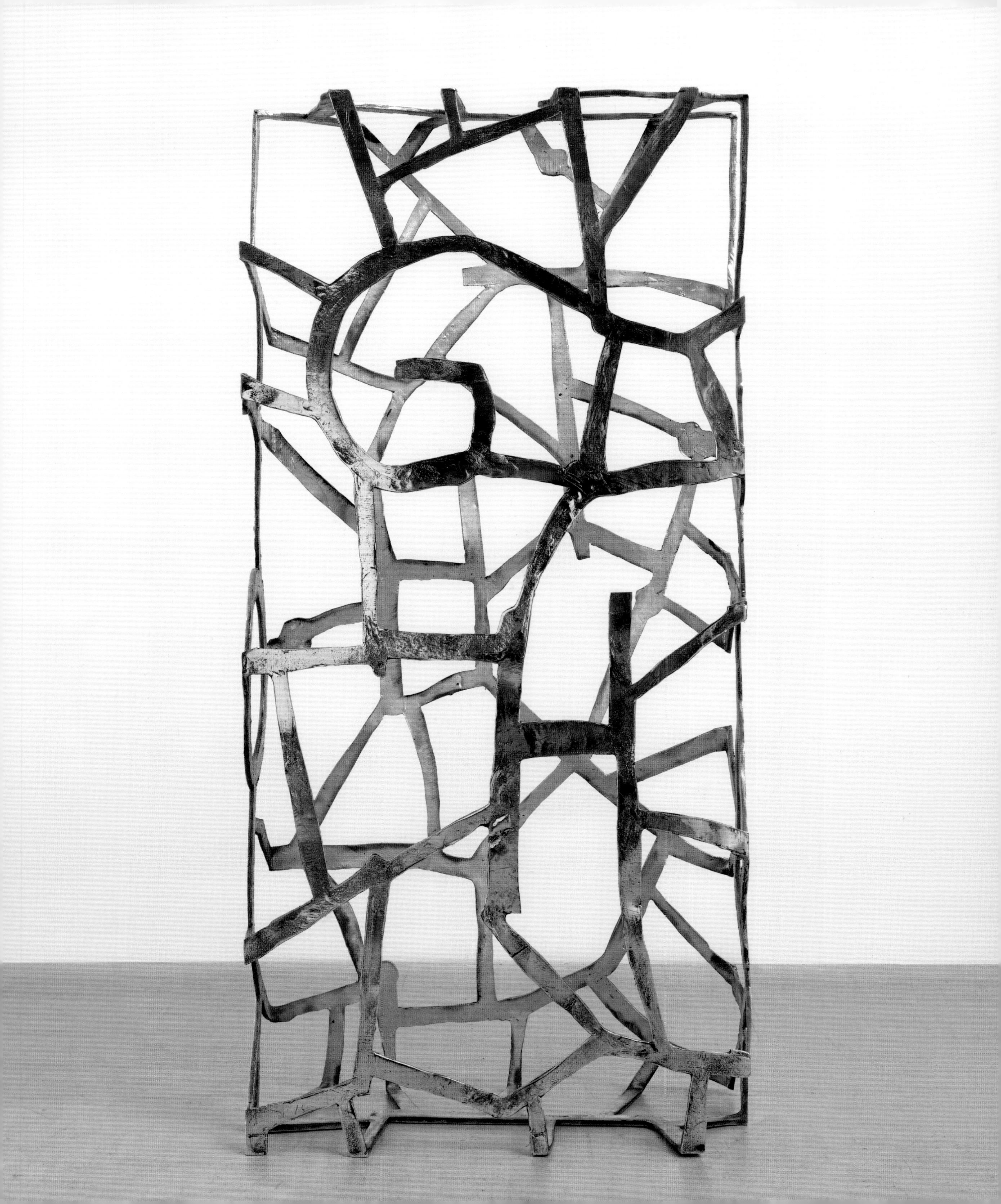

Sahand Hessamiyan

Geometry and art: shaping visual cultures of the Islamic world

My approach to geometry moves fluidly between its structural beauty and the spiritual complexity it embodies. It forms the structure of the universe, from the position of the planetary bodies to the intricate forms found in organic matter in nature. Mankind's homage to its surrounding has been to emulate it – in construction, weaving, or even sacred patterns drawn on the ground. I have always been drawn to the power of this form, especially to the way it reflects in architecture, hence many of my works have involved taking apart the structures of buildings and studying the fundamental building blocks.

My inspiration primarily comes from the complex, almost labyrinthine elements that are synonymous with traditional Iranian structures. My research has led me to study both the private quarters inside residential structures – which are spaces of sanctum – and the understanding of how the honey-combed *muqarnas* are designed and constructed inside the corners and domes of religious buildings. Questions of ornamentation and their symbolism drive me to understand how we merge the sacred and the profane to find balance and harmony – both driving forces that stabilise chaos.

My introduction to this came early, at the time when I was a student of sculpture at Tehran University (2000–2007) and began looking at architecture closely for one of my projects. This was a transformative experience, as I grasped the many aspects contained in this discipline and the countless possibilities of creation it offers. From then on, I focussed most of my studies and works on elements drawn from architecture, at the core of which geometry lies. My experiments over almost two decades have led me to delve deeper at a conceptual level, and to understand the formal load-bearing structures that support such creations. These were endeavors into a more minimal, perhaps even transcendental understanding of the material. It is majestic how metal, concrete, and plaster are able to create spaces of silence, tranquillity and reverence. And like the unmappable nature of the universe, and the infinite possibilities within geometry itself, each work I make channels further questions and potentials.

My work is an expression of my wonder and the sheer joy of what I am able to create with my own hands. I work across varied scales – what usually starts as drawings on paper or maquettes in construction paper, usually ends up with a life of its own; the resulting sculptures becoming separate entities: evolved, different, but always tied to the same narrative. No matter what the end result is, or how complex the final sculptures turns out to be, to me it remains preliminary experiments in learning the secrets of geometry and the universe we live in.

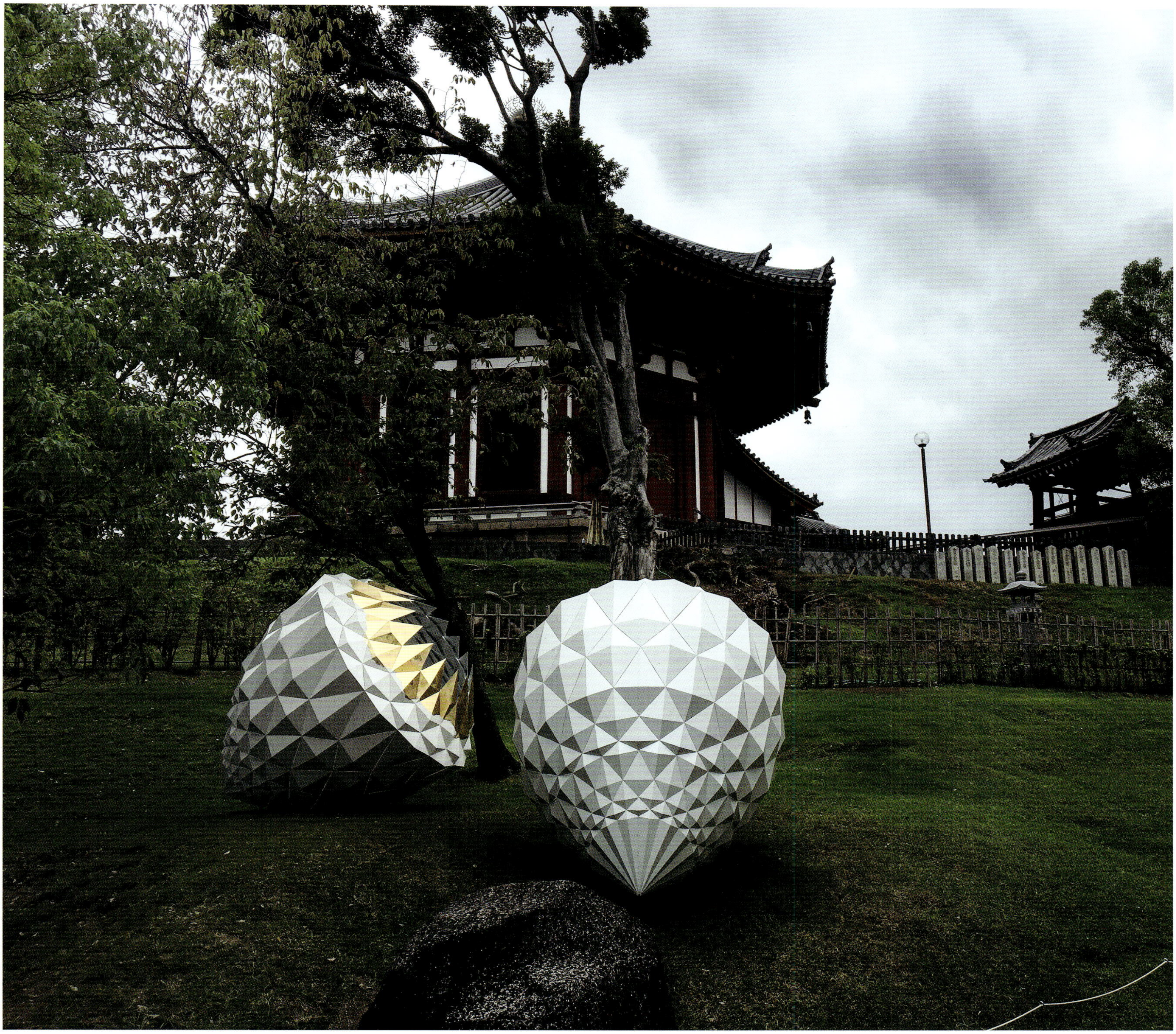

Forough, 2016
Stainless steel, gold leaf, electrostatic
paint, 256 x 256 x 300 cm each

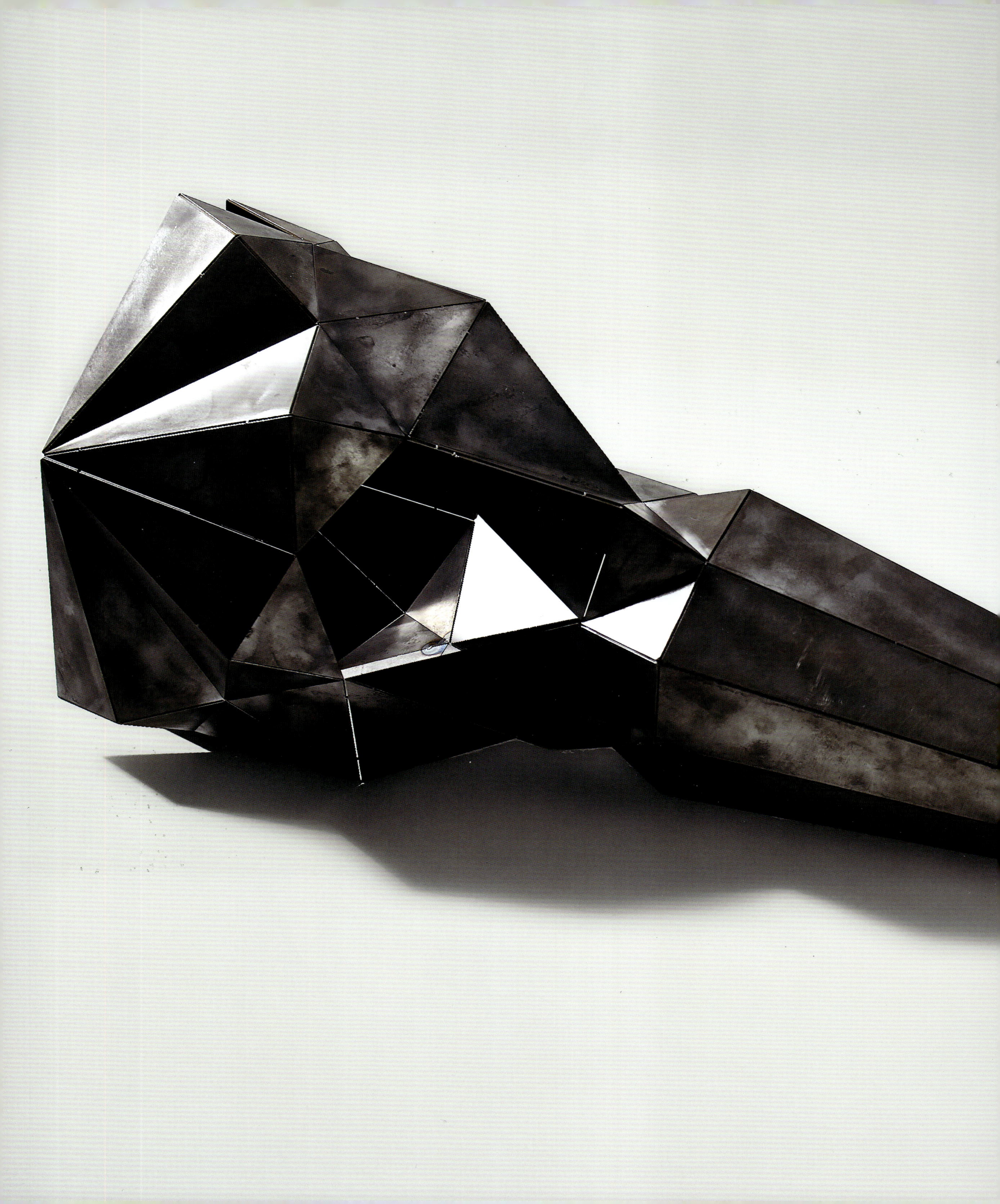

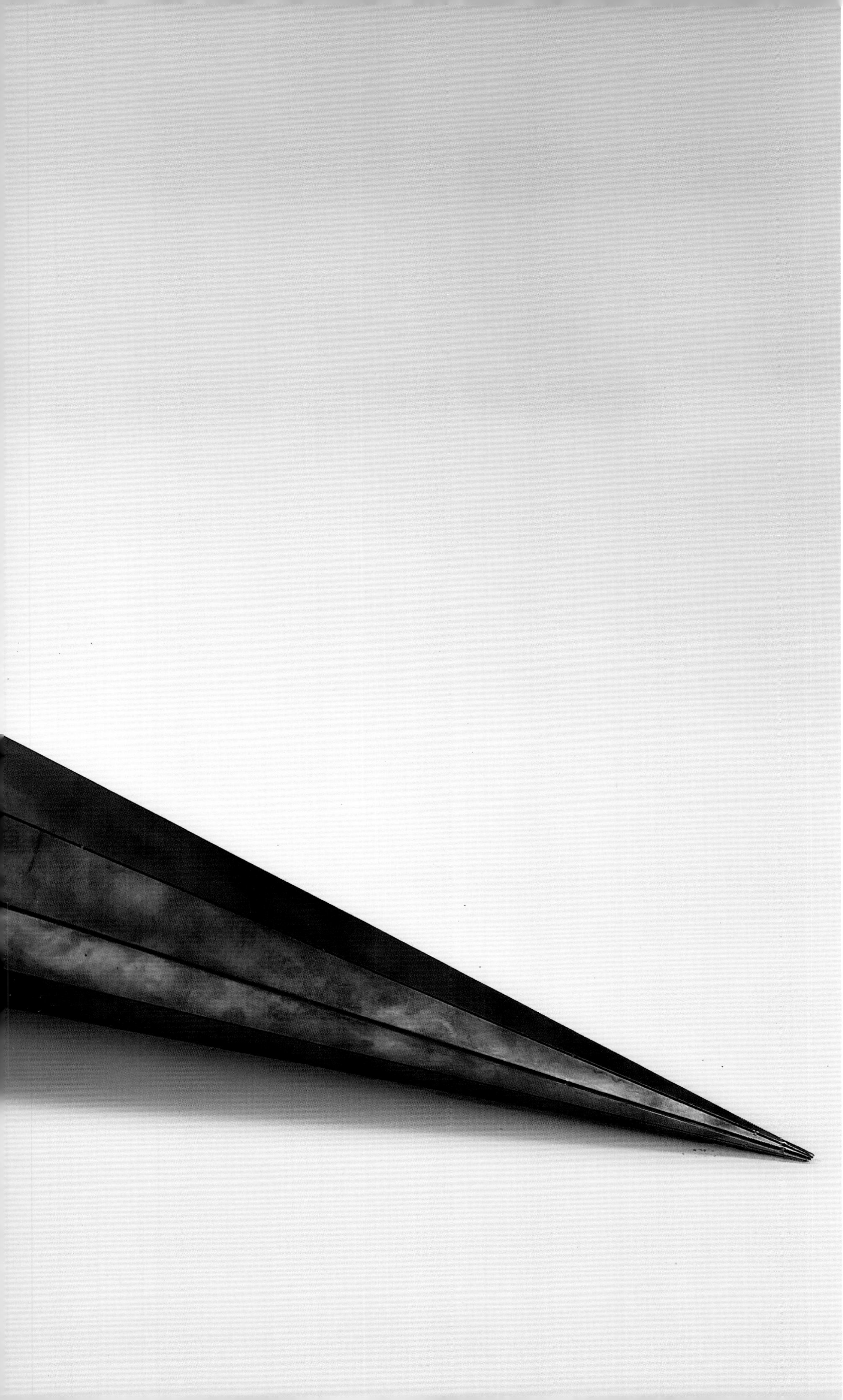

Nail, 2012
Steel, 115 x 40 x 26 cm
Edition 1/3

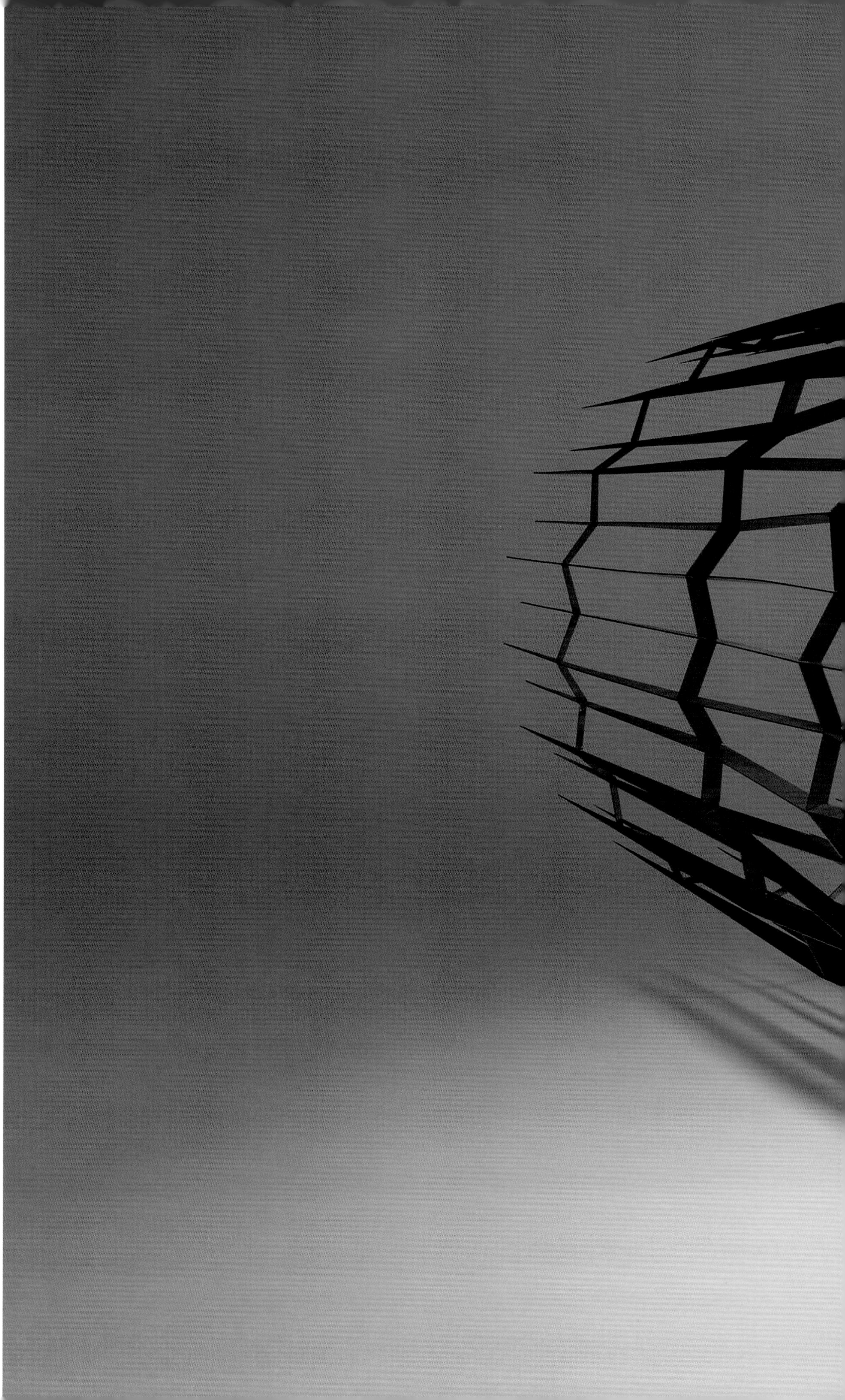

Khalvat (prototype), 2014
Stainless steel, 100 x 60 x 60 cm

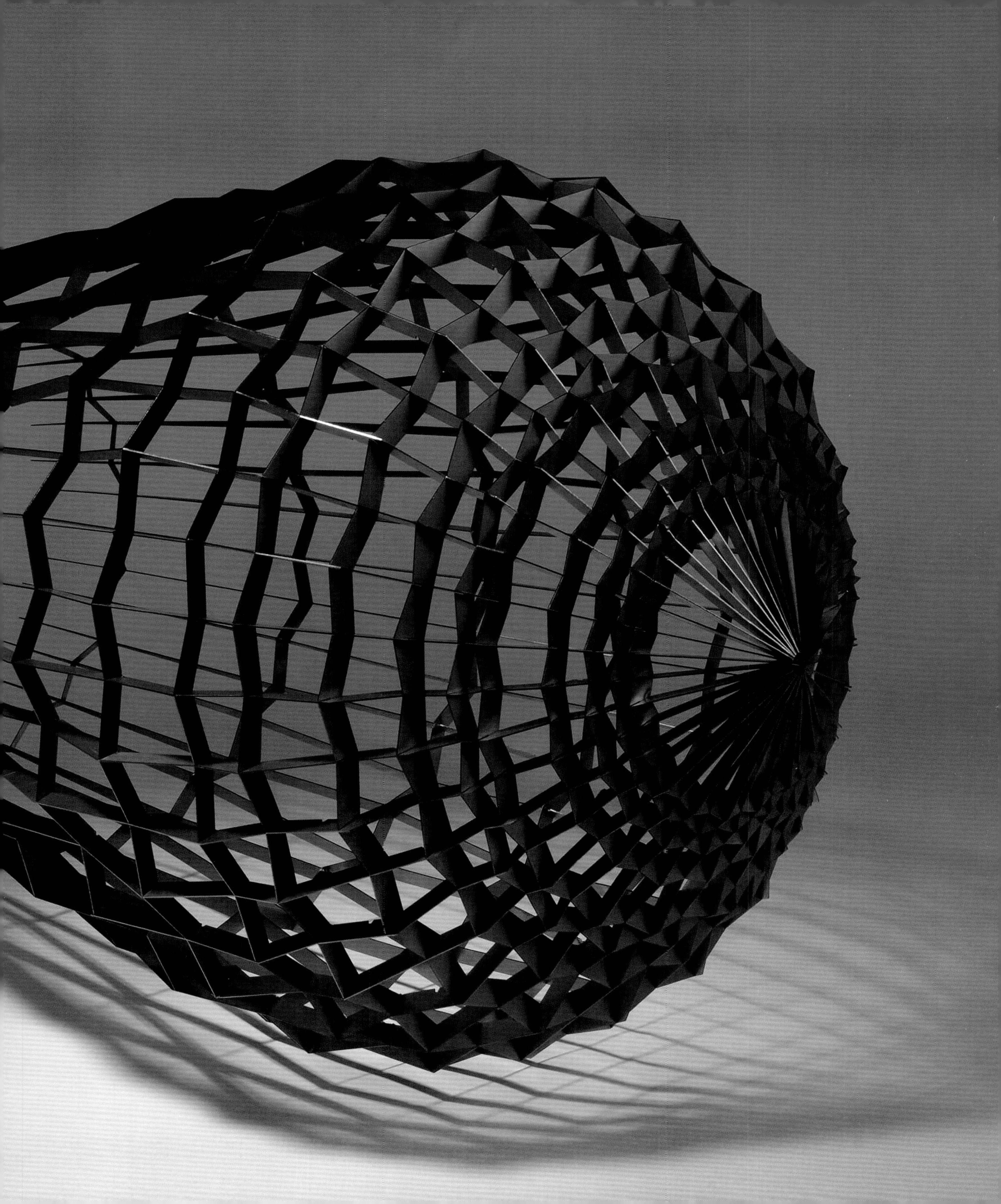

Mohamed Abdul Latif Kanoo

As an artist with a profound interest in simplifying forms to their most essential basis, in stylisation and communication of the essence, I have long held a fascination for Islamic pattern. Wishing to address the core concept of faith – namely the deity and His manifestation in the human mind, I decided to devote one of the most significant aspects of my current art production to an installation that references the 99 names of Allah. In my other works I similarly reduce shape and form to their most essential, thereby arriving at their basic core. In this particular installation I have made it the height of my exploration whereby geometry becomes part of an important, yet transformative, element of the narrative.
Here, I have used a robust wooden frame with an embroidered *shemagh* fabric bonded to it, painted in an individual colour thus combining both colour and texture. Each single unit or component of the 99 names, measures 1 m x 1 m and is 7 cm deep – mathematically symbolic and significant numbers in themselves.
The *shemagh* fabric itself is iconic of the region in that it is an instantly recognisable personal item of headdress that identifies its (mostly male) wearer as being from the Middle East, in particular from the Gulf Region (including Iraq and Jordan).
Upon experiencing the magnitude and scale of the installation and its random mosaic of colour (not unlike Richter's windows in the Cologne Cathedral), there is a further yet gentle visual attraction to the weave pattern that entices the viewer to approach the installation more closely, and which ultimately reveals the embedded embroidered pattern. This perspective of alternating between nearness and distance is revelatory in any work involving pattern. The installation itself intends to intrigue the visitor to question why the number 99, and to enquire about the embedded weave pattern as part of the overall design.
To date, the installation has been presented in a circular three-dimensional form, 13 m in diameter, 3 m high, and yet the individual 99 components could be further transformed to be presented in other configurations. For example, another option is a three-dimensional set up of a square box comprising of 4 sides, each 5 m high and 5 m wide, with one slot left deliberately empty to represent the Oneness and perfection of Allah which must never be duplicated in human craft.
A multitude of geometric forms could in this way be achieved, offering both the discovery and infinite possibilities of geometric play.
The mathematical and symbolic value of geometrically oriented work is limitless.
While the Islamic faith has, for centuries, offered sublime expressions of what can be accomplished, my own practice revolves on the modern, current and contemporary interpretations, often with an ironic twist or some different perspective, which injects a conceptual or thought-provoking dimension.
My work aspires, and is dedicated, to the genius of geometric simplicity.

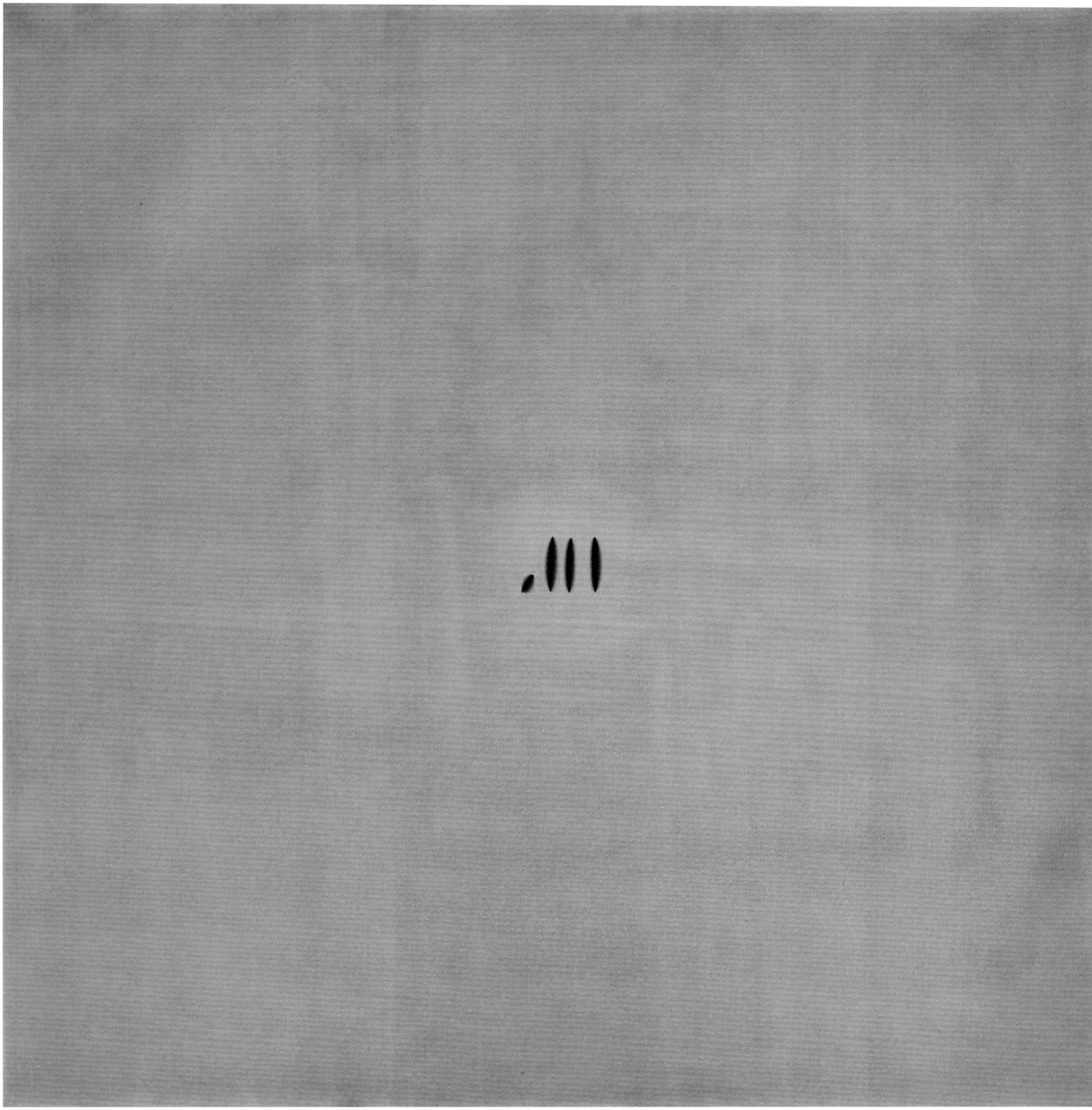

Allah, 2009
Acrylic on canvas, 130 x 130 cm

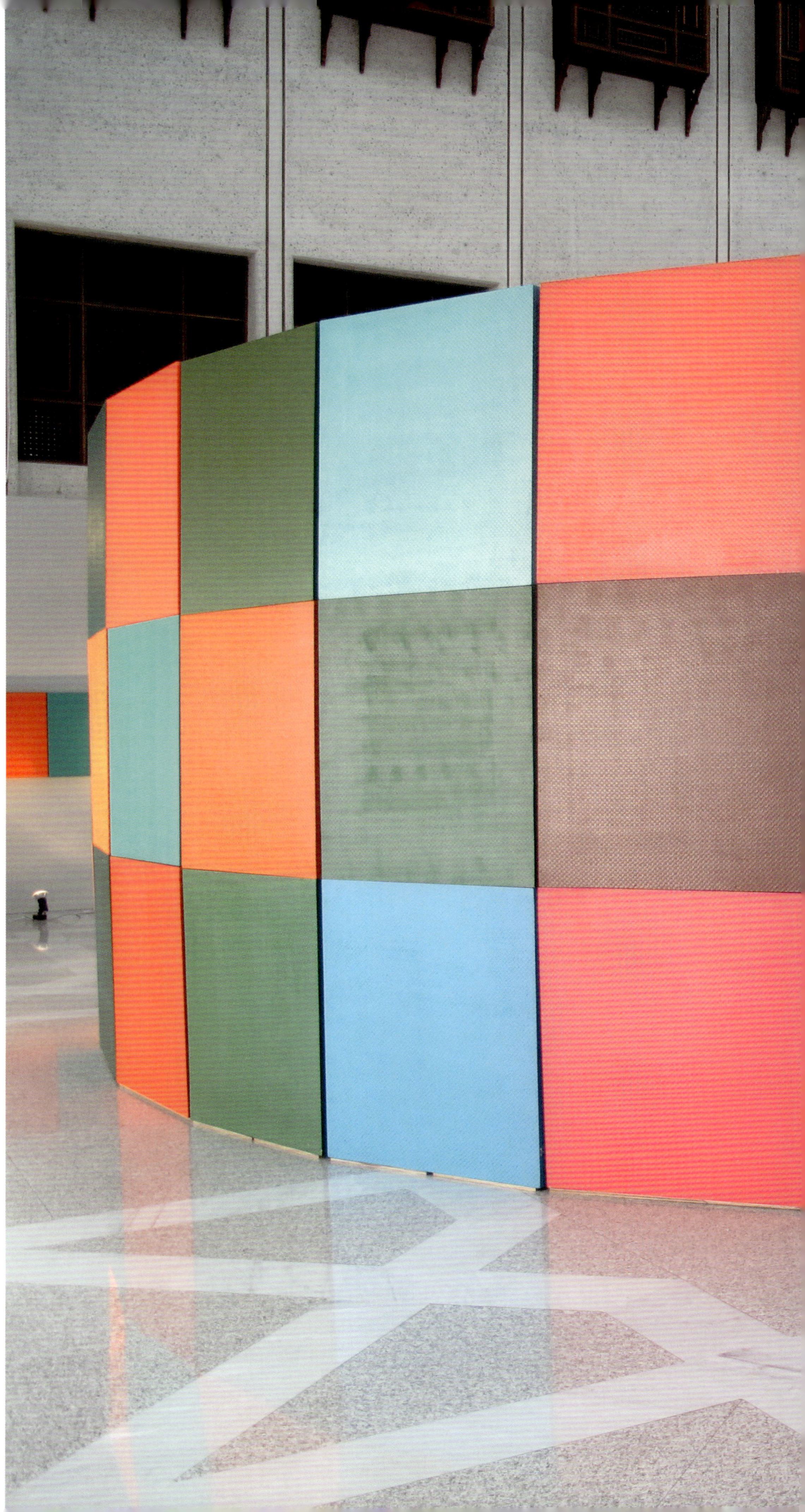

"99"- formed of 99 "Shemaghart",
2009
Untitled pieces in mixed media,
100 x 100 x 7 cm

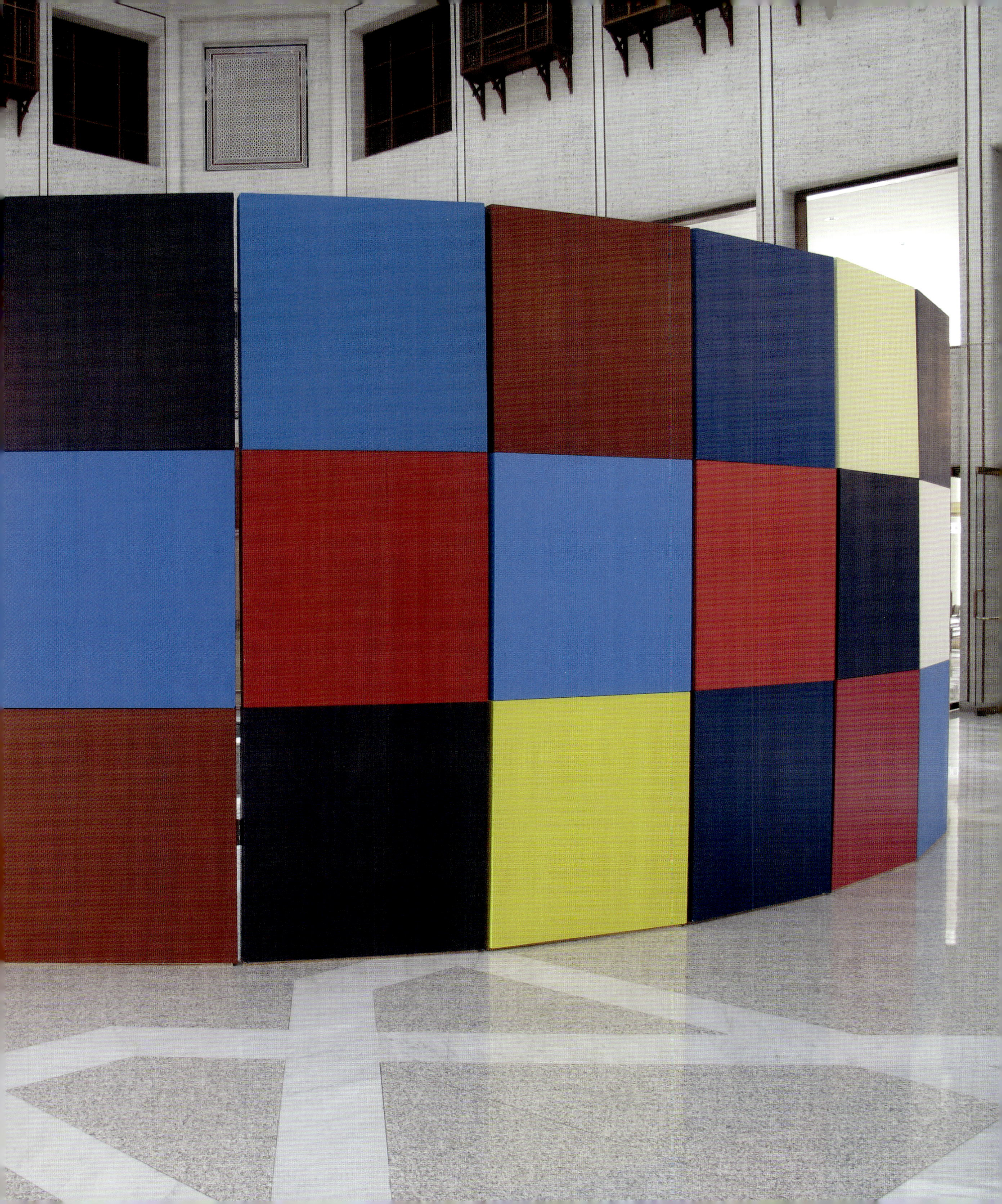

Ahmed Mater

I started out as a physician but turned to the arts as a young man. My main aim has been to scrutinise the realities of contemporary Saudi Arabia. Forging an ongoing, complex mapping of the Kingdom, my practice has synthesised and documented collective memories to uncover and record unofficial histories. My work is often research-led and mostly conceptual, but in more recent times I have also been keen to explore the geometry at the heart of universal laws. Growing up in Abha, a city in the fertile mountainous region close to the border with Yemen, my early years were geographically remote from the Kingdom's capital. The perspective granted by this physical distance exposed me to the modernising world beyond the border. I witnessed the most seismic period in Saudi history – namely, the Kingdom's oil boom cycle. Growing up, I witnessed the intense conclusion to a decade of momentous economic and political upheaval. I feel myself placed at the intersections of the past, present and future, tradition and innovation, heritage and globalisation; even religion, faith, economic power and modernisation. Using photography, film, sculpture and performance, my practice maps, documents and analyses of these changes, considering the psychological impact on the individual, the community, society and the world. *Desert of Pharan* (2011–2016) is a five-year photographic encounter with Mecca, its inhabitants and histories. *100 Found Objects* (2014) is a reverent collation of displaced artefacts and a significant contribution to 'thing theory', where reaped materials manifest a panoply of neglected stories.

I embrace the paradoxes of science and faith, enmeshing the two to explore their connections and contradictions. Like a general medical practitioner, I use broad investigative techniques to assess the condition of my environment, and diagnose its unofficial socio-political histories and realities. My scientific training has also inspired me to increasingly delve into the grid system of geometry and its effect on the visual arts. In *Magnetism* (2009) iron filings whorl and whirl around a black magnet, evoking the congregation of pilgrims that throng the Ka'aba, making manifest the immutable pull of Islam's holiest site.

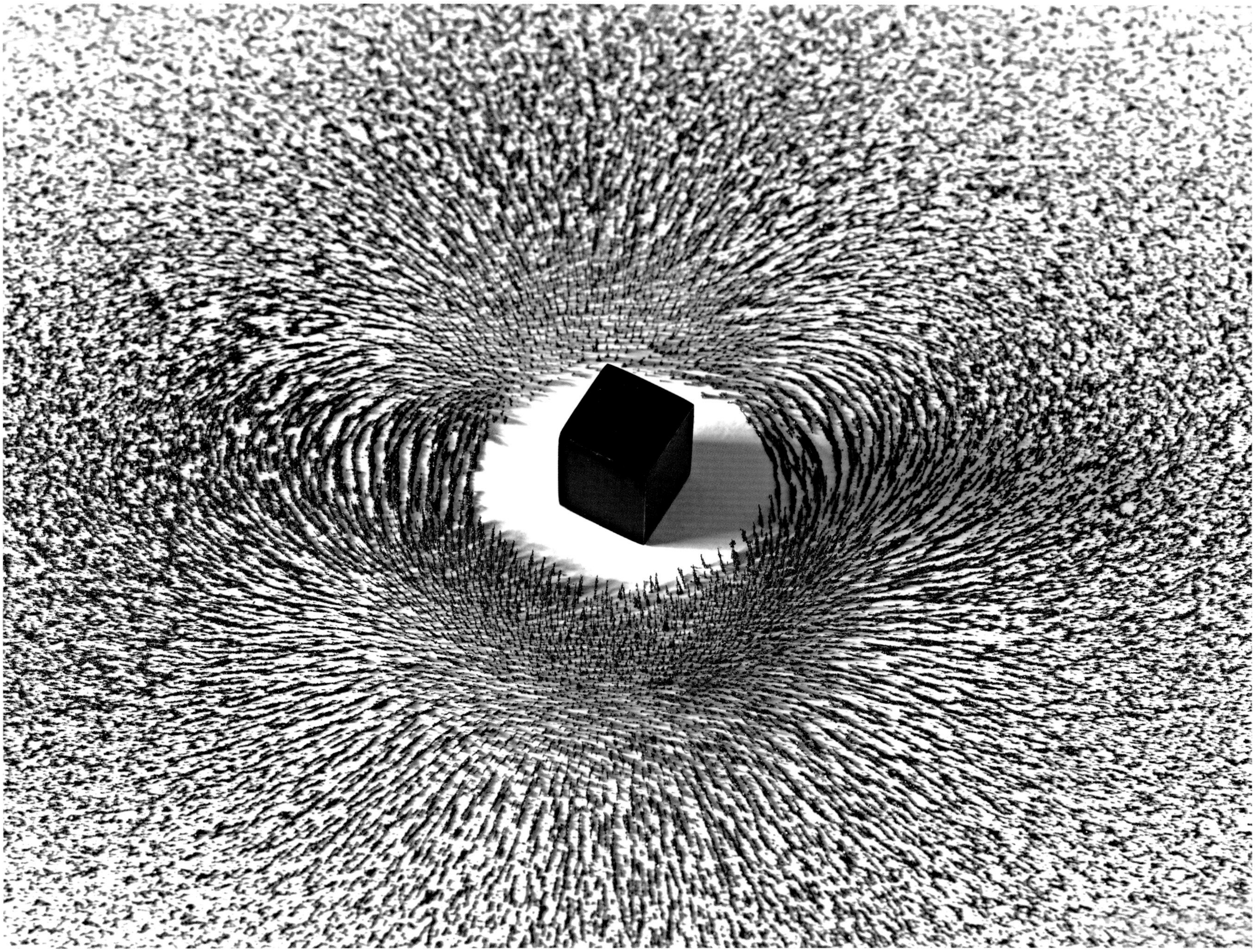

Magnetism IV, 2012
Diasec mounted lightjet print on Kodak
Premier paper, 180 x 240 cm

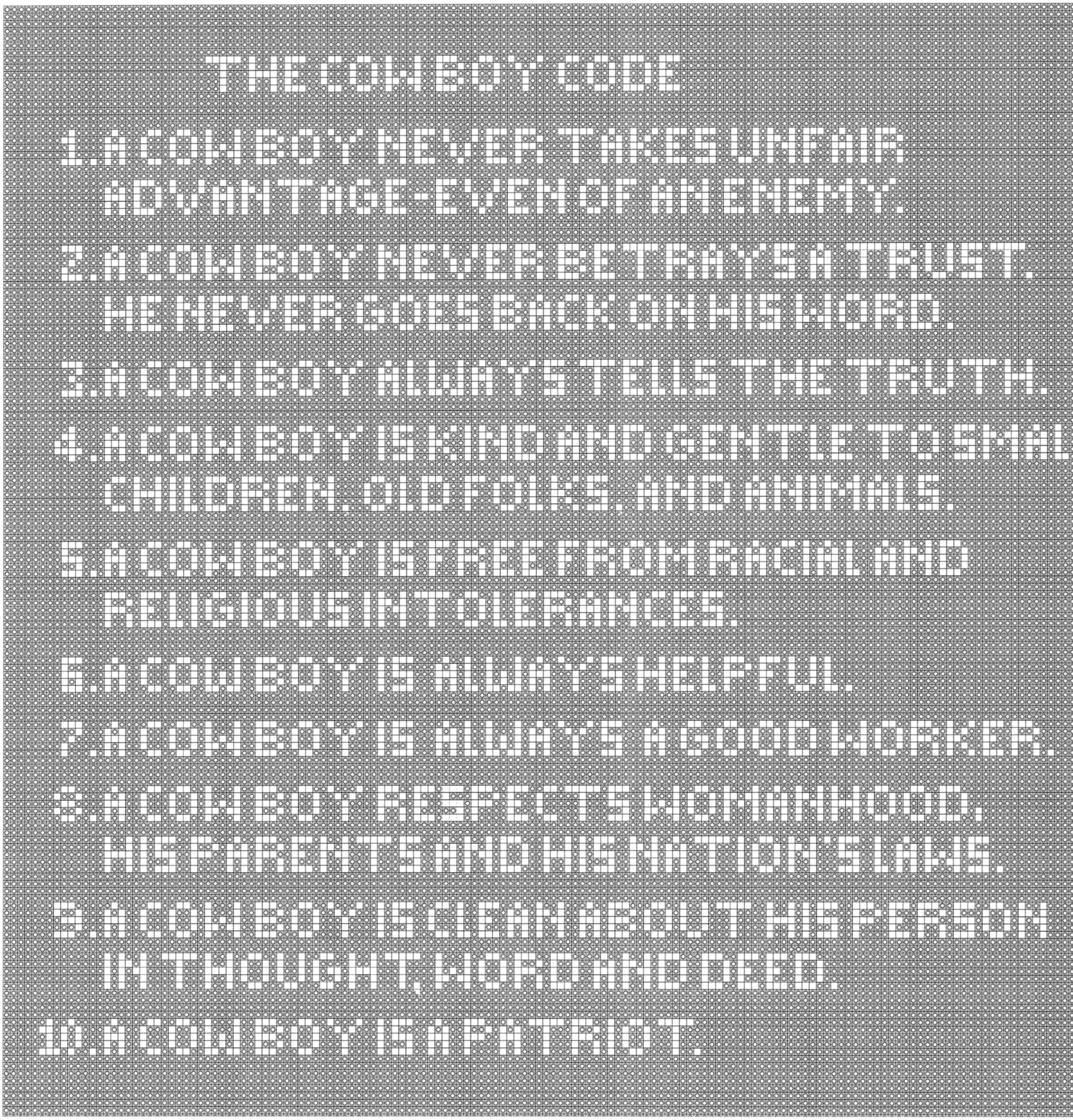

Cowboy Code (Hadith), 2012
Plastic toy gun-caps glued together
into sheets, 415 x 800 cm

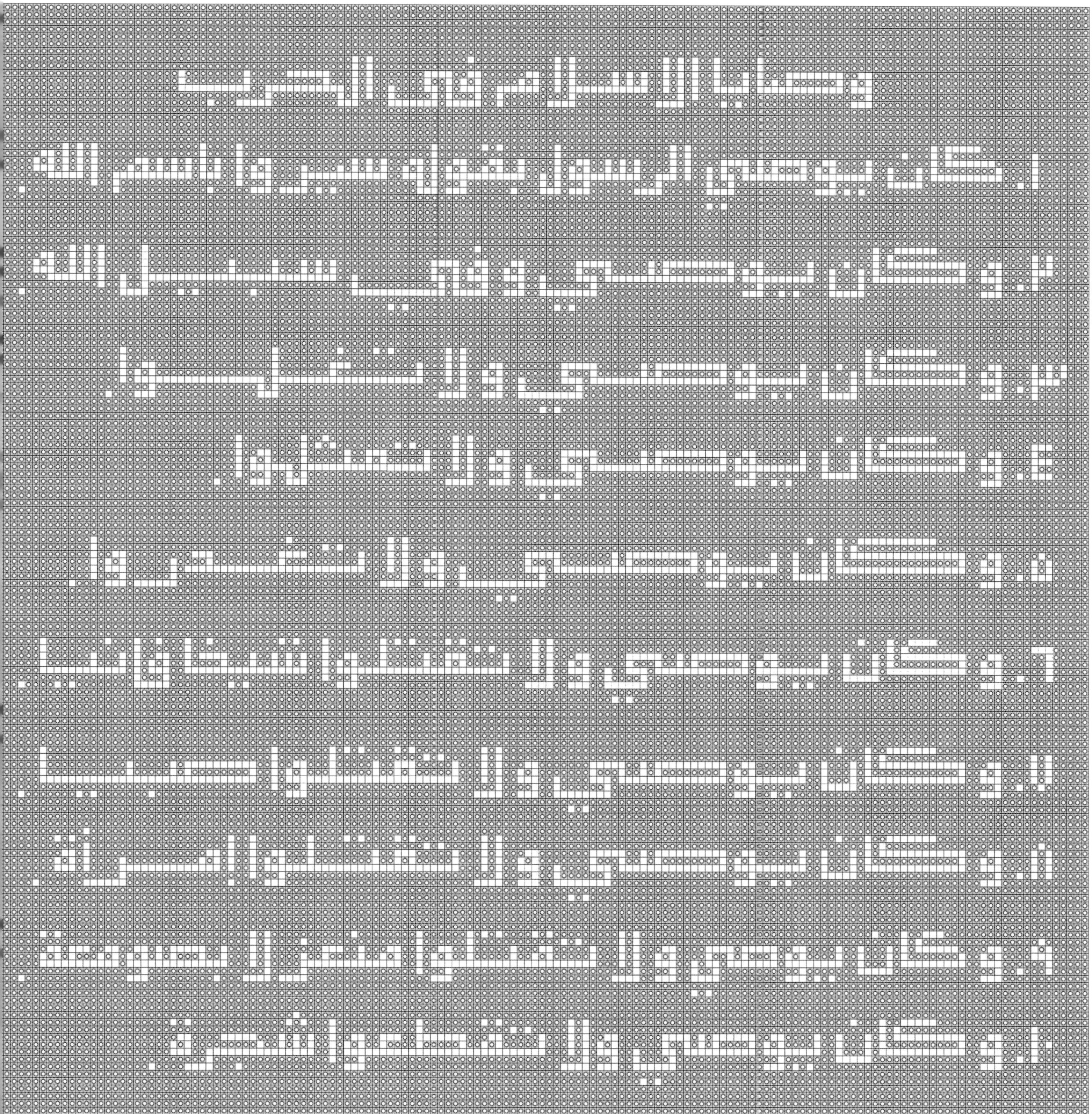
وصايا الإسلام في الحرب
1. كان يوصي الرسول
2. وكان يوصي بالغزو في سبيل الله.
3. وكان يوصي ولا تغلوا.
4. وكان يوصي ولا تمثلوا.
5. وكان يوصي ولا تغدروا.
6. وكان يوصي ولا تقتلوا شيخا فانيا.
7. وكان يوصي ولا تقتلوا صبيا.
8. وكان يوصي ولا تقتلوا امرأة.
9. وكان يوصي ولا تقتلوا
10. وكان يوصي ولا تقطعوا شجرة.

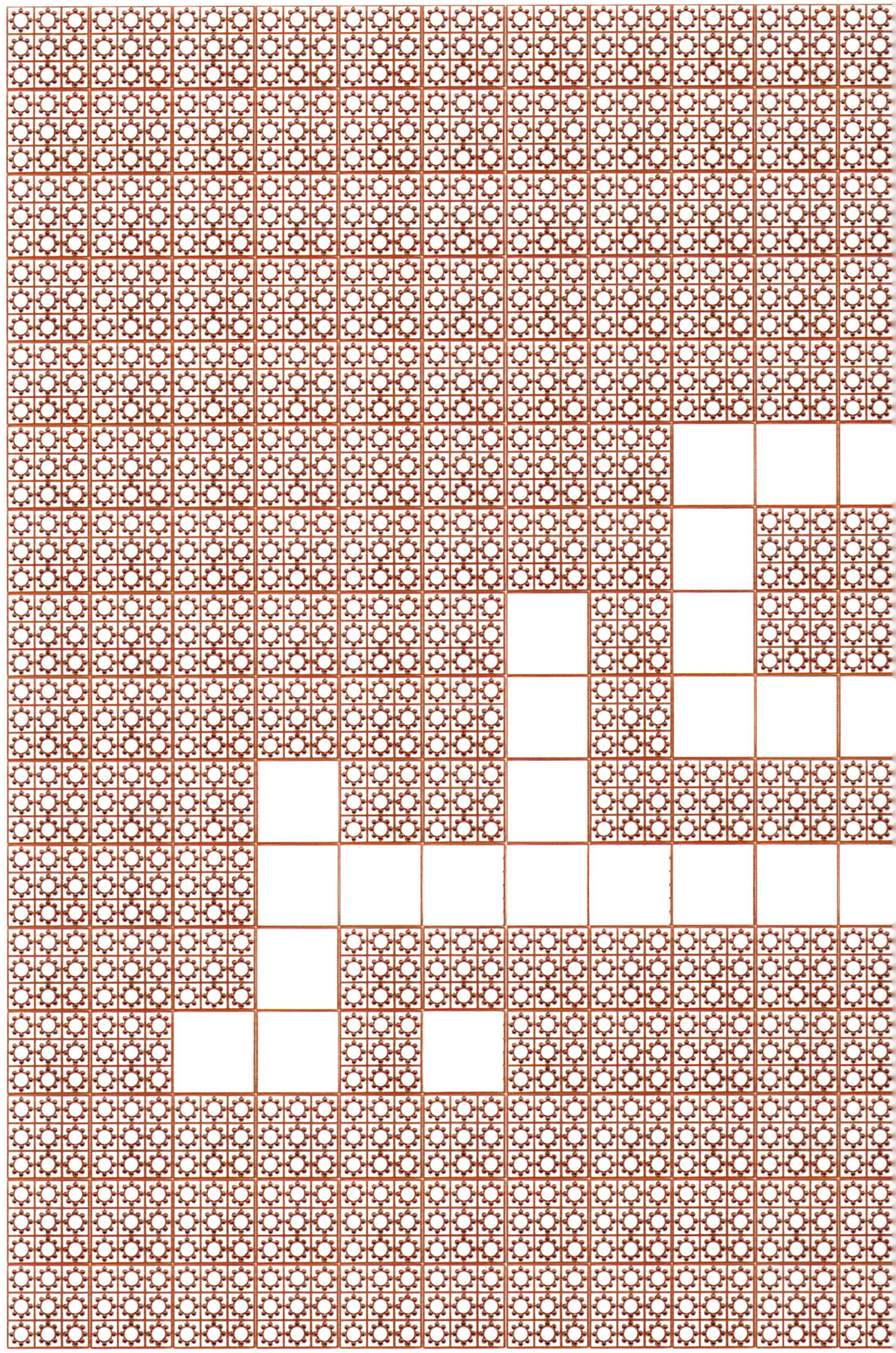

Allah O Akbar I, 2011
Plastic toy gun-caps glued together into sheets,
100 x 150 cm

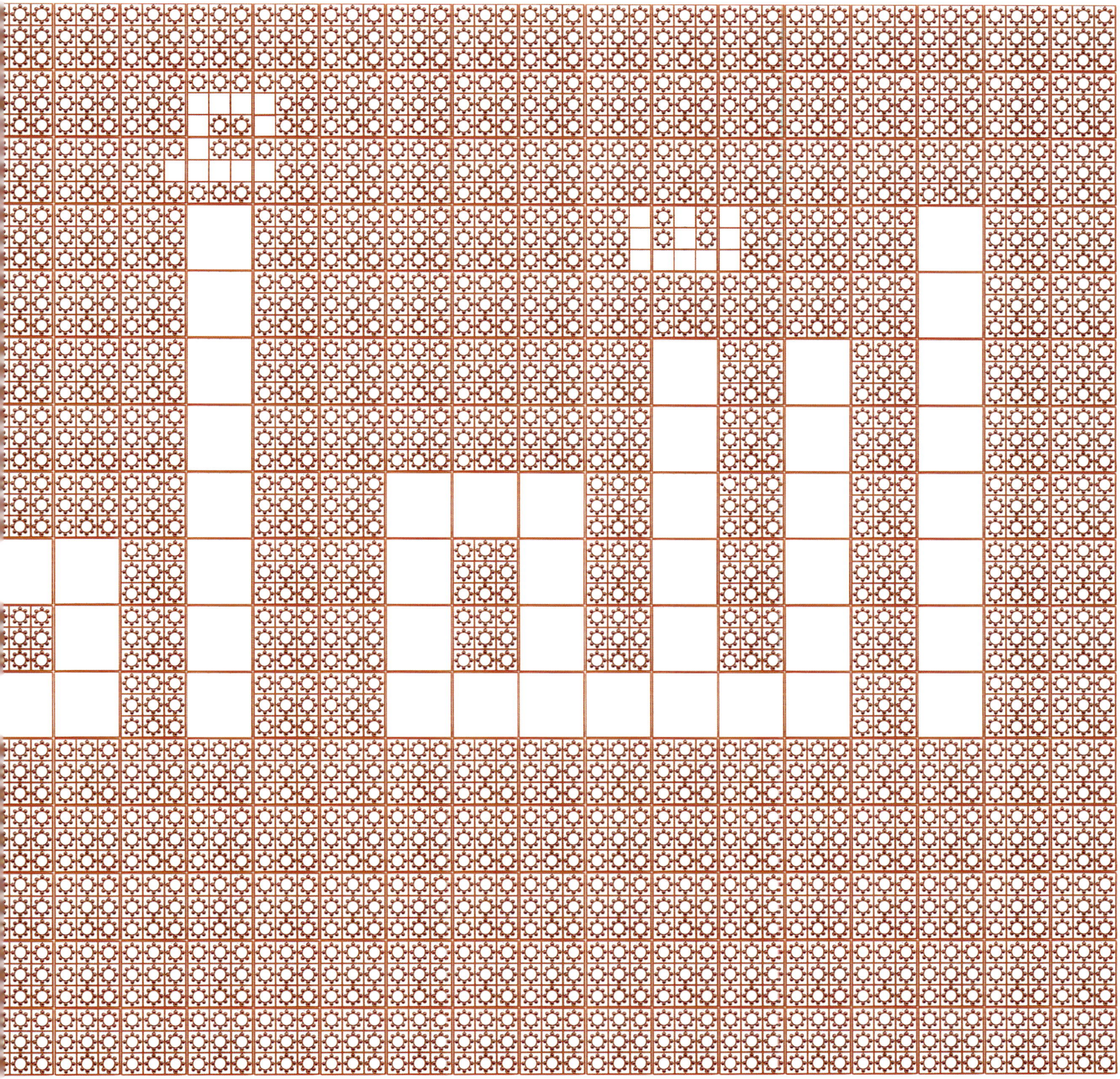

Mehdi Moutashar

Long before I became an artist, my dialogue with nature as a child and in adolescence, on the banks of the Euphrates in what was once ancient Mesopotamia, played a significant role in how I treat space. My contemplation of palm groves, the interplay of light and dark caused by the moving mesh of palm branches, the quick drawings I made in the sand with date-stones, the ever-present bricks, which I later discovered were the first objects created by man whose proportions have remained unchanged for millennia, all strongly influenced the growth of my imagination and the formation of two major axes in my work: the importance of geometry and the rejection of illustration. You might also say that my then growing interest in scientific disciplines such as maths, physics and chemistry, also comes from this same source.

The discovery in Paris of geometric abstraction and minimalism, as well as my acquaintance with the work of Matisse, Max Bill and François Morellet, with their regard for Arab-Muslim art, far removed from anything to do with decoration, led me gradually to base the totality of my work on the concept of measurement, within a global philosophical approach to space where the ground, the walls, ceilings, open spaces and horizons all arise from the same unity: in other words, geometry in its most literal sense: measuring the earth.

Whatever my materials and techniques (wood, metal, brick, crayon, collage, elastic thread) in a given context, whatever the form (murals, constructions, installations), for me it is always the appropriation of space through measurement, with geometry as the alphabet of this measurement.

The carpet weft is open to infinite possibilities; the square pivoted at 45 degrees and the polygon star, the play of parallel angles, the cut resembling the slant of the calligrapher's reed, and most especially the interlacing of these forms, the path of a continuous line in space developed by the multiplication of the angles of orientation; all these elements make up the language of a three-dimensional geometry which connects me fundamentally to the Arabesque as well as to calligraphy, both of them hanging on the notion of measurement.

Houé (2010) is a monumental construction whose strata are a homage to the brick, and whose form combines two letters of the Arabic alphabet, one aerial, the other helical, bending in and out at the same time, along with some more recent works, in which the vibration of a simple elastic thread stretched between two points experiments with a new way of drawing, show clearly the central theme which runs through all my explorations: the ever changing relationship between the finite and the infinite, between plane and volume, between continuity and break, and between time and space.

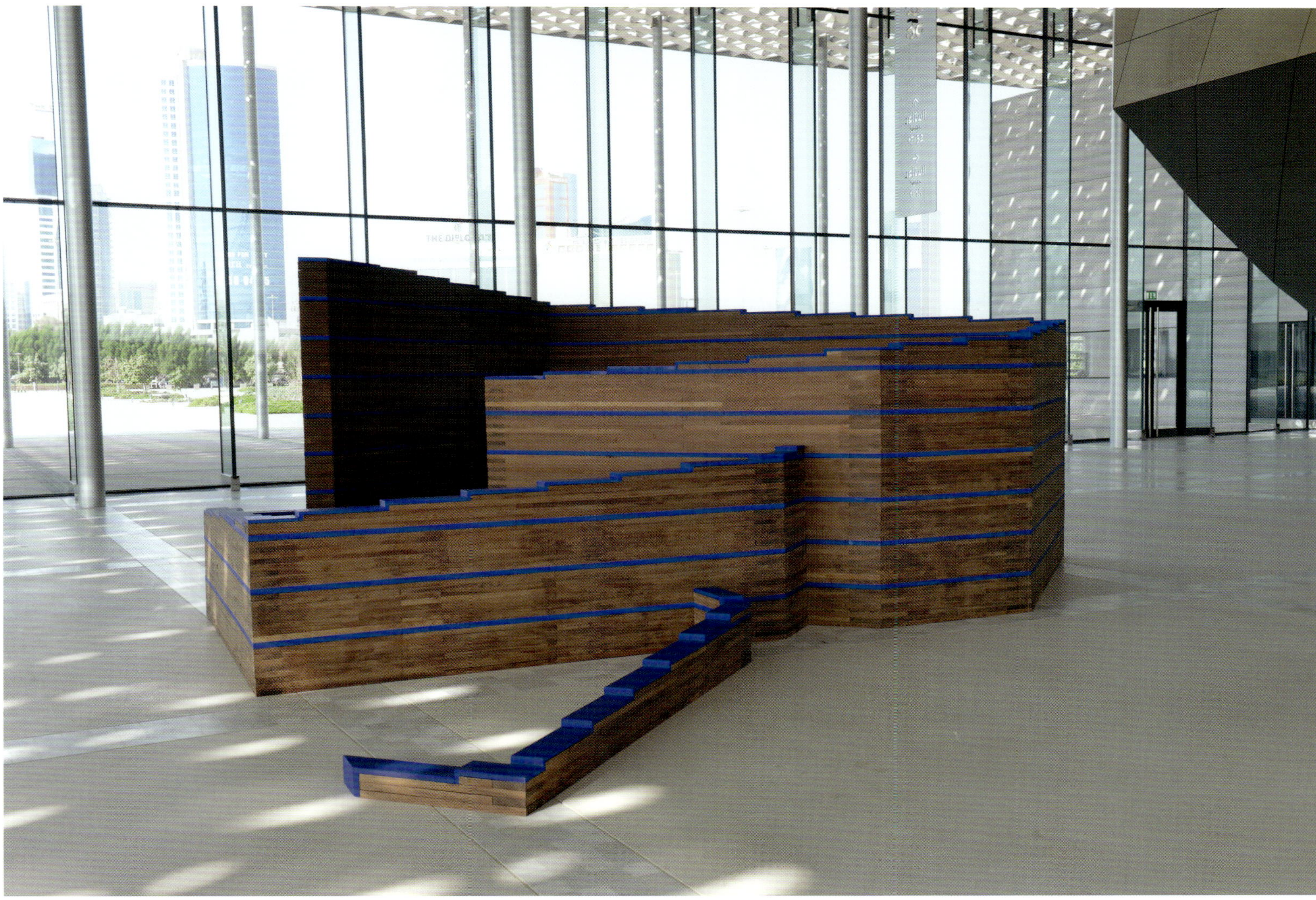

Houé, 2010
Wood and painted wood,
225 x 750 x 440 cm
Photograph taken at the National
Theater of Bahrain by Saleh Al Aradi

Deux plis à 60° et deux carrés, 2012
Painted steel and elastic wire, 136 x 116 cm
Photo Jean-Luc Maby

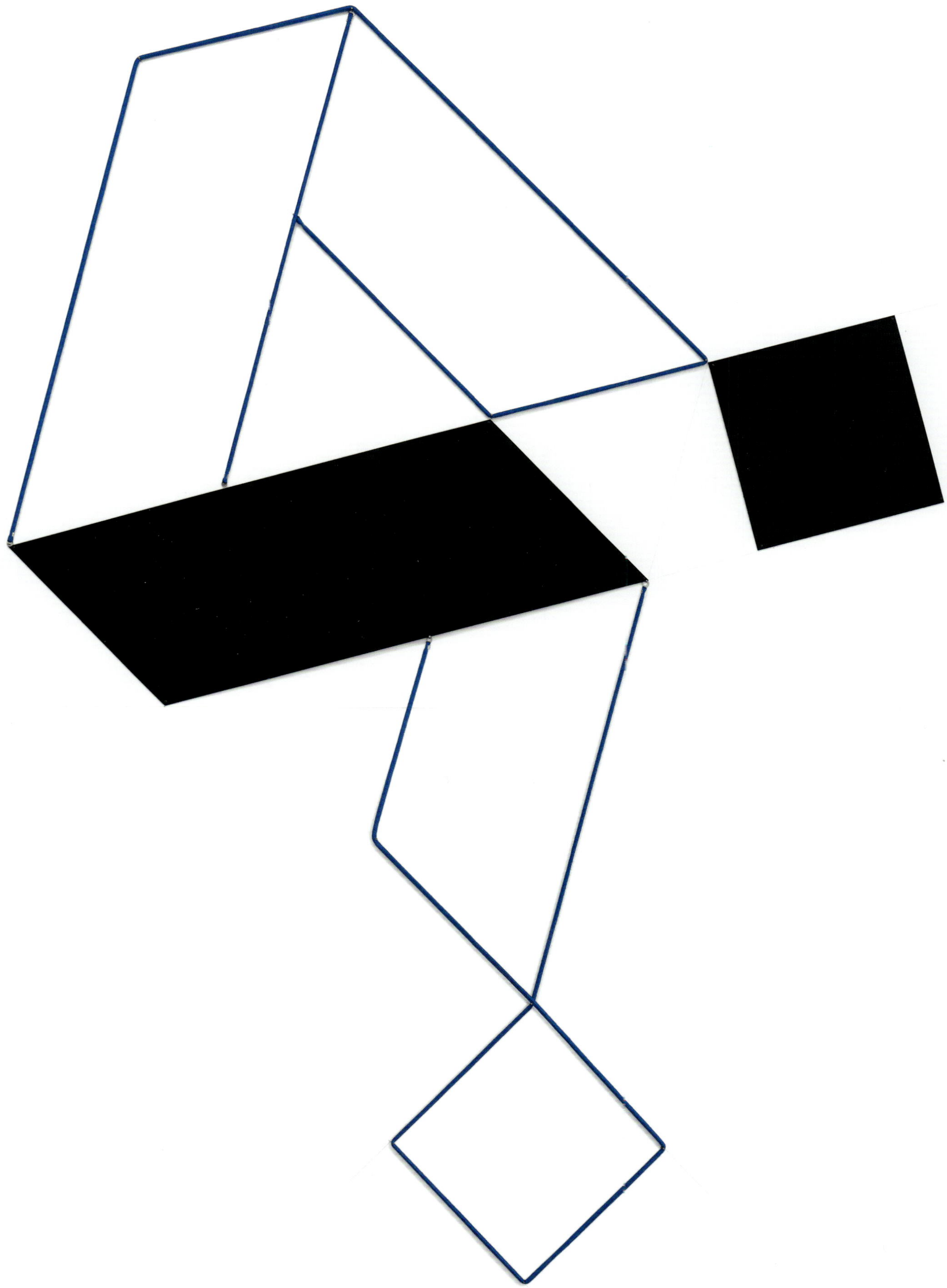

Trois carrés dont un pivotant à 45°, 2015
Acrylic on wood, elastic wire, 150 x 150 cm

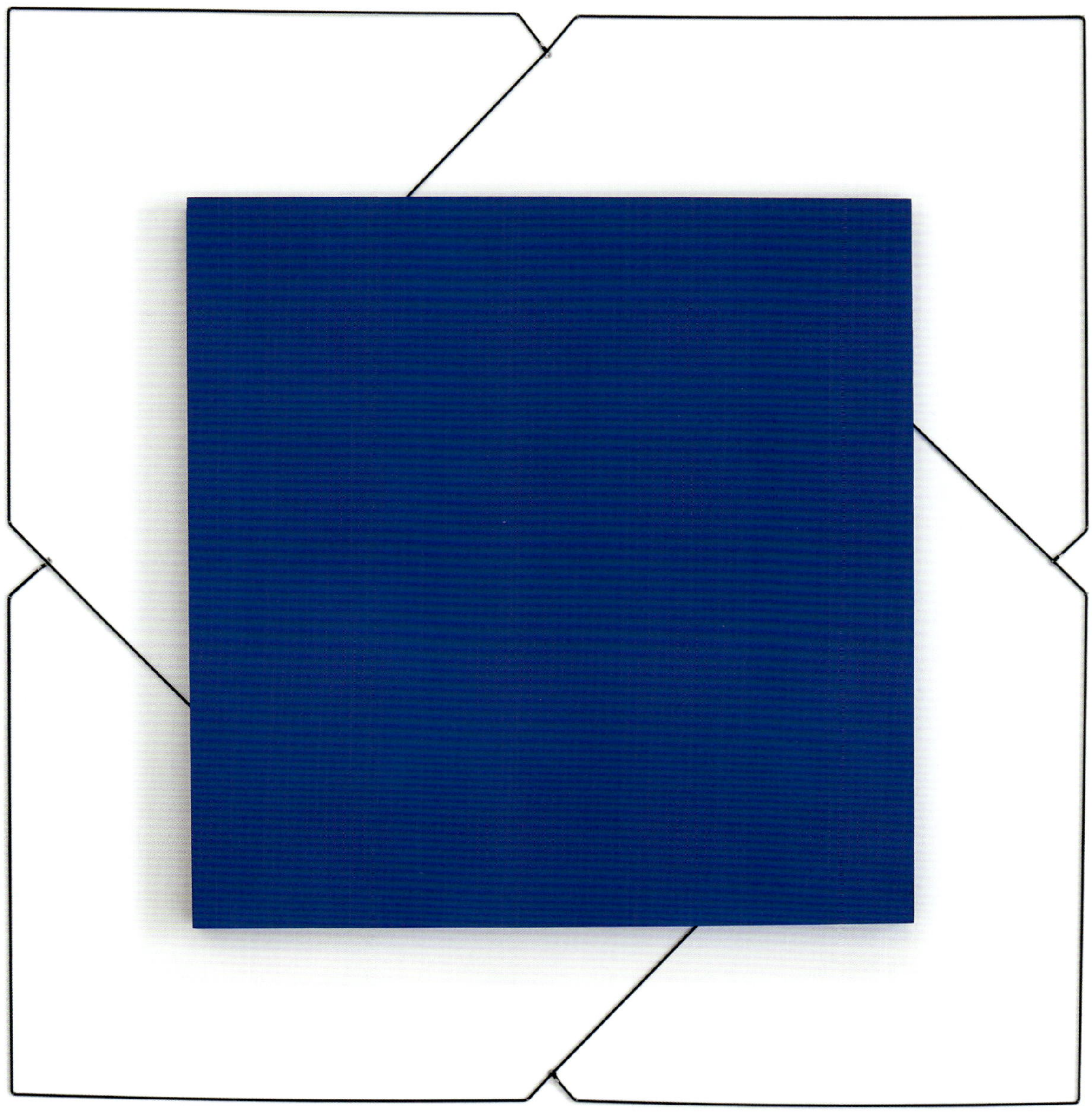

Mouteea Murad

Words out of time and space

The task of distinguishing one's self is an exhausting idea for a contemporary artist. Exploring the self can be time-consuming and distracting. Values and ideas from society might lead to misconceptions and the abuse of aesthetic values. I have therefore focussed my energy on researching Islamic artistic heritage while seeking to present it in new ways, allowing my work to become a catalyst to express myself and substantiate my words.

Historically, Islamic ideas of aesthetics and beauty have manifested themselves in thought, ideas, language, art, architecture and all facets of life. Islamic art was utilitarian art and the artist was a craftsman who focussed on the greatness of God, The Creator, and used the magic of artistic influence to attract souls. Although our society has evolved, and works of art have different roles and meanings, I still believe that the role of art should focus on depicting the greatness of God, The Creator. Thus my art shows my personal connection with God.

While the recognition of beauty brings happiness, my role is to present and add beauty to the magnificence that already exists. The soul is a divine essence only present in humans, transcending notions of time and space. The process of creating allows me to know myself on another level, digging deep for reality and truth and consequently getting to know the universe and God. For whoever knows himself will know God. Thus I consider the time I spend working as worship.

Sufi scholars preach that art needs not only to derive beauty from one's own values and aspirations, but also from what is finest and superior, those being the qualities of God, The All Mighty. I have that in mind when I create, whether in order and visual accuracy or in chaos. I place beauty into two categories: a materialistic beauty, attained by the senses and subject to social pressures and human nature, and a subjective, perfect beauty, perceived through an enlightened mind rather than capricious senses. That kind of constant and absolute beauty is what I am trying to attain.

I belong to the old school of Muslim artists who think that reaching God, The All Mighty, is the ultimate purpose of art. Everything started with Him and everything should ultimately come back to Him. This justifies my concentration on abstraction, repetition of lines, colours and shapes where expression is absolute. Abstraction in Islamic art is the ability to withdraw the whole from its parts and find its meaning regardless of time and space.

I try to highlight the importance of the content, not the subject, and present the particularity of an Islamic heritage that is rooted in global civilisation.

I have purposely moved away from sketching towards modulating more geometric forms, seeking creative power and value in an attempt to reach the absolute. While it's impossible to portray the absolute or God himself in portraiture or representative style, I tend to express him in abstract lines, colours and brush strokes to showcase the value of the matter rather than its looks. My role as an artist is to mold these forms in a geometrical, mathematical, and logical form characterised by balance, proportionality and harmony. I make art using a precise algebraic calculation, in order to represent philosophical ideas and spiritual meanings in a special kind of rational sequence.

Many secrets and mysteries lie within the folds of my paintings. They unfold for some viewers, and conceal themselves for others.

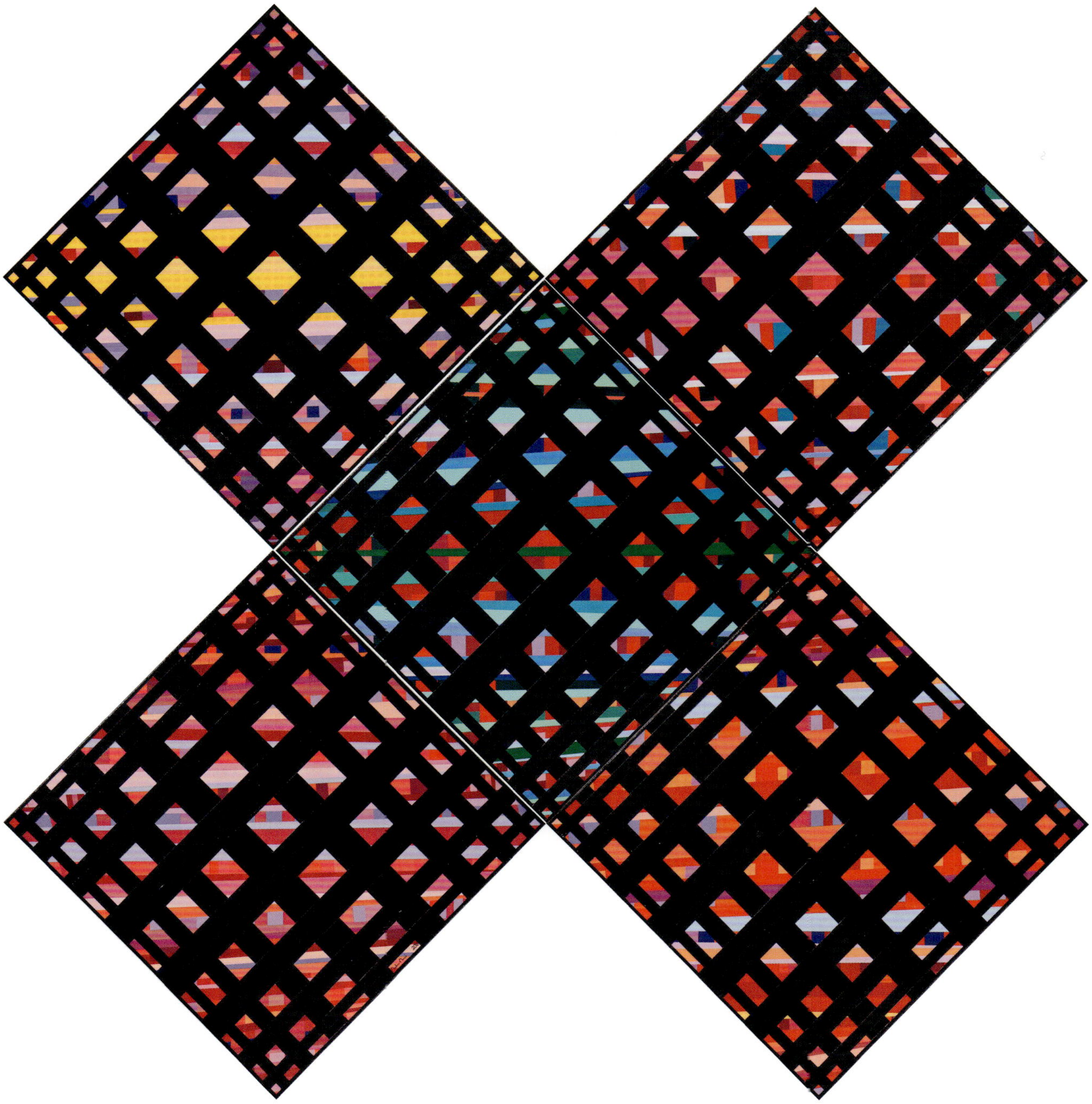

Trial No. 124 - When We Go On
in Time and Space, 2016
Acrylic on canvas, 282.5 x 282.5 cm

Trial No. 132 - Trance at Sunset, 2016
Acrylic on canvas, 185 x 200 cm

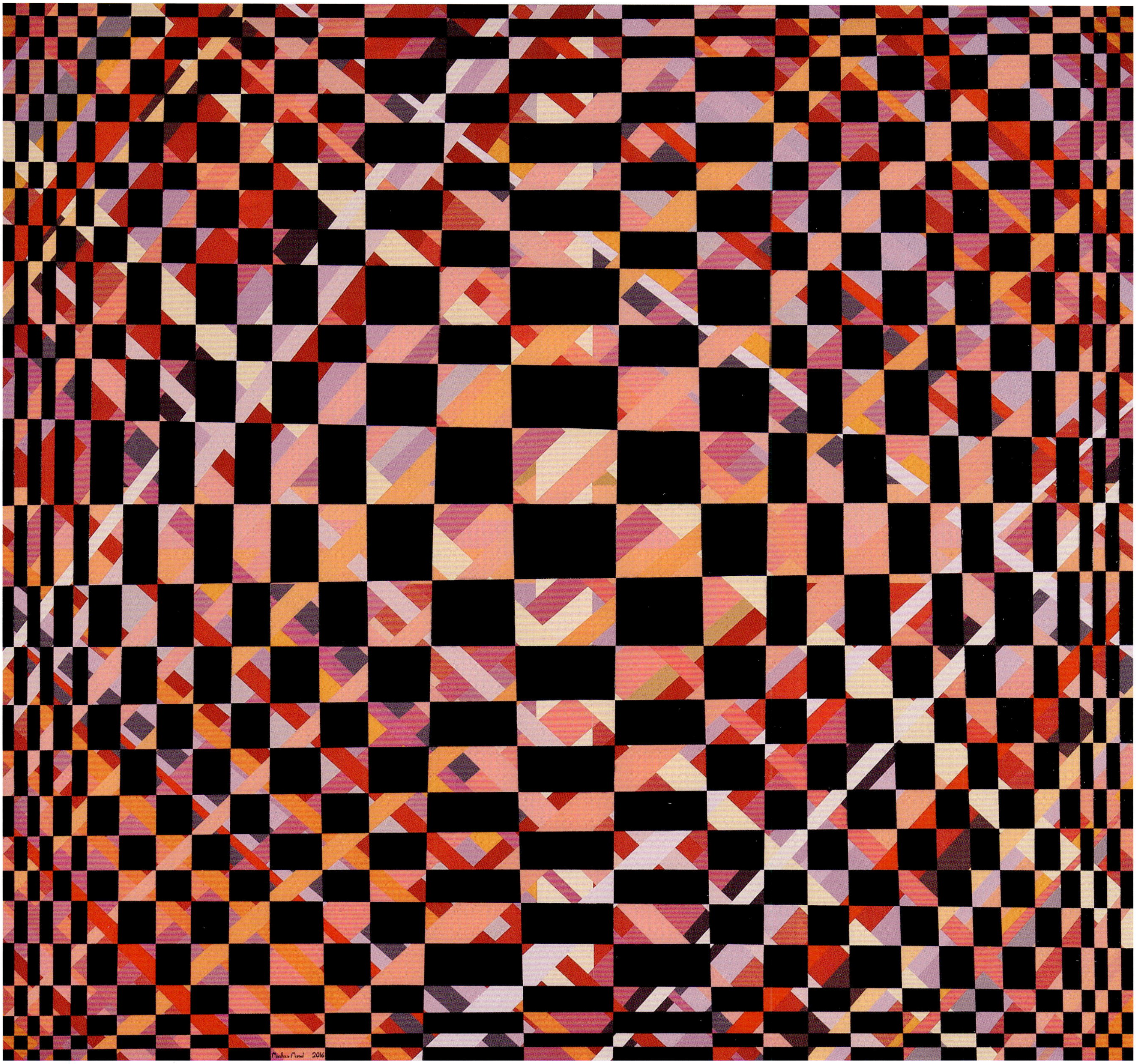

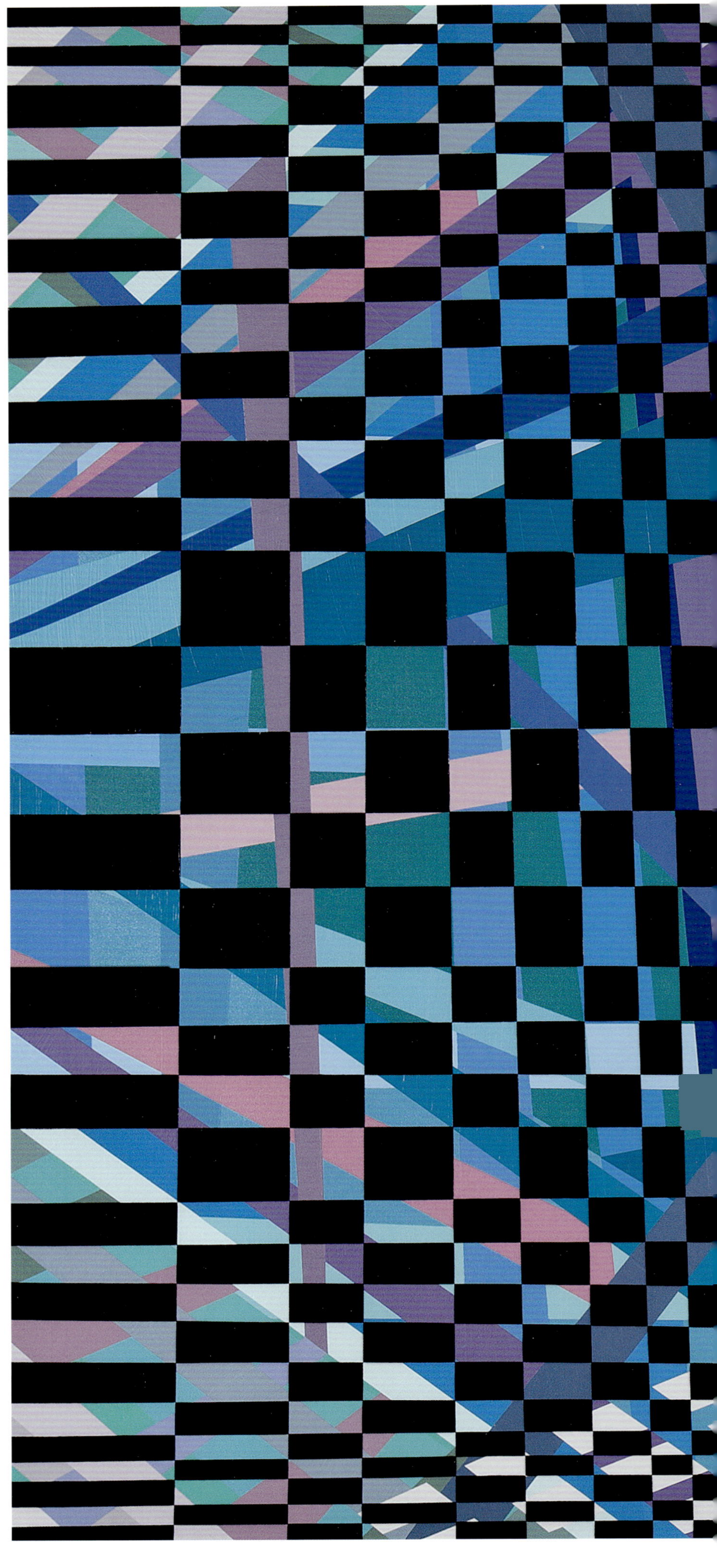

Trial No. 134 - Tunes of the Migrant Birds, 2016
Acrylic on canvas, 185 x 250 cm

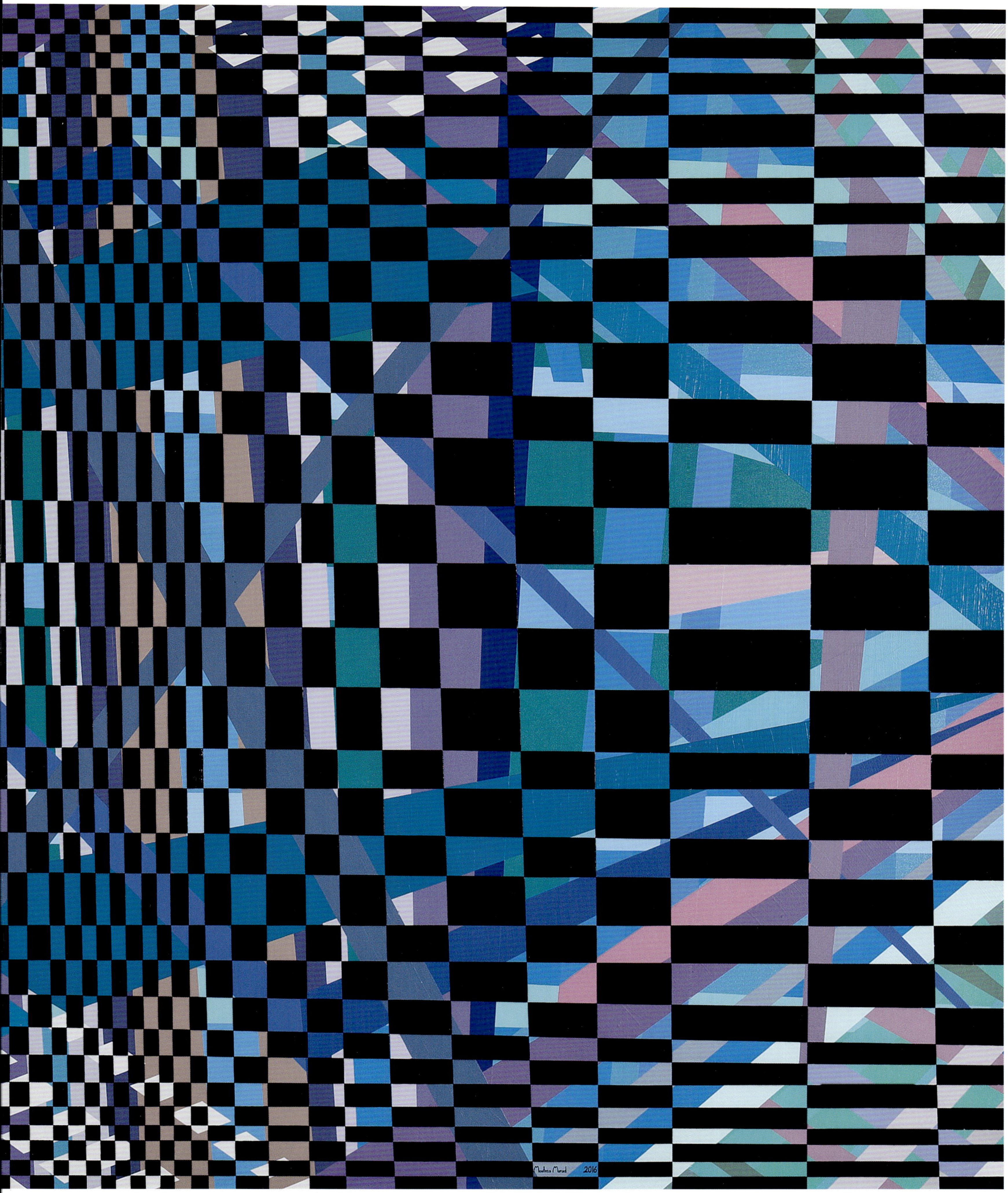
2016

Naqsh Collective

Art has always defined and documented the vast cultures and civilisations throughout history. Women uniquely distinguished the art in Palestine and the Levant through embroidery, which reflected the congruence of art, colour, design and exemplary geometry.
As an architect and a graphic designer, embroidery drew us with its rich motifs, disciplined geometry, and its consistent precision in expressing and archiving the history of Palestinian women on their dresses. Each dress will tell a different story according to where its maker came from. Each city or village carved its own pattern, unit of embroidery, consistently from one dress to the other, documenting their roots and origins through a needle and many colourful threads.
At Naqsh Collective, we feel that we inherited the different units of embroidery from our grandmothers who preserved them for us, the next generation to see and enjoy them.
We took it upon ourselves to expose the beauty of each unit, its graphic angles, geometric shape, and the story of each ancestor it represents, while adding our own touch and flavour, showcasing the flexibility of embroidery to adapt to time with its innovative patterns.
Highlighting each unit, you will see the bird, the tree or the grape leaf sewed in a perfect, yet simple minimalist pattern. These patterns are closely associated with the ones found in mosques and castles throughout the Islamic history. As you look further, you will note how Islamic art influenced embroidery, as they both portray the surrounding plant environment without the human body, through the use of motifs and geometry.
As artists, we are mesmerised with taking each unit of embroidery outside its normal realm, studying its every angle digitally on the computer screen before it materialises on the different media we use. We stumble upon the limitless possibilities to craft these units on stone, copper, wood and several other potential media. We start with the story, the narrative, the origin, what exemplifies that village or city before selecting the proper material, as it is important for us as designers to tell the right story, with our ancestors' native language.
Let us take the *Jaffa "Yafa"* series for example. In it, we delved into the beautiful nature and culture of old Palestine, examining many pictures of the 'Old town'. Nermeen transformed these pictures into detailed minimal sketches. These sketches were drawn using the amazing units of embroidery that tell Yafa's stories to the diaspora who never saw or experienced such beauty.
Another example is *wihdeh* or 'unit'. In it, I dared to utilise one of the most important elements of embroidery, taking it out of its familiar context, placing part of my architectural soul, sewing the Palestinian stories with architectural media, making every piece immortal and immune to time.

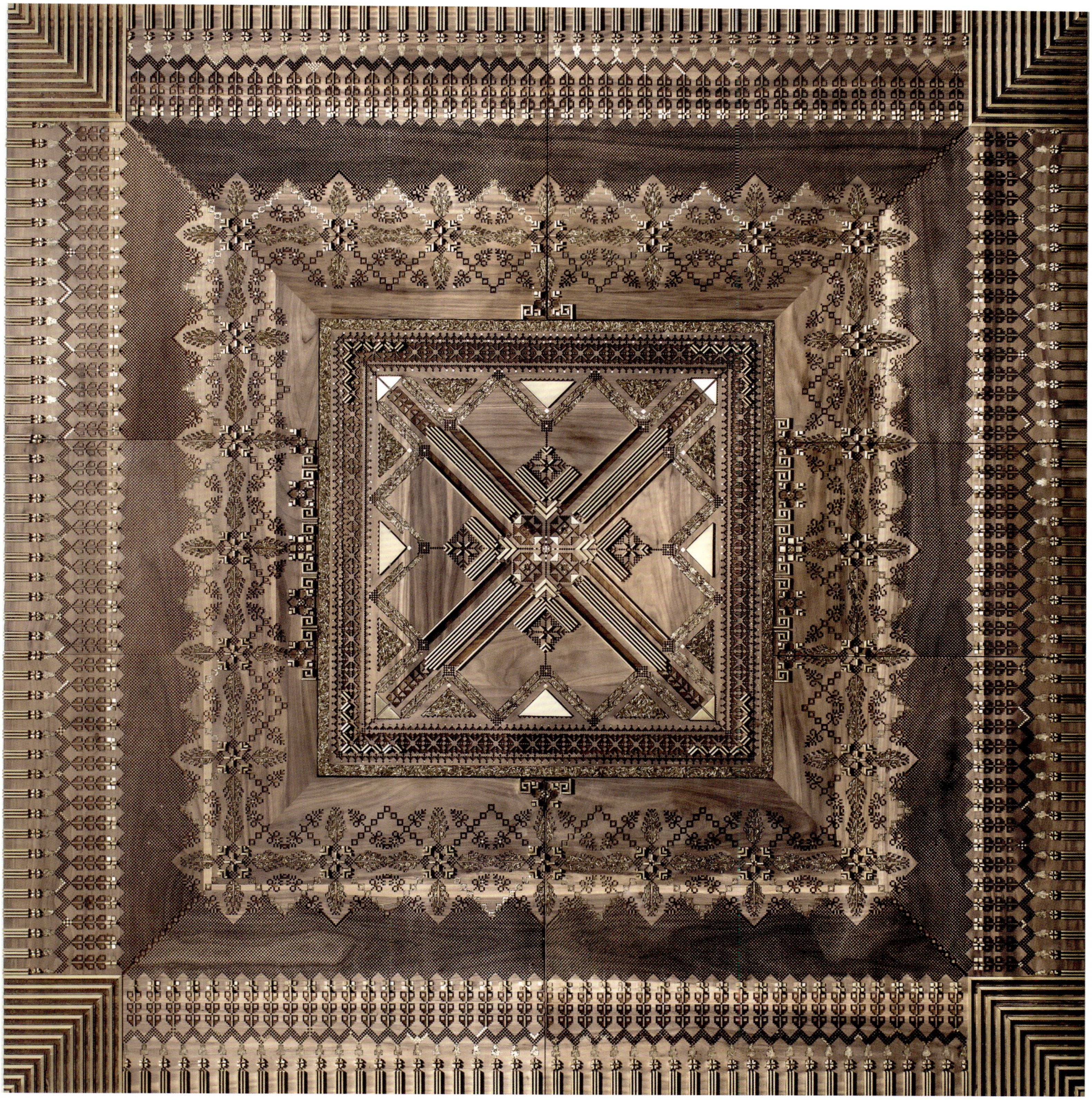

Bridal Cushion, 2018
Solid walnut wood with brass, 200 x 200 cm

Leap of faith, 2018
White industrial marble with brass,
220 x 240 cm

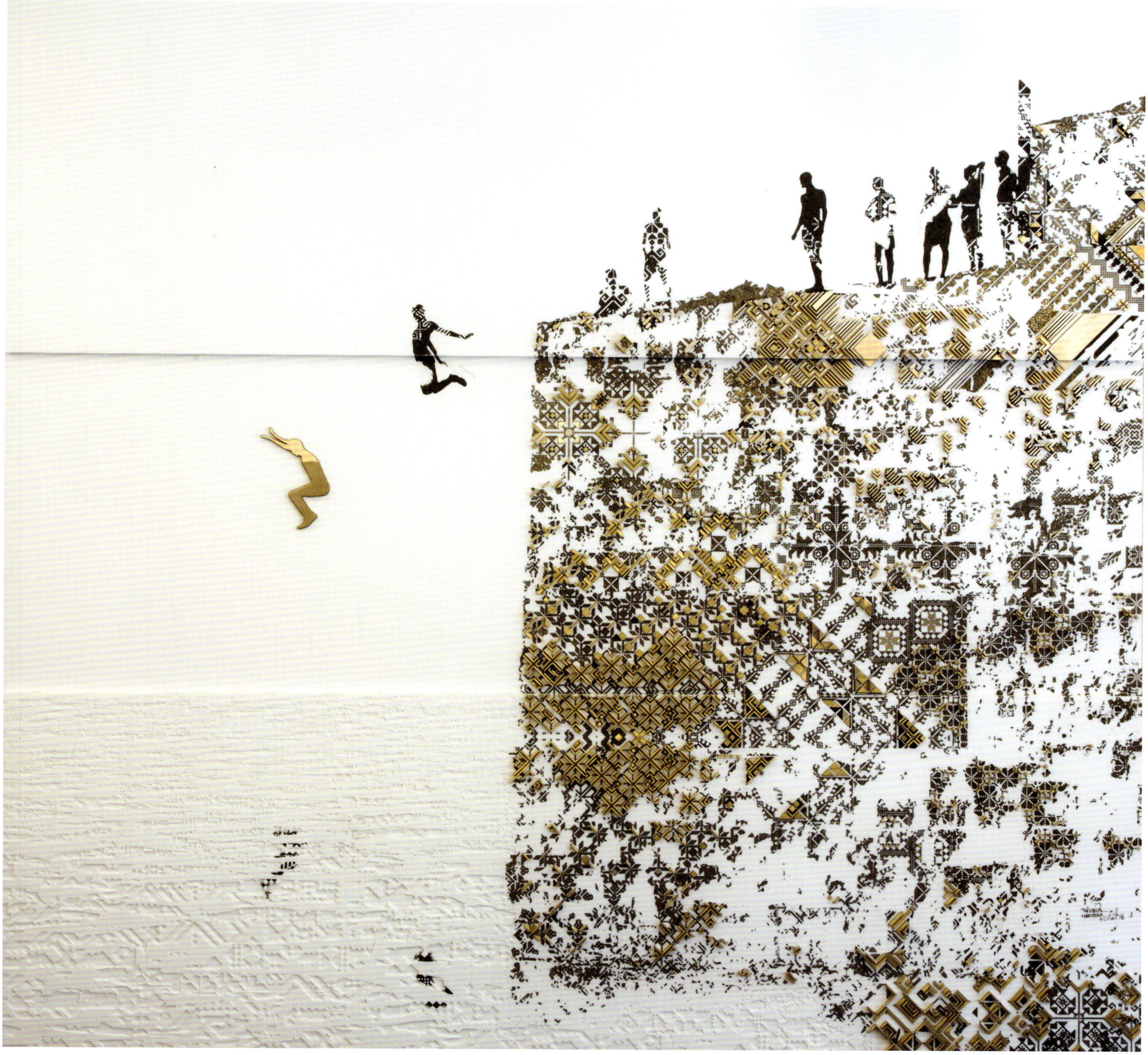

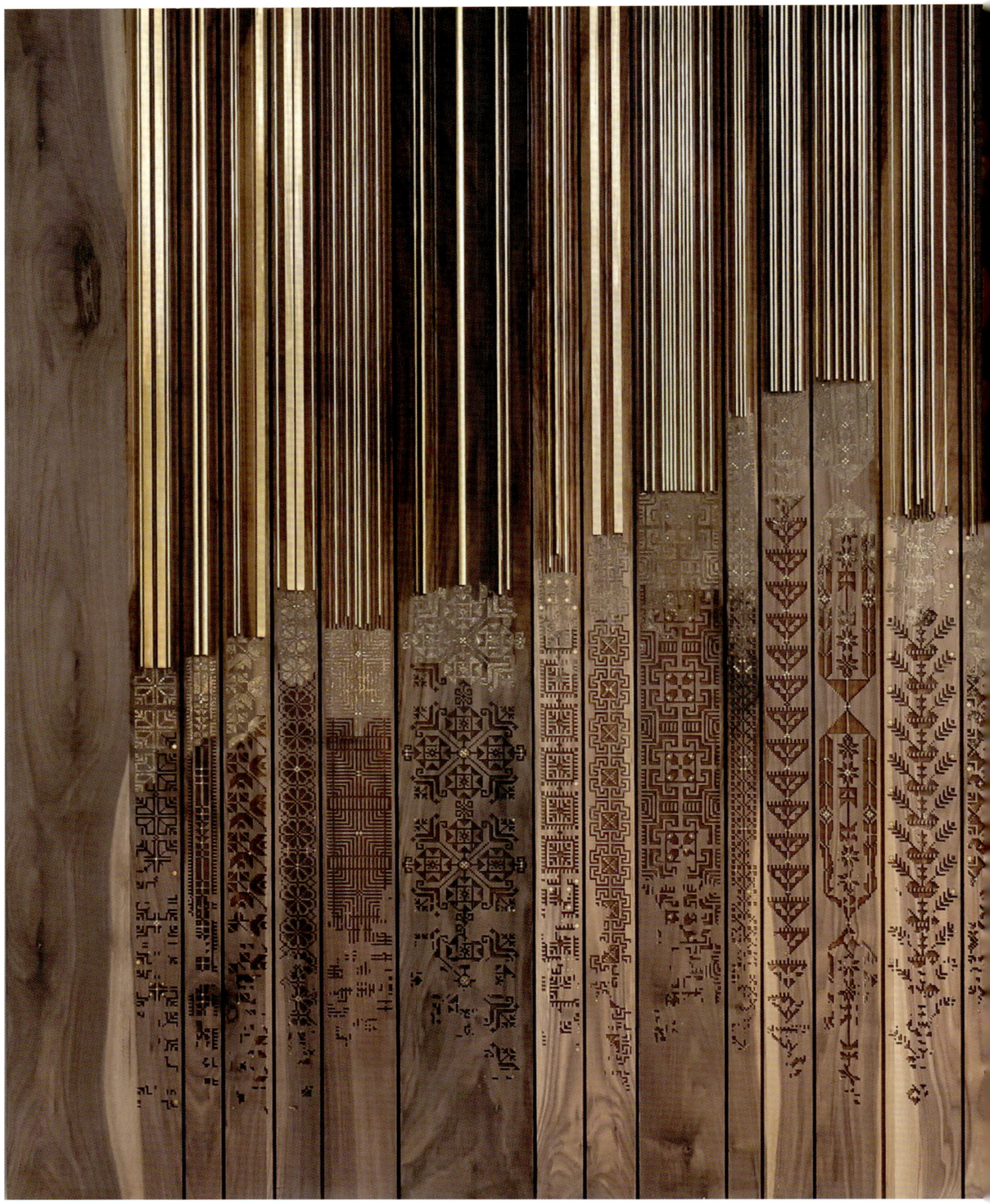

The Shawl, 2015
Solid walnut wood with brass,
225 x 375 cm

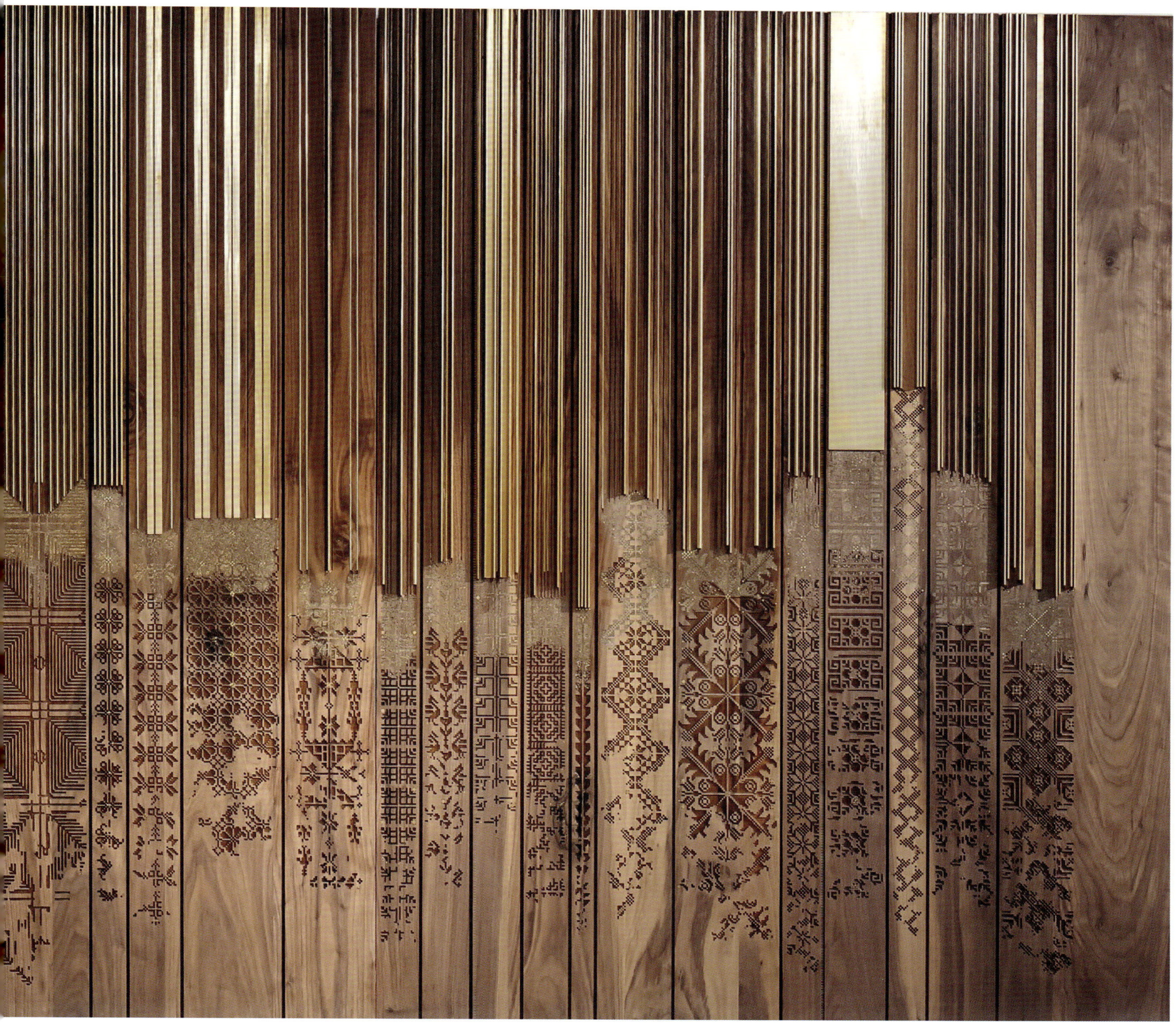

Nima Nabavi

My practice is influenced primarily by – and stems directly from – the work of my grandfather, who was a geometric artist for over fifty years in Iran. For as long as I knew him, he was always engaged in deep explorations of the underlying grids and the source of patterns from which the infinite tessellations of Islamic art and sacred geometry emerge. His work was more akin to a spiritual and mathematical quest than an artistic practice – as though he was truly trying to decode parts of nature's algorithm. "The whole universe is in these grids", he would often tell me.
Two years after my grandfather passed away, I was suddenly struck with an intense curiosity about his geometric work. I started drawing my own grids based on residual memories I had of conversations with him about the mathematical rhythms of these linear constructions.
Little did I know then that I was about to be drawn into the same portal that he had walked into half a century earlier. With each grid I drew, new questions arose and new geometric directions presented themselves for further study. Each new piece built on the one before it, incrementally intensifying with complexity, engulfing my mind deeper into patterned thoughts. I was beginning to see what pulled my grandfather in so deep.

My work is all individually hand-drawn with just pens and rulers. The majority of my pieces include intense repetitions of basic building blocks – like a thin black line – drawn in accordance to predetermined parameters, to create gentle geometric effects. I am intrigued by intense, detailed work that culminates in very subtle results and variations. Each piece I draw usually contains several thousand lines, each often as small as an inch long (approximately 2.5 cm), and usually separated by distances of at most 1/16 of an inch (1.5 mm). Repeating these iterations over tens of hours on each piece, I learn more about how the lines interact under the specific conditions and use that knowledge to inform the deepening complexity of the next series I work on.
Contemplating and calculating the order and placement of the lines is an engrossing mental challenge, and the slow execution of the actual drawing is heavily meditative and deeply satisfying. Like my grandfather, I am very fascinated by the universal appeal of the geometric language of symmetry, order and tessellation. While engaged in the work, I often feel like I am scratching at the surface of the underpinnings of natural phenomena, getting a glimpse of the mechanics that run the universe.

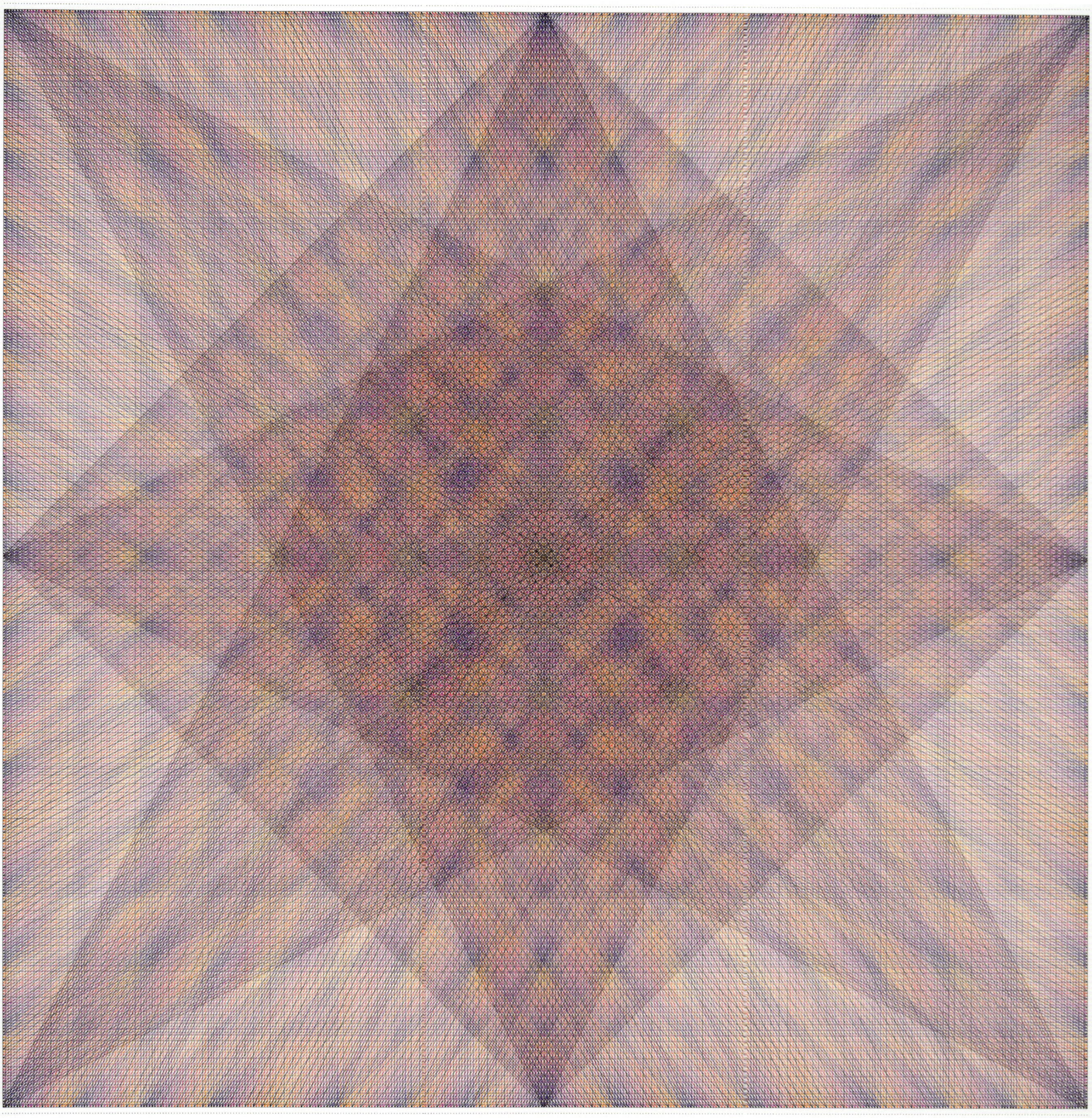

2018.08.23 (3.2.3), 2018
Ink on archival paper, 61 x 61 cm
Jameel Art Foundation Collection

2018.07.16 (2.4.8), 2018
Ink on archival paper, 20.3 x 20.3 cm
Jameel Art Foundation Collection

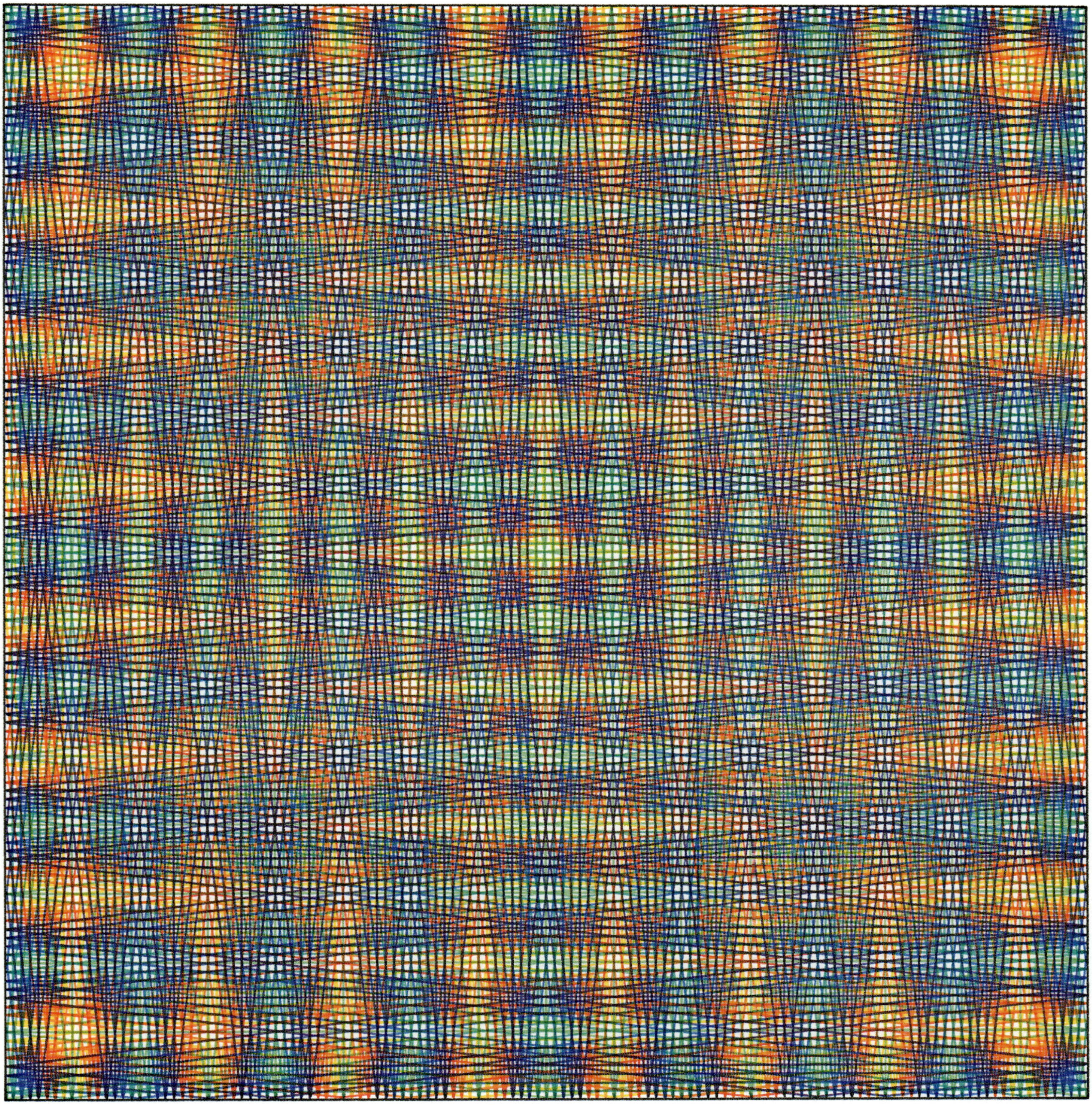

2018.04.06 (1.13.16), 2018
Ink on archival paper, 40.6 x 40.6 cm
Jameel Art Foundation Collection

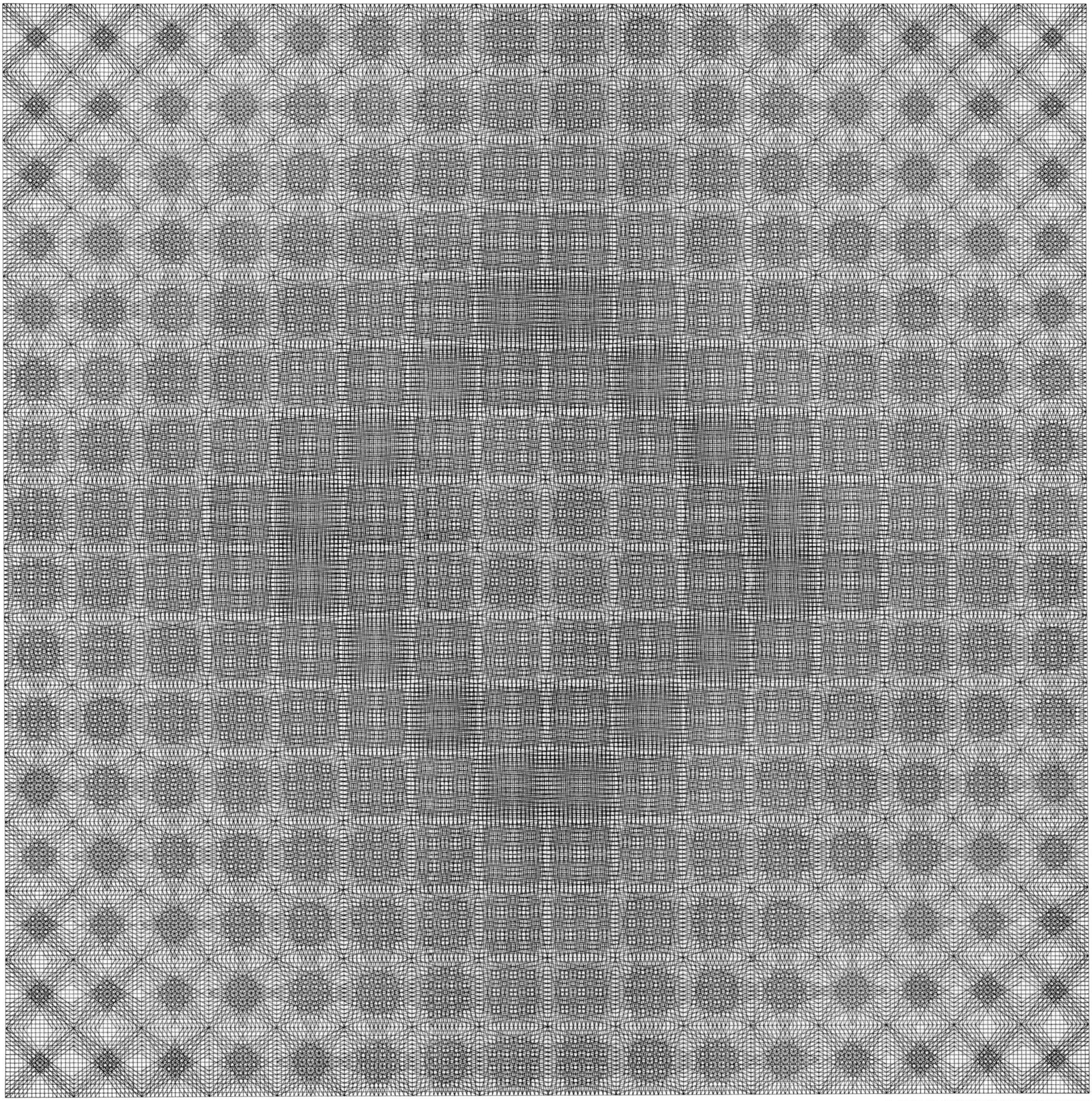

Timo Nasseri

I take my inspiration from mathematics, geometry and patterns and I underline their interrelationship in terms of repetition and aesthetics in my drawings and sculptures.
My practice is one that tackles the subject of infinity and that aims to solve puzzles, whether they are historical mysteries or the explorations via mathematical theorems to discover an overarching order in the chaos of existence.
With many of my works, the influence of Islamic art, its mathematics and philosophy, makes a most striking first impression; I use my artistic practice to invent, to generate form and images through a process which is a synthesis of reason, intuition and imagination in a keen desire for comprehension of the world – or simply understanding the limitations of being human.
My work is also deeply inspired by Islamic ornamentation, specifically the vaulted, honeycomb-like architectural detail of the *muqarnas* found in the ceilings of many Islamic structures. I like to flatten these three-dimensional patterns and reveal the algorithm behind their beauty, rendering it with precision and grace in white ink on black paper. I am intrigued by the idea that the drawings alter their meaning based on whether the audience knows this backstory or not.
I believe that a key for understanding is needed, just as in maths, a formula is needed. Without knowing what pi or co-sign means, you're not able to read the language. But if you have this intelligibility, I believe that it could also be a formula for understanding the world more widely, as well as fantasies such as an alternative gravity in a parallel universe.
I also explore in my work the universe's infinite nature and the endless possibilities held within by drawing constellations on star maps. The night sky has long been a tool for navigation and a source of inspiration in the Middle East – constellations have led many explorers to success or ruin, depending on the path they followed.
The promise of so-called universal disciplines such as geometry, science and music is that by their mathematical origins they can surpass particular languages and be accessible to anyone. My work aims to hold on to this wild potential while also bringing them down to earth. My drawings and sculptures are sensorial representations of unlimited possibilities of the imagination and of existence created out of chaos – the experience of infinity within us.

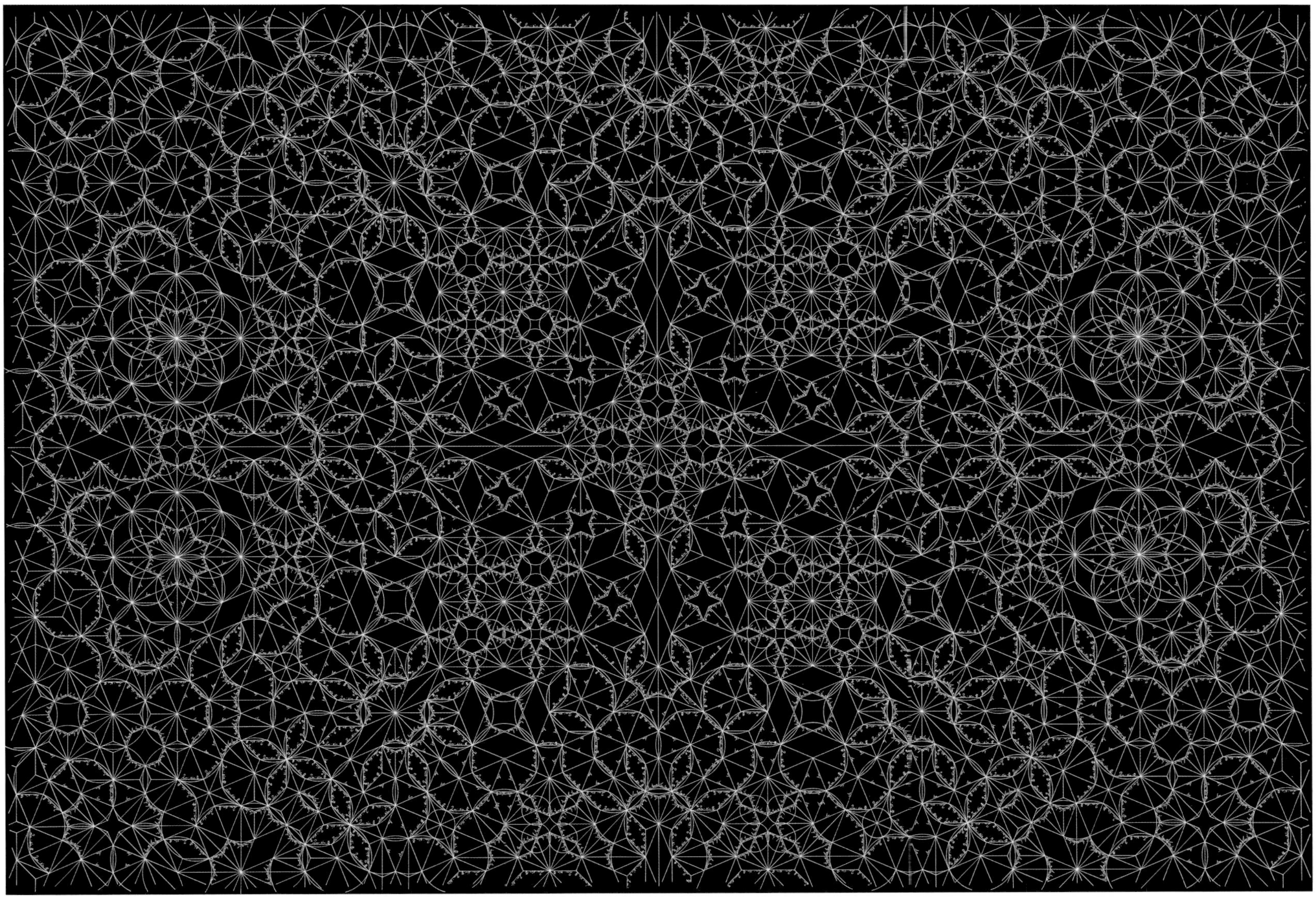

One and One #47, 2017
White ink on inked paper, 108 x 159 cm
Courtesy of the artist and Ab Anbar Gallery

Epistrophy 8_1, 2017
Stainless steel, 217 x 217 x 80 cm
Unique
Courtesy of the artist and Ab Anbar Gallery

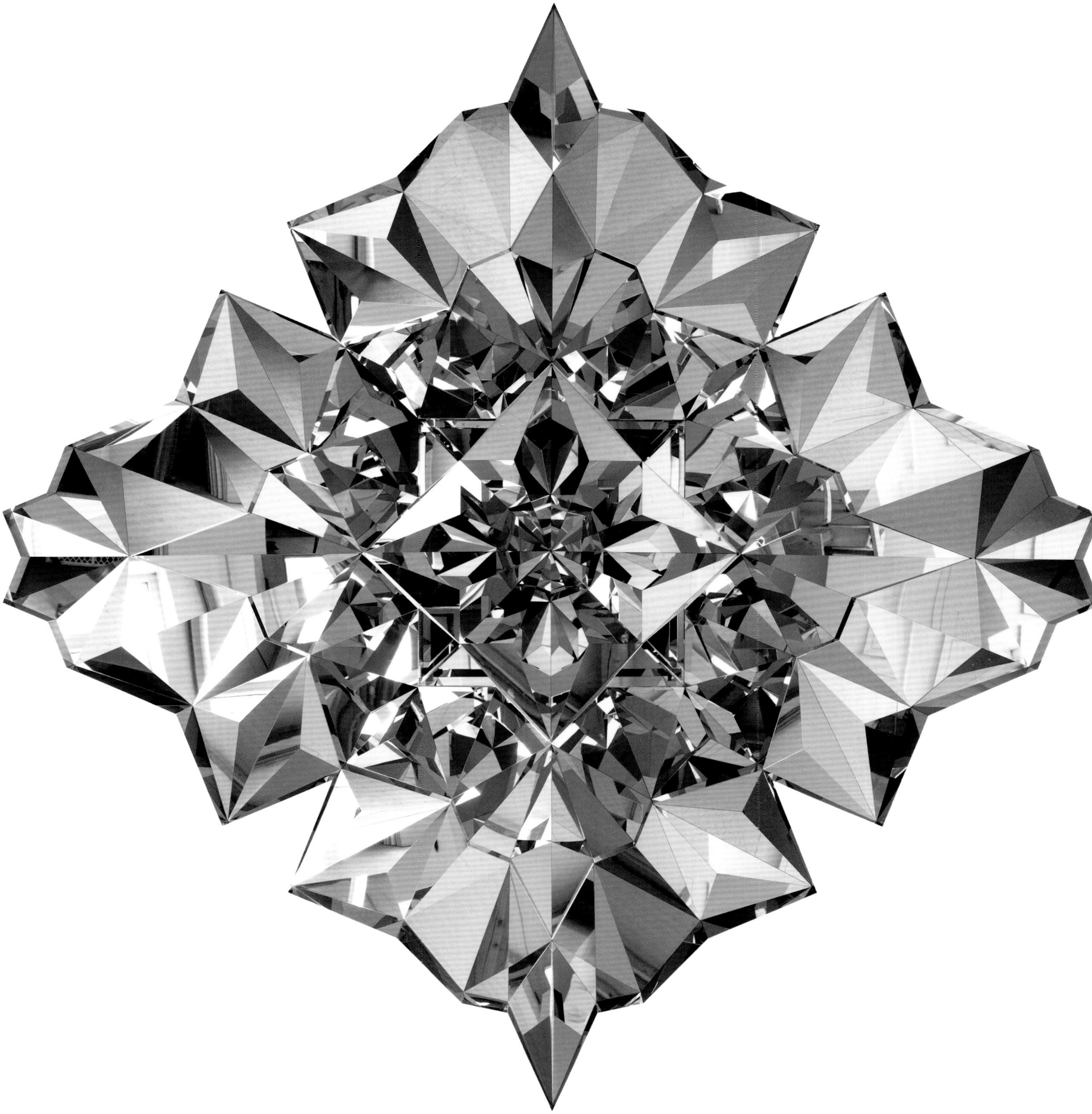

Pion, 2015
Brass, wood, latex, 65.5 x 65.5 x 65.5 cm
Edition of 3 + 1 AP
Courtesy of the artist and Ab Anbar Gallery

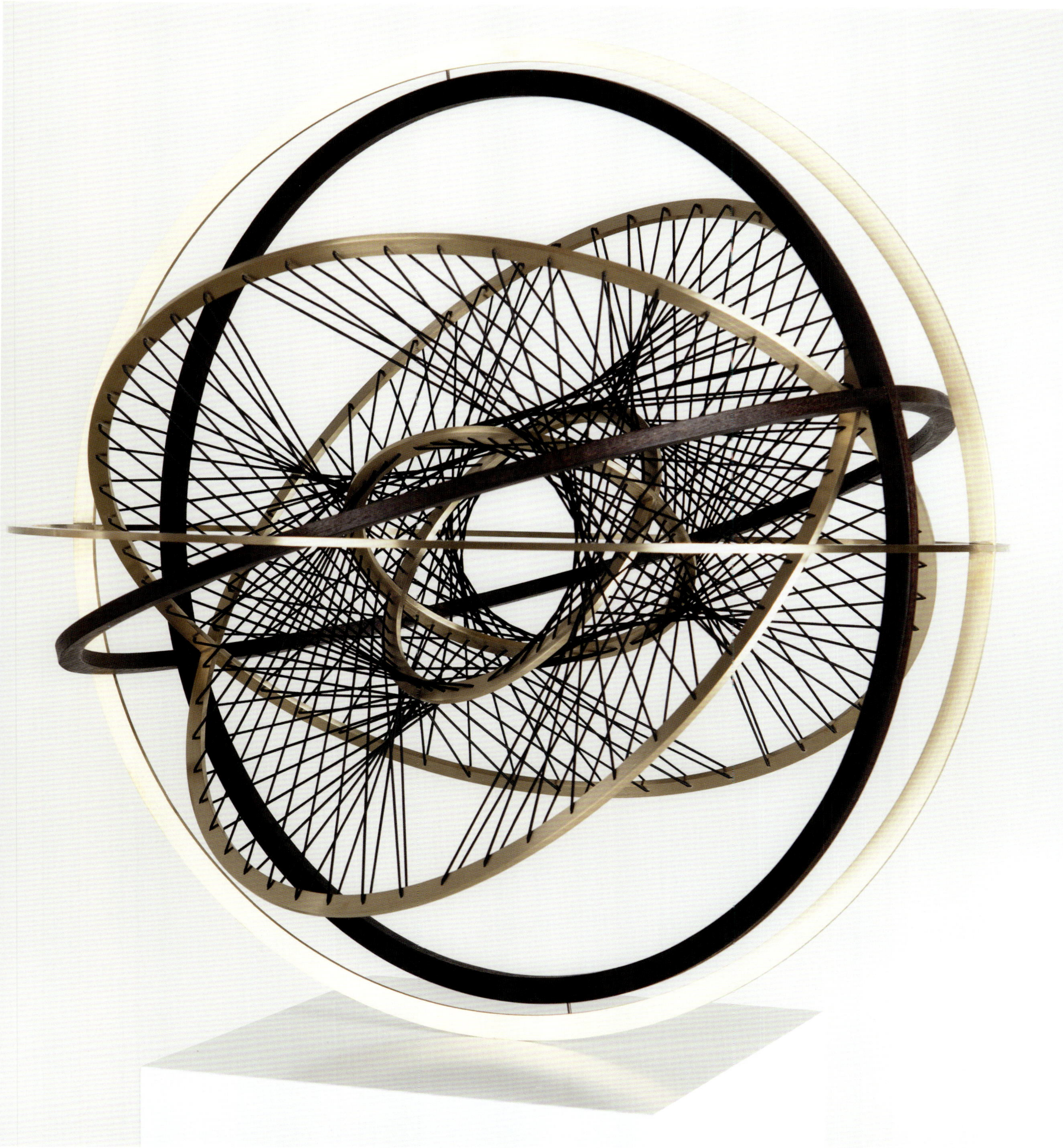

Mahmoud Sabri

In the late 1960s, Mahmoud Sabri experienced a total change of direction on life and art, coming away from his previous political and social notions and moving towards a scientific understanding of the universe. He stripped his art down to scientific equations and explored the infinite creative possibilities that he believed had transformational possibilities. Spurred by the space, technological and scientific advances of the 1960s, Sabri saw quantum physics and Einstein's Theory of Relativity, as a basis for creating art and linking the two together. In 1971 his ideas were formulated and published in a manifesto entitled *Quantum Realism – an art of the techno-nuclear age* and the art he produced following this principle was exhibited with the launch of his manifesto in Prague in the same year; it would sadly be Sabri's last exhibition before his death. The artistic language of the new art (colour, form and structure) is derived from the system of line-spectra associated with different atoms and the relations linking spectral-lines, energy-levels and electrons. "In the 1980s," he said, "my work changed its direction by focussing on the analysis of the structure of the atom. This transition from molecular to atomic structure manifested itself in a further change of artistic language. In Phase 1, only selected visible spectral lines were involved; these were translated into colour areas and treated as the distinctive colour characteristics of atoms/molecules.
In Phase 2, both visible and invisible spectral lines were involved and treated as the distinctive colour characteristics of atoms and space-time… These drawings are to me (as the mathematical equations are to a mathematician) a means of verifying the reality of the artistic structural solutions as well as grasping their possible deeper meanings and implications."
Sabri believed that Quantum Realism addresses the uniqueness of our age in a new form of relation between humans and nature, or a new form of perceptual activity. He saw the old perception of mass-object-form as being gradually negated and replaced by a new perception of energy-process-structure. The new artistic creativity provided Sabri with the possibility of unifying art and science, and looking at the fundamental laws governing nature as a basis for his avant-garde art. His dramatic transition from the figural to geometric and mathematical forms meant that the latter half of his work bore closer resemblance to the mosaics of his native Iraq than he had anticipated, and while never abandoning his concern for the socio-politics of the region, this latter evolution took him to more universal and philosophical concepts.
Roxane Zand

H2O-O2.4NG (Air and Water), 1969
Oil on canvas, 140 x 130 cm

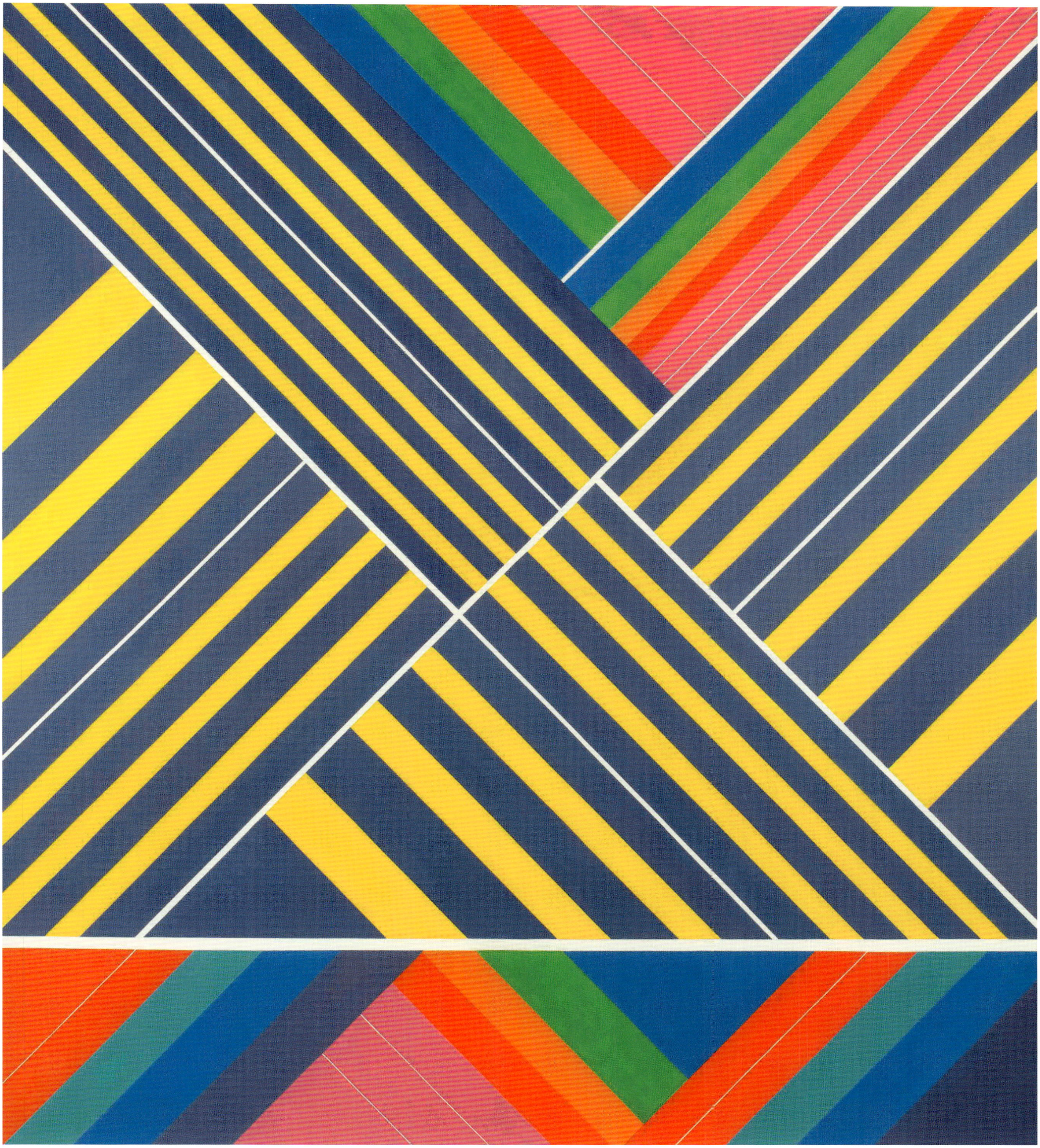

Elements of Water, Salt and Vinegar, 1969
Oil on canvas, 140 x 130 cm

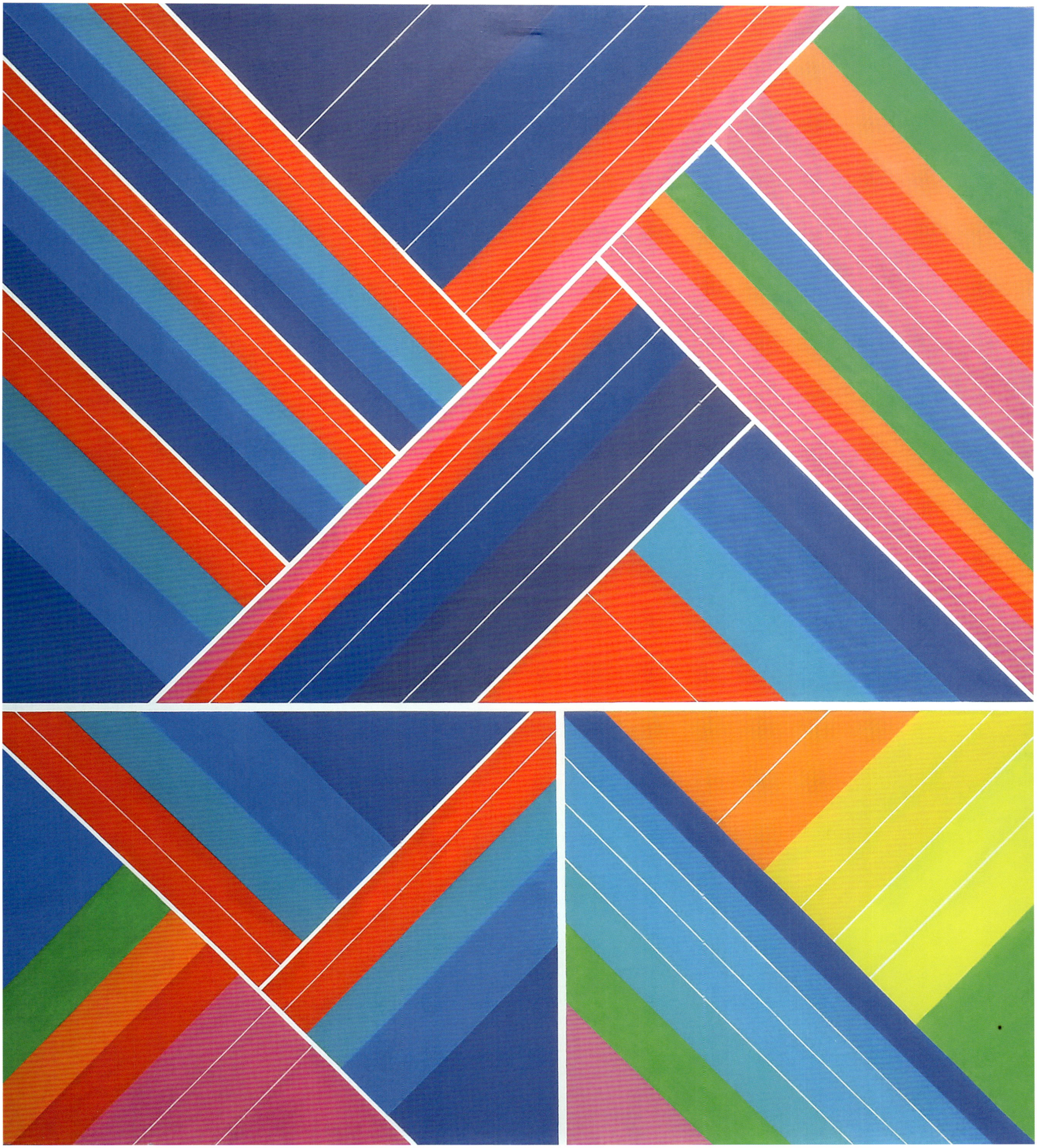

Samir Sayegh

Thoughts about the role of geometry in my artistic work take me back to my childhood days; to nature, to an orchard full of different trees and plants, to days when one had to listen to the order of seasons, to the moments when flowers bloomed and fruits ripened, moments of pollination and moments of harvesting.
I realise now that a hidden role of geometry was behind my first imaginings, penchants and knowledge of life and art.
The dialogue between straight and sharp angles that are at the basis of Kufic calligraphy had a stunning aesthetic value in such early times, while the secret geometry in square Kufi made me wonder about the dialogue between the black, which is the body of letters, and the white, which is the space between them.
What does the equality and symmetry between these opposites represent? Are they night and day? Presence and absence? Existence and the hereafter?
Yet, as I observed the forms of this Kufi style and followed the path of its composition and construction, this led me to a state of fullness and wisdom.
Thus, geometry started to reveal its explicit role to me, when I began to combine ornamentation and calligraphy in a single work of art.
The role of geometry was no longer confined to the rules, styles and systems of creating circles, squares and triangles. It became an attitude, a philosophy, and a comprehensive vision of art, human beings and existence.
Geometrical abstraction became a manifestation, an absolute or creative translation of the concept of unification [*tawhid*]: *unification is abstraction*. Unification, in essence, not only treats the hereafter as one, but considers the hereafter and existence as one too. There is no duality in unification, for nothing remains in the end but the only one.
Geometrical abstraction, or what we call Islamic geometrical ornamentation, embodies the path of this unification, as well as its essence, whereby this ornamentation is based on an indivisible 'unit' that replicates or reproduces itself in mathematical systems to create a geometrical grid and ornamental work. If we call this unit *part*, then we would necessarily call the grid or ornamental work *whole*. As we contemplate the relation between the part and the whole, it becomes clear that the part conveys in its essence the image of the whole, and the whole necessarily carries the image of the part. From there comes the expression of the small universe that embraces the large universe.
Here, geometry started to play a spiritual and Sufi role as I considered calligraphy as an art of form; the form of spirituality or mystic energy that resides within *par excellence*. This mystic spirituality, inner energy or abstraction arises by instinct and by consciousness, as described in the spiritual vision and Sufism of the unity of being and the *complete* human being.
It is striving to connect with the Absolute.

KĀF, 2018
Acrylic on canvas, 150 x 120 cm

MIM, 2017
Acrylic on canvas, 150 x 100 cm

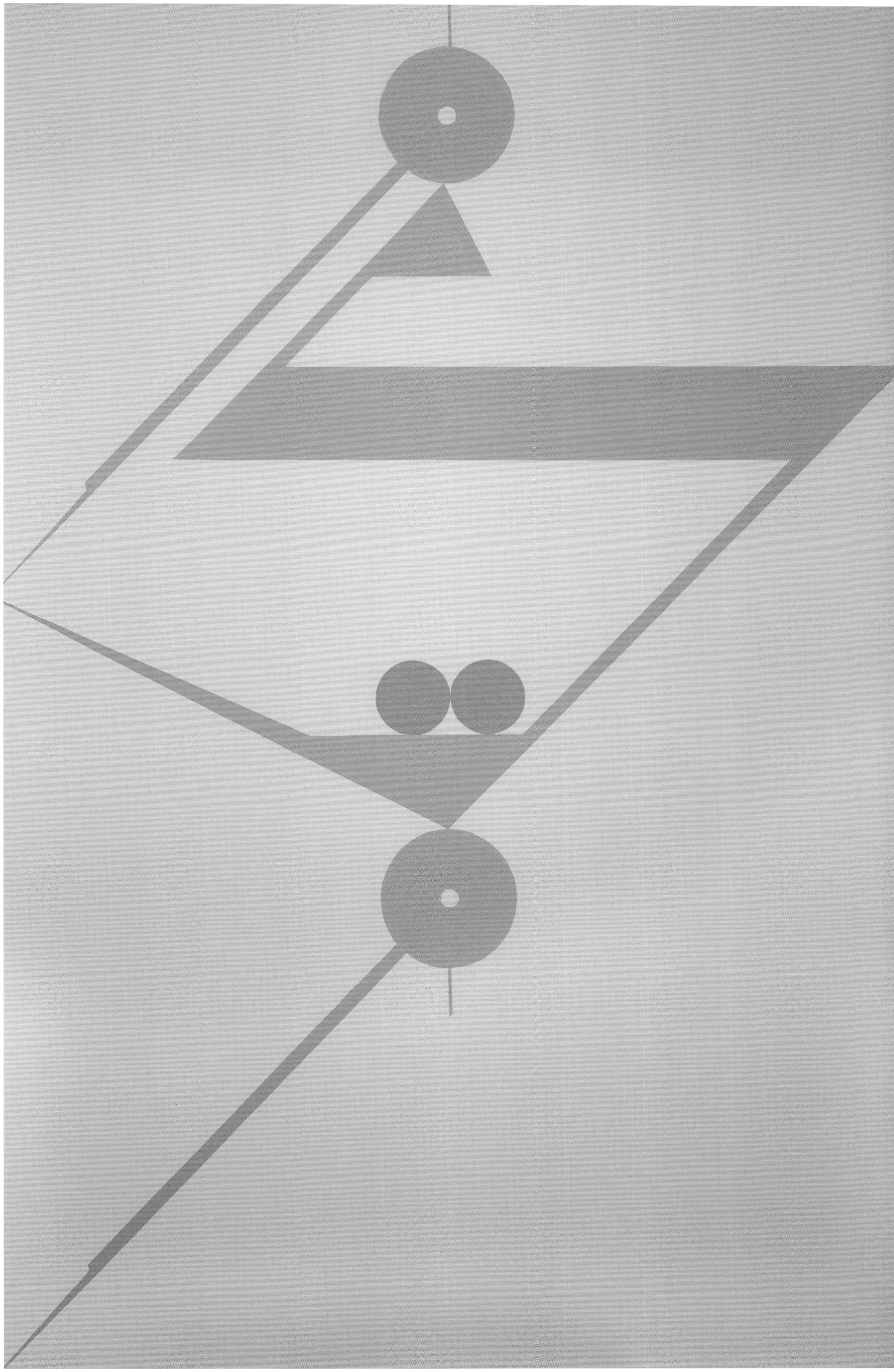

SHAUQ, 2018
Acrylic on canvas and gold leaf,
120 x 100 cm

Philip Taaffe

Ultimate Reality is at once Absolute and Infinite, the source of all being, of all consciousness and of all life. Itself beyond form, it speaks to mankind through revealed forms which, while externally bound and limited, open up inwardly towards the Boundless. Through revelations of this Word or Logos come into being the sacred traditions which although outwardly different are inwardly united into a Centre which transcends all forms. They are, however, the bridge from the periphery to the Centre, from the relative to the Absolute, from the finite to the Infinite, from multiplicity to Unity.
– Seyyed Hossein Nasr*

Emancipatory signs: geometry in Islamic art
Geometry in Islamic art is essentially a direct answer to the Divine in the form of praise and thankfulness for endowing humanity with the intelligence and creative imagination to summon these extraordinary pictorial inventions. What has come down to us is a source of profound inspiration. As artists, we should be honoured and challenged by these astonishing historical achievements. I feel a sense of humility and awe at the seemingly endless levels of productive craftsmanship and the precise engineering required for covering those vast walls and arches and cupolas throughout the entire geography of the pan-Islamic world.
Extensive scholarship, dating back at least to the early nineteenth century and up until the present day, has enabled us to look at the cultural specificity and the mathematical precepts involved in the development of geometry in Islamic Art. The *girih*, a codified form of geometric patterning with algebraically defined elements, appears toward the end of the seventh century. Curiously, from my own practical standpoint, this is also around the same historical moment that the art form known as orizomegami, involving the careful staining and folding of paper, seems to have come into existence in Japan.
From 2008 to 2012 I produced approximately two dozen paintings that combined the orizomegami technique with Islamic geometry, an example of which is reproduced in this publication (*Epiphania,* 2010).
Artists working from some allegiance to the Western tradition in painting, for example, aim to make something to be physically experienced by another person: it is a raw, freely chosen, interpersonal relationship between the maker and the viewer, so it is close to what a musical composer does, or a poet, or a dancer – it is coming out of one's inner being. On the other hand, the anonymous collective of craftsmen and architectural engineers responsible for constructing Islamic edifices labour in deference to the Ineffable. Although these might seem to be quite diverse motivating factors, the most important parallel here is that art has to do with expression, with summoning an inner state, shaping a personal experience.
I have a fairly unwieldy set of concerns that go into determining what I do in my paintings.
I like to consider the history of the decorative as it relates to patterns of cultural migration: the Byzantine period, and its influence on the formation of Islamic Art, for instance.
I have also immersed myself in the annals of natural history through scattered, intuitive, non-systematic research methods. All of these things are filtered through my own sense of cultural urgency. For me, an important function of geometry in Islamic Ornament is what Oleg Grabar referred to as mediation: a bridge to a world of rumination on the Divine.
In 2012 I prepared a statement as an introduction to a performance of Sufi music by the Pera Ensemble of Istanbul, at the Bohm Chapel in Cologne, Germany, during an exhibition of my paintings. I thought it might be appropriate to include here, as it has been previously unpublished:

"The cause of religion must serve to liberate and nourish the human spirit. The divinity we find within and around us needs to be celebrated as the source of our most profound joy. The Sufic tradition within Islam certainly offers some of the world's most magnificent manifestations of our relationship to the Divine. I believe in the importance of music and dance and poetry and visual art as our most powerful weapons in the continuing struggle against all forms of religious authoritarianism."

* From the foreword of *Islamic Patterns: An Analytical and Cosmological Approach* by Keith Critchlow, 1976

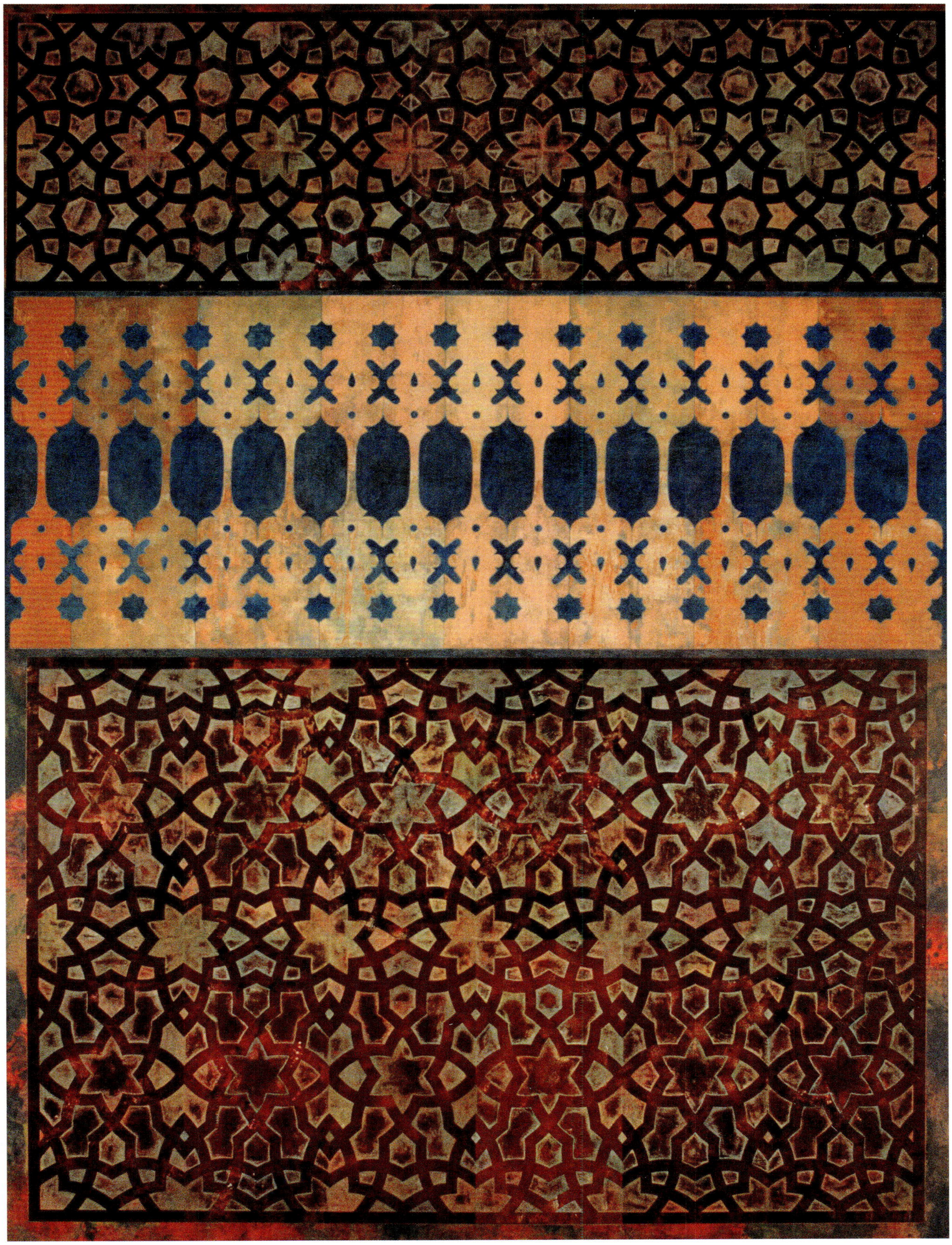

Screen with Double Lambrequin, 1989
Mixed media on linen, 369 x 285 cm
Broad Art Foundation, Santa Monica, CA
Photo by Claudio Abate

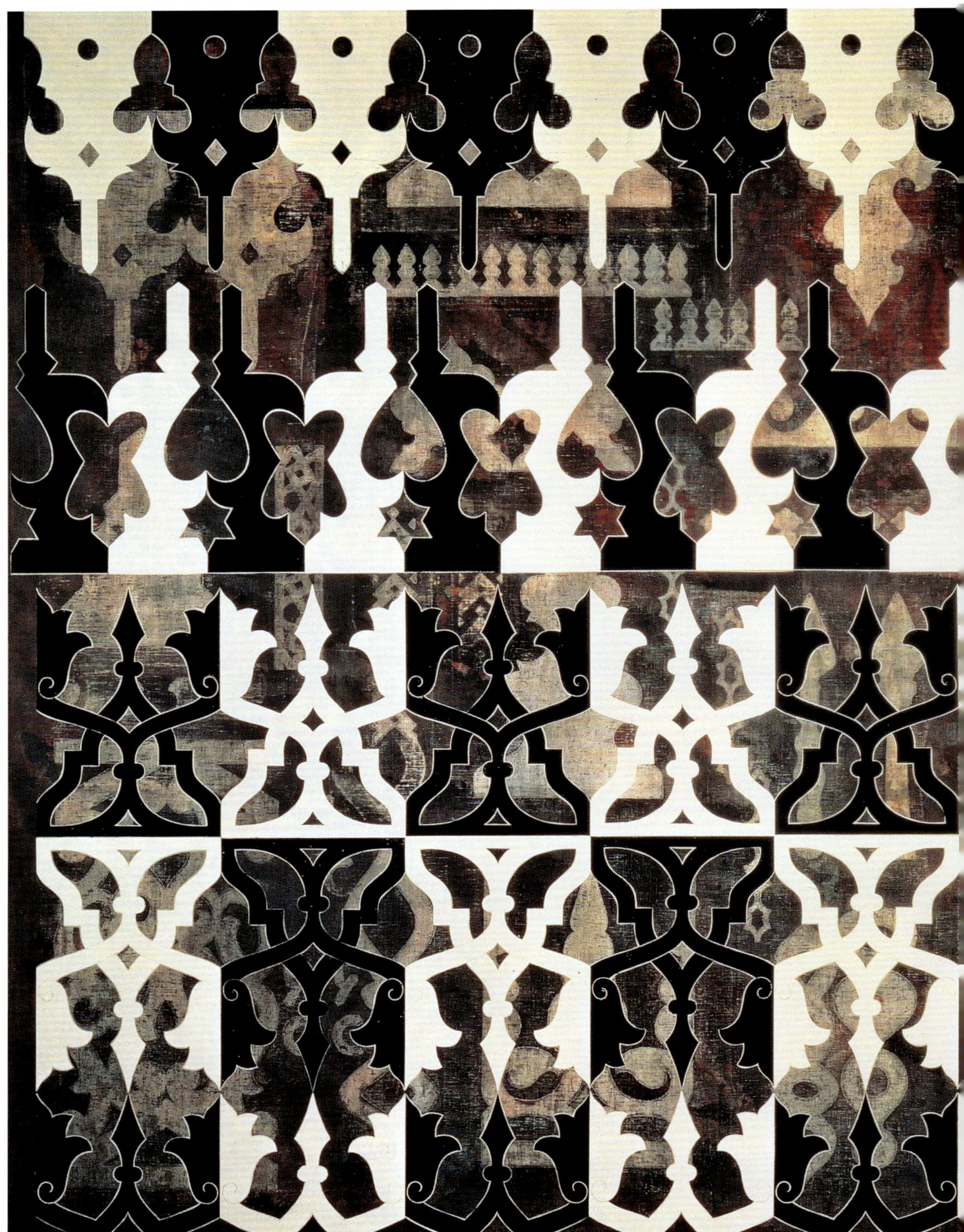

Al Quasbah, 1991
Mixed media on linen,
228.5 x 460 cm
Appletree Collection

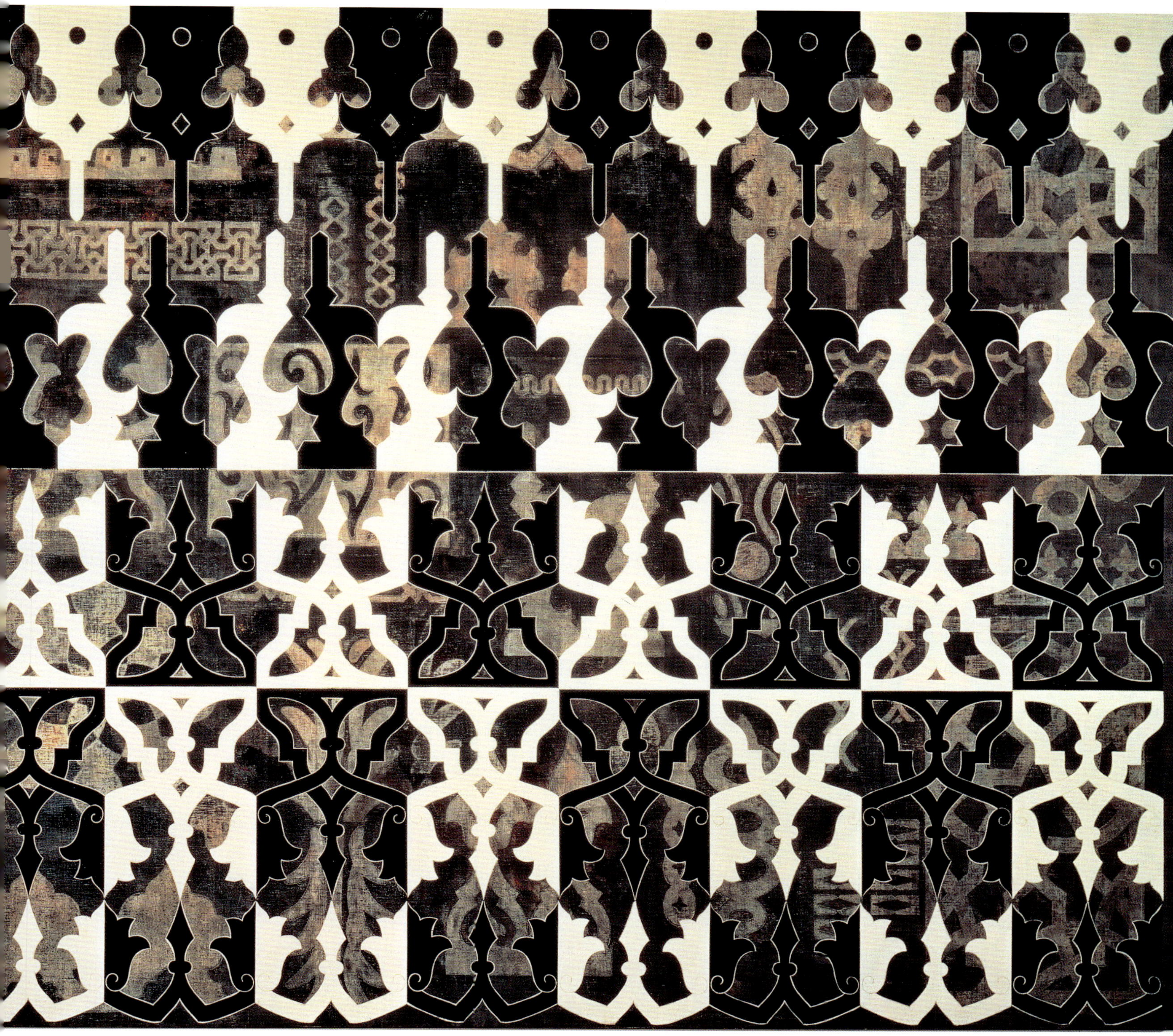

Epiphania, 2010
Mixed media on linen
Triangle: base 329 cm, height 285 cm

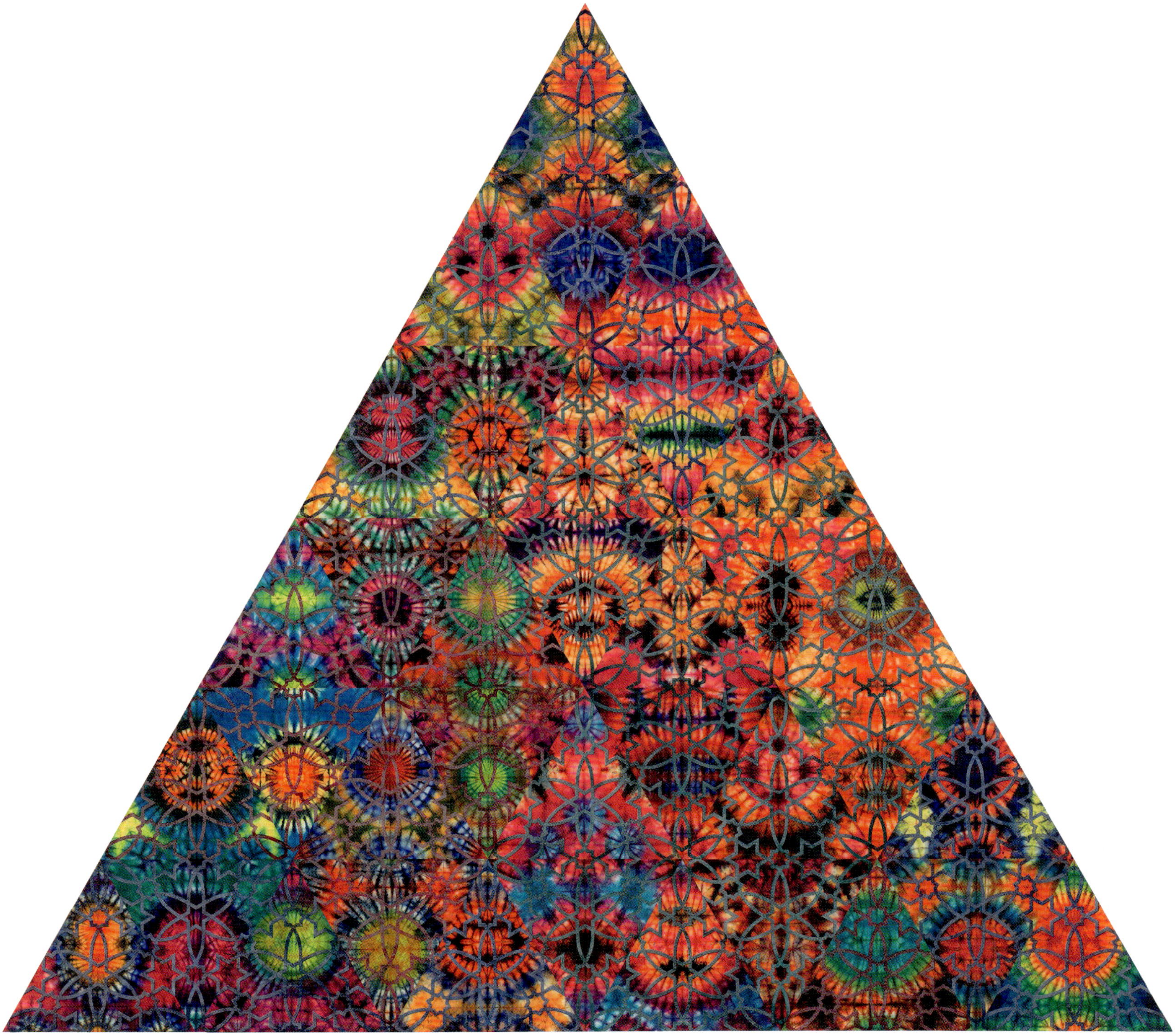

Gebran Tarazi

Ceiling Light Season: the picture as ecosystem
Around the end of the 1980s, Gebran Tarazi, working in the family boutique as a craftsman and colourist – objects and light fittings, but also woodwork and decoration – gradually saw a new, imperious destiny beckoning, one born of his own savoir-faire. A conscientious worker who carefully varied each panel of the ceiling light with different lines and chromatic surfaces, he would make the radical shift of status from, as he was fond of putting it, that of the craftsman who knows what he is doing to that of the artist who does not. The ceiling light would make the transition to the table – the writing desk, even – and very soon to that of the picture, when it became clear that Tarazi was unquestionably 'in the process of making modern art'. Thus could the ceiling light rise above our heads again and the picture be (re)born of this ascent. This would be the sign of a fundamental inversion in terms of the events to come and the twelve series (or 'seasons') that would serve as cyclical, thematic chapters in the artist's attempt to exhaust the Qayem-Nayem motif: the picture, blessed as it may have been with the seal of modernism, would never conform to a Western doxa backed up by the theoretical celebration of American Abstract Expressionism and the writings of art critic Clement Greenberg, which froze the picture outside time in an absolute present.
Tarazi makes the *picture* something much more important than the *paint*. His colour ranges are burdened with no 'dramatisation' or painterly lyricism. They depend, rather, on the light of day striking them, and on the concentration of our gaze, but above all on our ability to imagine the fully fledged ecosystem the picture harbours – its living space. In linking the experience of the picture directly to that of the ceiling light, or of the chequered pattern or the mosaic under our feet, Tarazi – for a time a collector of Caucasian carpets, whose full splendour he dreamed of revealing by hanging them on the wall – no longer saw himself as the interior designer he was predestined to be by the family he aspired to emancipate himself from. Rather he considered himself the shaper of a counter-history of ornament in which the fear of the void – the *horror vacui* – of the Orientalist vulgate was replaced by the attraction of concentric forces, arrangement of surfaces and spatial potentialities. Whence the fact that in most cases the pictures of the twelve seasons contain a frame treated as if it were an internal element of the work: a frame often decorated with infinitesimal gradations of colour, all but invisible to the naked eye, at least at first glance; a conception of the frame that denotes an urge to index the picture space in terms of the space around it, or which secretly welcomes it. Thus each picture's 'secret garden' has less to do with its inner structuring – its geometric code – than with its ability to *create place*. An ideal place at once everywhere and nowhere, taking shelter in the privacy of a meditation on the number and the adaptability of the chromatic figures making up a painted ceiling in the region of Susa, in Morocco – viewed looking upwards, in search of a modernism *turned upside down*.

Qayem-Nayem Season
The Qayem-Nayem motif: two rectangles standing vertically (Qayem) and two others lying horizontally (Nayem) which come together at right angles around a central square and give rise to another square – the basic unit, the classic theme in the universal language of *ornament*. This is how Gebran Tarazi represented that theme in its raw, undisguised form, between his forty-fifth and fifty-ninth years; between 1988 and 2003, when he threw himself into a (seemingly) frantic attempt to exhaust the optical, geometric and chromatic possibilities of the Qayem-Nayem matrix. A resolve that makes you think of a mathematician or a physicist in search of the ultimate formula; in retrospect, though, Tarazi looks more like an architect intent on building the family house according to its receptiveness to the host of potential positions, in one and the same lifetime or one and the same *cosmos*, of the sun, the moon and the stars. Far from having its roots solely in the traditional Islamic arts, the Qayem-Nayem reflects a cultural and symbolic syncretism we can as readily identify in Chinese civilisation as among the Etruscans of the pre-Roman era: its formal associations link it to all kinds of heraldic crosses, swastikas, traceries and other labyrinthine and spiral-like forms. Sprung, then, from a metaphysical syncretism tied to our symbolic unconscious, or from a *migration of motifs* tied to our geometrical unconscious – but also from trade and the circulation of goods and craft skills – the Qayem-Nayem, embedded in the context of the arabesque, illumination, tapestry and wood or copper engraving, became a talisman for Tarazi: exhaustion of possibilities via combination, but also via movement.
In a stance not far removed from the sacrificial, the artist submits to the preconditions of a stylistic degree zero invested with an immutable, endlessly déjà vu base unit to which he claims to be able to bring countless other, scarcely imaginable 'visions'. The Qayem-Nayem's characteristic Russian doll, square-within-a-square structure is intended to be simultaneously inclusive and expansive: every form that can be a part of it is also a form of which the Qayem-Nayem can be a part. A form rooted in the unconscious of a whole group of civilisations and especially in quaternary cosmic symbolic systems (the four rivers of Paradise, the four seasons, and so on), but which also asserts itself – in the endless calculations of our artist-mathematician – as destined to a kind of roaming across the chessboard of motifs and colours 'available' to these same civilisations. The Qayem-Nayem, or the transcultural talisman, the migratory bird and the temple gate (in a kinetic dream).
Morad Montazami
Curator and Director of Zaman Books

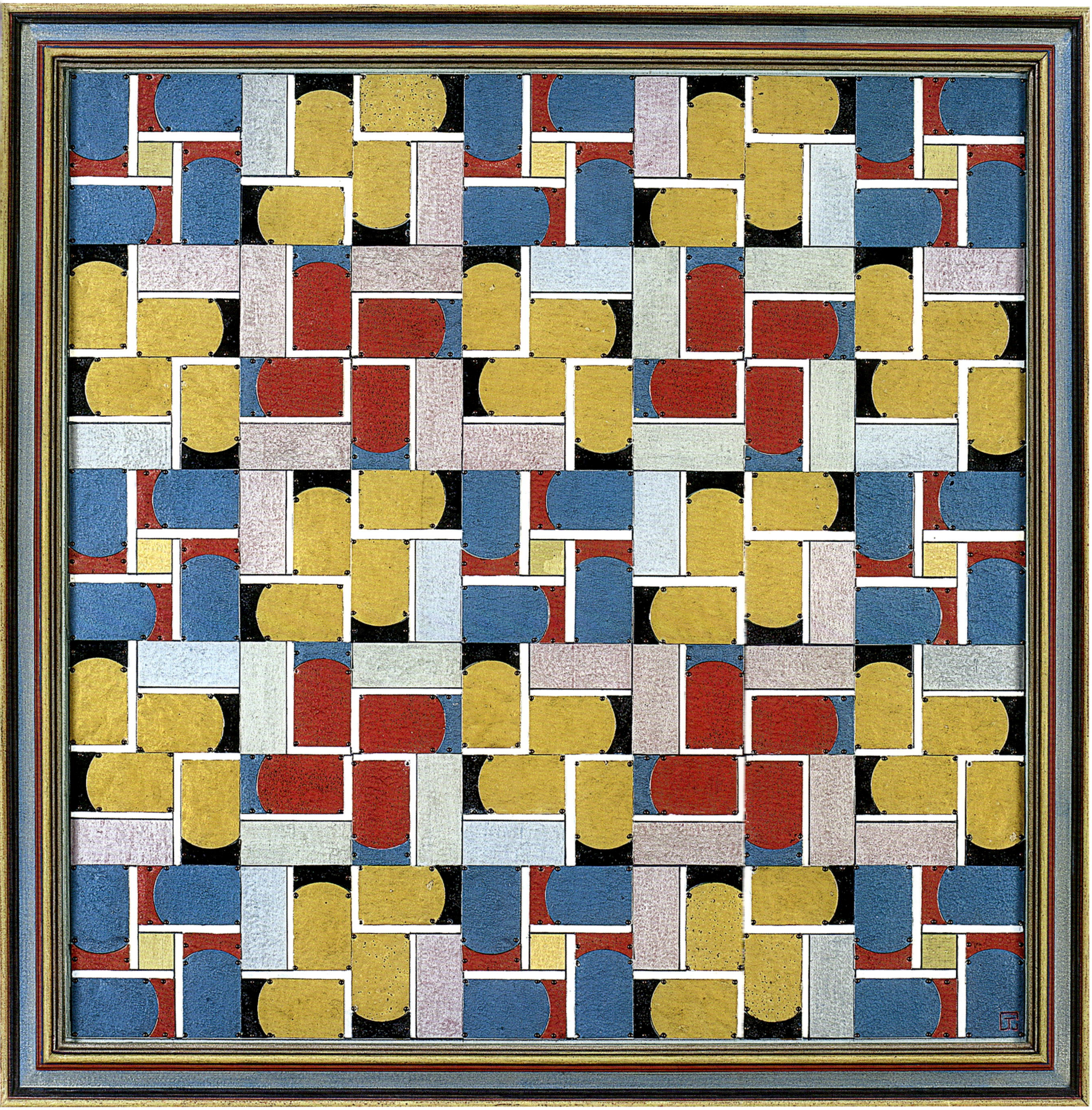

Untitled, 1999
Metallic and acrylic painting on metal and wood, 68.2 x 68.2 cm

Untitled, 1999
Mixed media on wooden modules,
75.5 x 75.5 cm

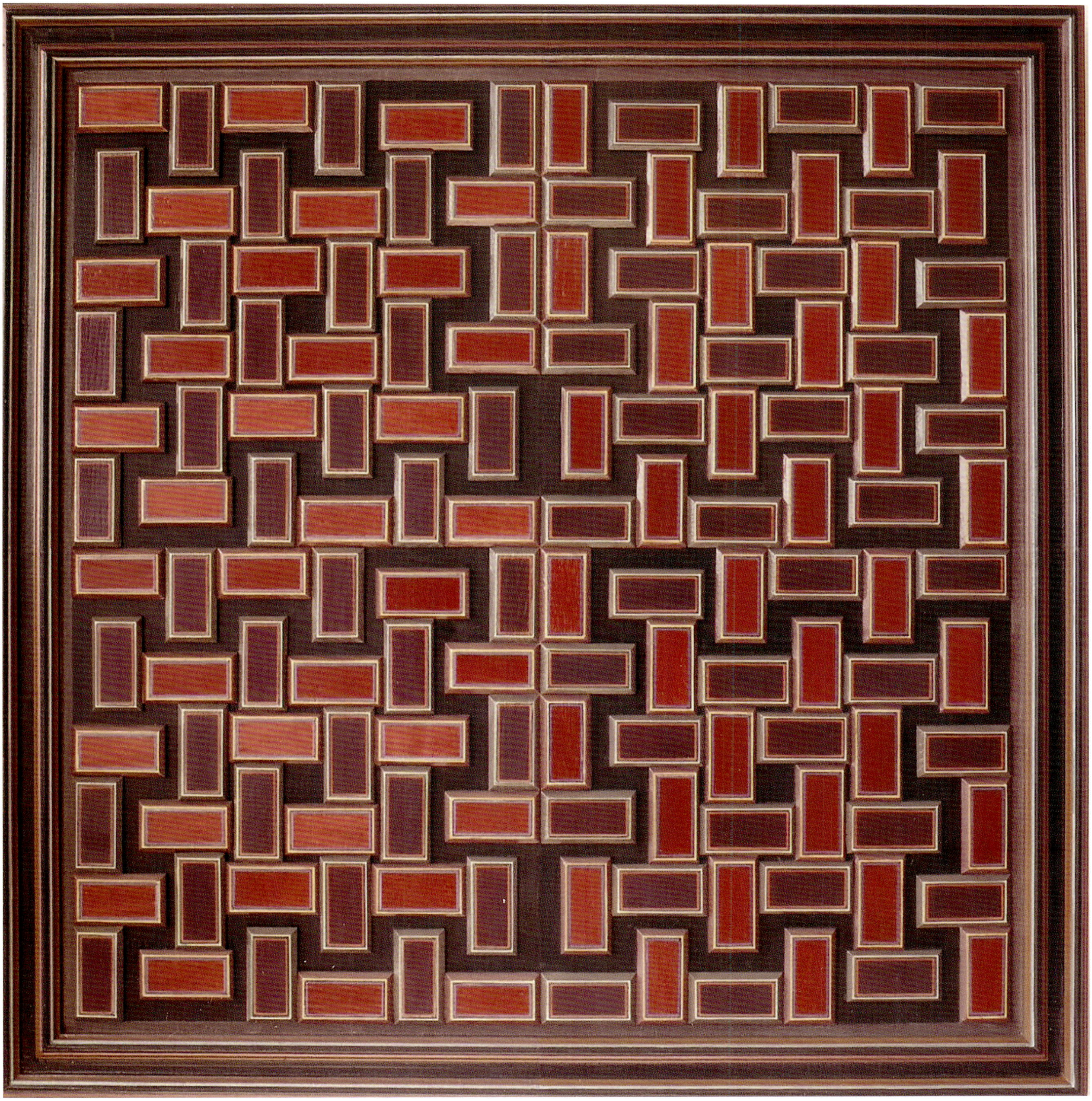

Untitled, 2001
Acrylic on wood, 91.5 x 91.5 cm

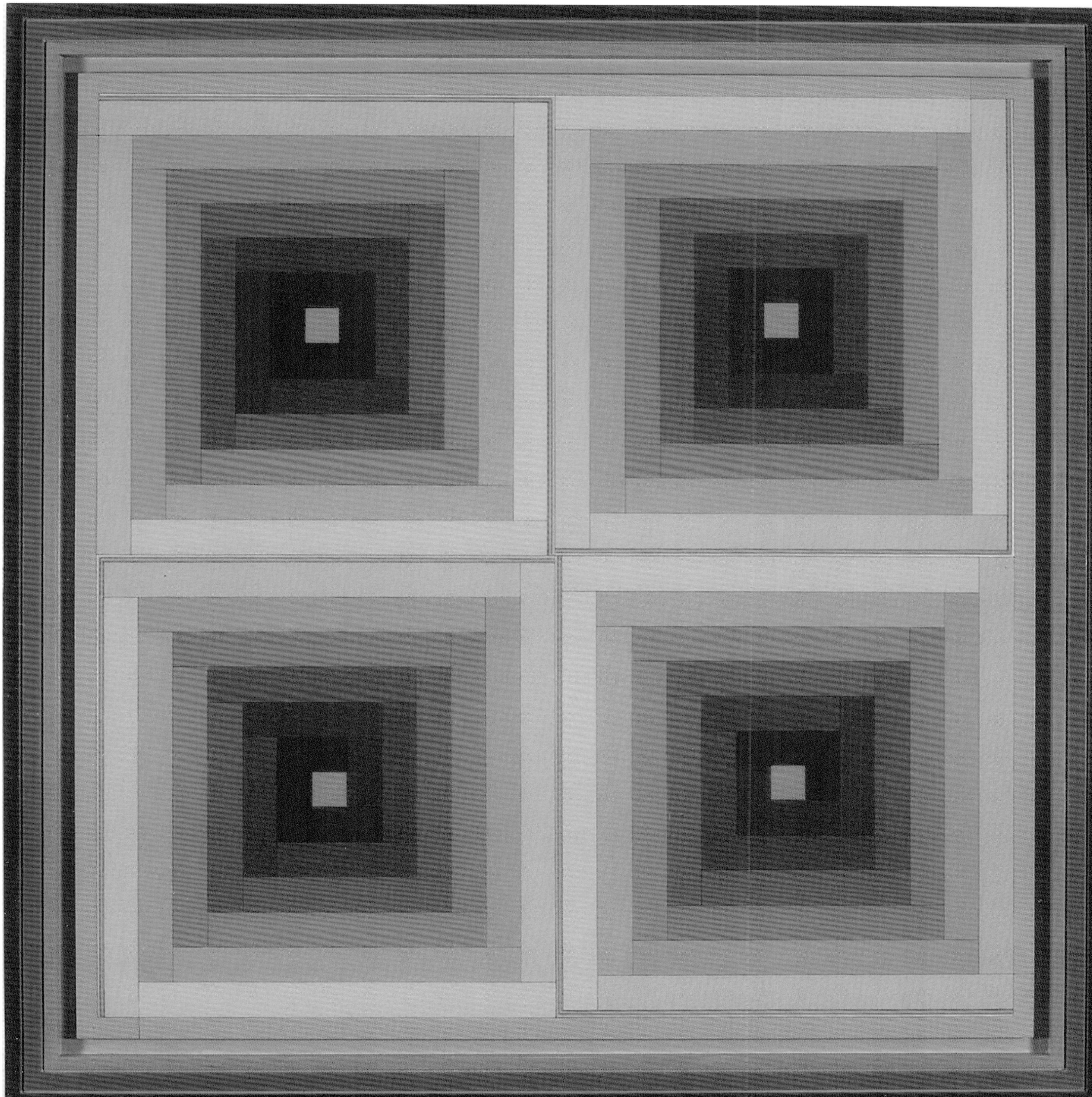

Biographies

Ebtisam Abdulaziz was born in Sharjah in 1975, where she continues to live. Trained in mathematics and science, she is a multidisciplinary artist and writer. Abdulaziz incorporates her unique perspective on mathematics and structures of systems to explore issues of identity and culture through installations, performance and works on paper. She creates codes and graphic language within her practice. She has exhibited as part of the UAE and ADACH Pavilions at 53rd Venice Biennale, 7th and 10th Sharjah Biennials; Kunst Museum, Bonn, Germany; The Mori Art Museum, Tokyo; Institut du Monde Arabe, Paris; Benin Biennial 2012. FotoFest Biennial, Houston, TX. She was part of the touring exhibition *Past Forward*. She has also exhibited at Cara & Smack Mellon Gallery, New York; at NYUAD and Guggenheim Abu Dhabi. Ebtisam has been listed as one of the 100 powerful Arab Women in 2013, and her work is held in a number of important collections, including that of the UAE Ministry of Culture, the Renault Collection, and Deutsche Bank.

Anila Quayyum Agha was born in Lahore, Pakistan in 1965. She has a BFA from the National College of Arts, Lahore and an MFA from the University of North Texas. Agha's work has been exhibited in multiple international art fairs as well as in over thirty solo shows and fifty group shows. Recent solo shows in 2014 – 2018, include the Grand Rapids Art Museum, MI, MOCA Jacksonville, FL, Cincinnati Art Museum, OH, Peabody Essex Museum in Salem, MA, National Sculpture Museum, Valladolid, Spain, Rice Gallery at Rice University in Houston, TX, The Dallas Contemporary Art Museum, TX, and the State Museum in Indianapolis, IN, to name a few. In 2005, Agha was an Artist in Residence at the Center for Contemporary Craft, Houston, TX. Agha relocated to Indianapolis in 2008 to teach at the Herron School of Art and is currently the associate professor of drawing. In 2009 Agha was the recipient of the Efroymson Arts Fellowship. She has received two IAHI grants (2010 and 2015) and two New Frontiers Research Grants (2012 and 2016) from Indiana University. In 2013 Agha received the Creative Renewal Fellowship awarded by the Indianapolis Arts Council. She won the two top prizes at ArtPrize 2014, in the international art competition held in Grand Rapids, MI. In 2017, Agha was the recipient of Cincinnati Art Museum's 2017 Schiele Prize which recognises the finest works of art and design by living artists. This year (2018) Agha received the DeHaan Artist of Distinction Award and will use the funds to create new work for her solo show in spring 2019 at Talley Dunn art gallery in Dallas, TX. Additionally, in August 2018 Agha unveiled her public art project titled *This is NOT a Refuge*, in the Open Spaces biennale in Kansas City, MO. Her work has been collected by both institutions and private collectors nationally and internationally.
Agha works in a cross disciplinary fashion with mixed media; creating artwork that explores global politics, cultural multiplicity, mass media, and social and gender roles in our current cultural and global scenario. As a result, her artwork is conceptually challenging, producing complicated weaves of thought, artistic action and social experience. She lives and works in the USA.

Zeinab Al Hashemi is an Emirati artist born in Dubai in 1986. She obtained a B.A. in Graphic Design from Zayed University in Dubai. She specialises in conceptual and site-specific art installations. Her focus is on visual story-telling, transforming it through the lens of experimental media and the use of new materials. Her technique involves the manipulation of contemporary techniques, but with subject matter that is rooted in the cultural traditions of her native UAE. In earlier series she has created mixed media works with design elements from popular culture, commercially available Emirati products and traditional materials.
Zeinab has held an art residency at London's Delfina Foundation, participated in the UAE Pavilion at the Shanghai Expo in 2011, and been shown both locally and abroad. She exhibited in *Poems from the Desert and UAE: A Work of Art* at Ara Gallery, Sikka Art Fair, *MinD Made in Dubai*, DUCTAC, and the F1 Project at Abu Dhabi Airport. Zeinab lives and works in the United Arab Emirates.

Lulwah Al Homoud was born in 1967 in Riyadh, and now lives and works in the UK. She was the first Saudi to obtain an MA degree from Central Saint Martins College of Art and Design (2000). Her area of research was Arabic calligraphy and Islamic geometry. She is known for developing a highly personal approach that merges calligraphy and geometry in uniquely intricate patterns, based on mathematical concepts. She trained under the renowned calligrapher Rasheed Butt.
She represented Saudi Arabia at the 2018 London Design Biennial. Her work has been exhibited and acquired by international museums, among which the Los Angeles County Museum of Art (LACMA), Jeju Museum of Contemporary Art in Korea, and Five Continents Museum in Munich, Germany, as well as The Greenbox Museum of Contemporary Art from Saudi Arabia in Holland.
Lulwah was the only artist from the Middle East in the inaugural exhibition of 36 renowned international artists at the Jeju Museum of Contemporary Art, Korea, in 2009.
Her work has been exhibited internationally in Russia, China, USA, Europe and the Middle East. She has had solo exhibitions at the Sharjah Calligraphy Museum during the art biennial in 2015, at the Islamic Art Festival 2015, and the 2016 Calligraphy Biennial at the Sharjah Art Museum, as well as nine other major solo exhibitions among them at ArtSpace Dubai, and Naila Gallery, Riyadh.
Lulwah's commitment to her Islamic heritage has led her to collaborate with the British Museum in 2007 to introduce Arabic/Islamic art and design to GCSE students. She has curated a number of international exhibitions since 1999, including the one at the October Gallery in 2003, and the first Saudi Arabian group show at London's Brunei Gallery in 2008. She has also curated shows in 2010 in Shanghai and Beirut.
She is Co-Founder of Cube Arts in London 2010–2017, and Dubai 2012–2015, an initiative for cultural exchange programmes promoting art from the region internationally.
She works with major museums in the region as an art consultant.

Rashid Al Khalifa was born in Bahrain in 1952. He studied at Brighton and Hastings Art College, UK, and has painted over a period of forty years. He has transitioned from Realism to Individualism, and now focussed on the dual concept of abstraction and colour fields. He has participated in numerous international solo and group exhibitions. Solo exhibitions include: Saatchi Gallery, London, UK (2018), Ayyam Gallery, Dubai (2018), Shuman Arts Organisation, Amman, Jordan (1997), De Caliet Gallery and El Kato Kayyel Gallery, Milan, Italy (1996). Group exhibitions include: the Venice Biennale, Italy (2017 and 2015), Third Mediterranean Biennale, Sakhnin Valley (2017), tRIO Bienal, Rio de Janeiro, Brazil (2015), Galerie Gmurzynska, Art Basel Miami Beach (2010), Taipei Art Exhibition, Taiwan (1999), Sharjah Biennial, UAE (1999), and Art America Exhibition, Miami, FL (1997). He is the first and current President of the Bahrain Arts Society.

His works are held in a number of private collections, and he lives and works in Bahrain.

Ahmad Angawi is a Saudi multidisciplinary creative artist from Makkah born in 1981. He holds a bachelor's degree in Industrial Design from Pratt Institute in New York and a Master's degree in Traditional Arts from The Prince's School of Traditional Arts in London. Angawi is currently the Associate Director of Al Makmad Foundation, a cultural institution that aims to conserve and revive the Hejazi heritage. He is also the Program Director of The House of Traditional Arts located in Al-Balad, the historical district of Jeddah. The school is an initiative by the Prince's School of Traditional Arts in London, and Art Jameel and acts as a hub serving the local and wider community of artists and craftsmen. Angawi was also a Consultant and Program Researcher at the Saudi Commission for Tourism & National Heritage (SCTH) along with Turquoise Mountain, a non-profit, non-governmental organisation regenerating historic cities, and spurring the sustainable development of the traditional crafts industries. Ahmad is a co-founder of Al-Hangar, an independent artists' initiative that provides a platform for dialogue and cultural exchange by way of exhibitions, community-oriented projects and educational programmes. Angawi has exhibited locally and internationally in solo and group shows, and was most recently featured in the inaugural exhibition of the Al Bukhary Galleries at the British Museum. He was part of *#Cometogether*, Edge of Arabia, London 2012; *We Need to Talk*, Edge of Arabia, Jeddah, KSA 2012; the 55th Venice Biennale in 2013; and other shows in Dubai and USA.

Dana Awartani was born in 1987 in Jeddah. She is a Palestinian-Saudi artist, having trained in contemporary and traditional modes of practice and thought at a Foundation Degree in Art and Design and a B.A. in Fine Art from Central Saint Martins. She followed this with a Masters degree at the Prince's School of Traditional Arts. Influenced by these two diverse routes, her works are continual acts of revival and performances, of contemporisation and linkages. She has exhibited at the Venice, Kochi, Jakarta, Marrakech and Yinchuan Biennales. She has also been exhibited at the Jewish Museum in NYC in 2016, as well as at the Institute of Arab and Islamic Arts in NYC in 2017; at the Mosaic Rooms in London in 2017. Her most recent solo show was at the Detroit MOCA in 2017. She lives and works between Saudi Arabia and London.

Rana Begum was born in Sylhet, Bangladesh and studied painting at the Chelsea College of Art and Design (1999) and the Slade School of Art (2002) in London. She is currently based in London. Recent solo exhibitions include *Space Light Colour,* Sainsbury Centre for Visual Arts, Norwich (2017) and Parasol Unit, London (2016). Her public art commissions include *No. 700 Reflectors*, at Lewis Cubitt Square, a temporary work for the Kings Cross Project (2017).
Rana's artwork *No. 274 Reflectors* was commissioned for the *Art at Westgate* programme and is located at the escalators, Middle Square. Rana Begum explores in her work the relationship between space, light and colour, blurring the boundaries between two and three dimensions.

Kamal Boullata was born in Jerusalem in 1942, and is considered a foremost Palestinian artist and art historian. He is a graduate of the Academy of Rome, and Washington's Corcoran Art Museum School. He works primarily in acrylic and/or silkscreen, and composes abstractions that address the ideas of division in Palestinian identity, and separation from homeland through utilisation of geometric forms. Known as a member of the Hurufiyya Art Movement, Kamal has experimented equally with calligraphic modes.
Public collections of his work include the British Museum, London; Alhambra Islamic Museum, Granada; Institut du Monde Arabe, Paris; Jordan National Gallery, Amman; New York Public Library, NY; Mathaf Museum of Modern Art, Doha; Bibliothèque Notari, Monaco; Barjeel Art Foundation, Sharjah; Zimmerli Art Museum, New Brunswick, NJ.
As a Fulbright Senior Scholar Fellow (1993 and 1994), he pursued research on Islamic art in Morocco and Spain. With a Ford Foundation grant in 2001, he wrote on post-Byzantine painting in Palestine. In 2012, he was elected as a Fellow of the Institute for Advanced Study in Berlin. He has exhibited widely, and lives and works in Berlin.

Monir Shahroudy Farman Farmaian was born in Qazvin, Iran in 1922. She trained at the University of Tehran, followed by Parsons, and subsequently Cornell University. She lives and works in Tehran, Iran. Her distinguished career has spanned more than six decades, and she is today considered one of the most prominent Iranian artists of the contemporary period. Her technique ('Geometric minimalism') incorporates traditional reverse glass painting, mirror mosaics, and principles of Islamic geometry with a modern sensibility. Creating unique works that lie somewhere between sculpture, mosaic-work, and installation, her practice defies easy categorisation.
Monir was the first Iranian artist to have a solo exhibition at The Solomon R. Guggenheim Museum in New York; she has exhibited extensively both in Iran and on the international platform. She has received numerous accolades, including at the Venice Biennale (1958). Her pieces have also been acquired by the most prominent museums in the world, including The Metropolitan Museum of Art, the Tate Modern, the Victoria and Albert Museum and Queensland Gallery of Contemporary Art, and are held in major private collections.
She is the subject of a substantial monograph, *Monir Shahroudy Farmanfarmaian: Cosmic Geometry*, edited by Hans Ulrich Obrist; the co-author of an autobiography, *A Mirror Garden* (Knopf, 2007); and the focus of a documentary film, *Monir*.
In 2017, The Monir Museum, under the auspices of Tehran University, opened in Tehran. It is the first solo artist museum in Iran.

Nargess Hashemi was born in 1979 in Tehran, where she still lives and works. She was educated at the Neyshabour Institute and at the Fine Art Department of the Art University in Tehran. She grew up in a traditional household and studied Ancient Persian. Hashemi's works are intimate observations of the dualities that permeate her daily life in Iran by using a diverse range of techniques and materials, including monoprinting, macramé, graph paper and acetate. Her style is continuously evolving, from largely figurative works of celebratory scenes, to her most recent works in which she uses graph paper to experiment with more abstract, geometric compositions.
She has had numerous solo shows in her home town, and exhibited internationally in Dubai, Abu Dhabi, London, Kuwait, and New York.
She has also participated in Iranian Spring (2004) at the Tehran Museum of Contemporary Art, was part of a USA touring group show entitled *Wishes and Dreams: Iran's New Generation Emerges* (2007), and *The Language of Human Consciousness*, Athr Gallery, Jeddah (2014). Her major collaborations include one with Ramin Haerizadeh, Rokni Haerizadeh and Hesam Rahmanian for a multi-room installation as part of *The Creative Act* at Guggenheim Abu Dhabi (2016) and *Forgive me, distant wars, for bringing flowers home* at Officine Grandi Riparazioni, Turin, Italy (2018). She was also part of Bread and

Salt's touring exhibition in Italy entitled *Good Morning....Good Night!* (2018). She is held in the collections of the Cleveland Clinic Abu Dhabi, the private collection of HH Sheikha Osha bint Khalifa bin Zayed Al Nahyan, Mohammed Afkhami, and the Farjam Collection.

Susan Hefuna is a German-Egyptian visual artist, born in Germany in 1962. She trained in multi-media at the Stadelschule in Frankfurt.
Her work is exhibited internationally, the most recent being at the Galleria d'Arte Moderna (GAM) in Milan with the show *But a Storm Is Blowing from Paradise*, in 2018; *Contemporary Art and the Islamic Tradition* at the Katonah Museum of Art, Katonah, NY; *The Creative Act: Performance Process Presence*, Guggenheim Abu Dhabi in 2017; *Angst Eats Soul*, PiArtworks Gallery, Istanbul; *But a Storm Is Blowing from Paradise*, Guggenheim, NYC; *The Barjeel Art Foundation: Debating Modernism Part III*, Whitechapel Gallery, London; *Cross border*, PATAKA ART MUSEUM, New Zealand; *Contemporary Art of the Middle East*, LACMA, Los Angeles, in 2015; *Common Grounds*, Museum Villa Stuck, Munich; *Sharjah Art Foundation* at Bait Al Serkal, Sharjah, in 2014; Osthaus Museum, Hagen; *Encounter* at the Katara Arts Center in Doha; *Notationotations*, The Drawing Center, NYC; *Buildings*, Rhona Hoffman Gallery, Chicago in 2012; *Drawing in the 20th Century* at MoMA, NYC in 2010. Hefuna's work was included in several Biennales: Sydney Biennale, Australia 2012, *Fare Mondi* Venice Biennale, Italy, in 2009; Seville Biennial, Spain, 2008, the 2nd Riwaq Biennale, Riwaq, Palestine and the Ninth Sharjah Biennial, UAE in 2007. In 2013 Susan Hefuna was awarded the international Contemporary Drawing Prize of the Daniel and Florence Guerlain Art Foundation in Paris. Her work addresses the intersection of location and identity. She lives and works between Cairo and Germany.

Sahand Hessamiyan was born in 1977 in Tehran, and holds a degree in Bachelor of Sculpture from the Tehran University Arts Faculty.
He currently lives and works in Tehran. Sahand's practice explores contemporary sculptural directions, which take cue from Islamic architecture and ornamentation, but are also based on scientific-mathematical calculations reflecting the laws of the universe. His works are primarily interactive, and link science and geometry to the abstract nature of spirituality, as a reflective attempt to discover the esoteric nature of Iranian culture through the dissection of its architectural form.
Sahand's selected solo exhibitions include *Majaz*, BLOK Art Space, Istanbul (2017); *Frame Reference*, Sam Art, Dastan's Outside the Basement, Tehran (2015); *Khalvat*, The Third Line, Dubai (2014).
He has taken part in numerous group exhibitions nationally and internationally (France, Brussels, London, Los Angeles), including the Venice Biennale (2015), and his works are included in important private and public collections such as the Delfina Foundation, the Samawi and MAC Collections.

Mohamed Abdul Latif Kanoo was born in Bahrain in 1963. He commenced art in 1989 as a self-taught painter. His early works are inspired by the Pop Art style of Warhol and Roy Lichtenstein.
His work draws inspiration from his Islamic and Gulf heritage and extends to applied and digital media, photography and Arabic calligraphy. He interprets popular culture whilst respecting the artistic limitations of his faith. In the aftermath of the 9/11 terror attacks, he has focussed on advancing an artistic platform that presents an alternative and positive view of contemporary Arabia.
His works have been exhibited within the region and internationally. He lives and works in Abu Dhabi.

Ahmed Mater was born in Tabuk in 1979. Growing up in the fertile south of the Kingdom, his life and work have been shaped by the seismic changes of the oil boom and rentier era – transformations which have diverged into unprecedented social shifts. In 2016, Mater became the first Saudi artist to hold a solo exhibition in the United States with *Symbolic Cities: The Work of Ahmed Mater* at the Smithsonian Institution's Arthur M. Sackler Gallery, Washington DC.
He has also had solo exhibitions at King Khalid University, Abha, Saudi Arabia (2004); Royal Embassy of Saudi Arabia, London (2006); Artspace, Dubai (2009); the Vinyl Factory Gallery, London (2010); and Sharjah Art Foundation (2013). His work has been included in group exhibitions at the British Museum, London (2006 and 2012); Mori Art Museum, Tokyo (2011); Institut du Monde Arab, Paris (2012); Victoria and Albert Museum, London (2013); Museum of Islamic Art, Doha, Qatar (2013); Louisiana Museum of Modern Art, Humleaek, Denmark (2013); Nelson-Atkins Museum of Art, Kansas City (2013); Ashkal Alwan in Beirut, Lebanon (2013); Biennale Jogja (2013); Centre Georges Pompidou, Paris (2014); New Museum, New York (2014); and Guggenheim, New York (2016). He participated in the Sharjah Biennial (2007 and 2013); Cairo Biennial (2008); Venice Biennale (2009 and 2011); and Kochi Muziris Biennale, Kerela India (2012). His work is part of major international collections including The British Museum, London; Victoria and Albert Museum, London; Los Angeles County Museum of Art, California; and Centre Pompidou, Paris.
Physician turned artist, Ahmed Mater is one of the most significant cultural voices documenting and scrutinising the realities of contemporary Saudi Arabia. He uses photography, film, sculpture and performance to map, document and analyse the tension of his country's rapid developments. His practice embraces the paradoxes of science and faith. Entwining expressive and politically engaged artistic aims with the scientific objectives of his medical training, he fuses the two realms to explore their connections and contradictions.
He lives and works between Riyadh, Jeddah and Abha, Saudi Arabia.

Mehdi Moutashar was born in 1942 in Hilla, in Iraq. He has French nationality and lives and works in Arles, France since 1974. He completed the Académie Supérieure des Beaux-Arts, Baghdad, and the Ecole Nationale Supérieure des Beaux-Arts, Paris, having arrived in Paris in 1967.
He was a Professor of art at ENSAD (Ecole Nationale Supérieure des Arts Décoratifs), Paris, from 1974 to 2008. He is still teaching in Paris. His work, revolving mainly around the cube and its permutations, is seen as situated somewhere between "the arts of Islam, and the geometric arts of the West". His recent exhibitions include: Galerie Victor Sfez, Paris (2016); *Lastic*, Galerie AL/MA, Montpellier, France; *Au-delà de la forme: Richard Serra / Mehdi Moutashar*, Palais du Tau, Reims, France; Art Dubaï (solo show), Albareh Gallery (2017); *Moutashar, Ligne et couleur, 1968 -1978*, Galerie Orsay, Paris; *Moutashar, Measuring Space*, National Theater & Albareh Art Gallery, Bahrain; *Bagdad Mon amour*, Institut des Cultures d'Islam, Paris (2018). Moutashar was the joint winner of the 2018 Jameel Art Prize.

Mouteea Murad is a Syrian artist born in Homs in 1977. His work sees a unification of spirituality and formalism, continuously drawing influence from the geometric forms and motifs of Islamic art. Murad began

his career as a painter working on monochromatic, expressionist compositions that depict the anguish of modern man. In 2007, his work took on a renewed outlook that redirected his painting style, exploring relativity, spatiality, and the visual dynamic of geometric forms.
The evolution of Murad's work is reflected through the gradual stages of abstraction in his compositions as he builds on the breakthroughs of previous movements, experimenting with automatic brushwork, the illusionistic perspective of Op Art, the symmetry of geometric abstraction, and the collapsing planes of Suprematism.
In his most recent series, his relationship with mathematics plays an integral role, with the Fibonacci numbers and sequence at its centre. His forms and lines are largely defined by algebraic functions and their geometric application within the work.
Murad lives and works in Sharjah, UAE. He received a Bachelor of Art from the Faculty of Fine Arts, Damascus in 2001. Selected solo exhibitions include Ayyam Gallery Beirut (2018); Ayyam Gallery DIFC (2017); Ayyam Gallery Al-Quoz (2016); Ayyam Gallery Beirut (2011); Ayyam Gallery DIFC (2011); and Ayyam Gallery Damascus (2010). His work can be found in private and public collections internationally, including the Jordan National Gallery of Fine Arts.

Naqsh Collective
Nisreen Abudail was born in 1976 in Amman, Jordan, Nisreen received her B.A. in Architecture from Jordan University for Science and Technology. An architect inspired by the minimalist style of our contemporary life, she began her career in Jordan. Architecture as a discipline allowed her to observe and practice art and design. As an aspiring artist, she started creating personalised jewelry, art pieces, and furniture. Soon she began to exhibit her work at local art venues. Following her move to the USA, she continued to develop her career as an architect and an artist where she exhibited her artwork in several local and national art shows. Returning to Jordan in 2009, Nisreen founded Naqsh Collective along with her sister Nermeen Abudail.

Nermeen Abudail was born in 1980 in Amman, Jordan. After graduating with a B.A. degree in graphics, Nermeen began her career working for prominent local and international agencies. She is now living in Dubai, working primarily within the branding industry creating identities and transcending brands. Along with her sister Nisreen Abudail, she founded Naqsh Collective in 2009, dedicating her artistic talent and passion for creative expression to create work embodying local culture with an international appeal.

Nima Nabavi was born in Iran in 1978, and is a self-taught artist who was brought up in the UAE. He received his Bachelor's degree from the University of Southern California and an MBA from New York University. After living in the United States for twenty years, Nima is now based in Dubai, where he dedicates himself to a practice driven by a mathematical approach and contemplative execution of intricate geometries.
1, 2, 3, his first solo exhibition, opened at The Third Line in September 2018. His work has been featured as part of the January 2019 Sharjah Islamic Art Festival.

Timo Nasseri is a German-Iranian artist, born in Berlin in 1972. He began his artistic career as a photographer, and in 2004 made the transition to creating sculpture. He received his diploma in photography from the Lette-Verein in Berlin. Inspired by Ibn Muqla, he uses the means of natural science to open up a perspective for the poetic and fantastic. He has had solo exhibitions at Sfeir-Semler Gallery, Beirut (2012, 2015 and 2019), Kunstfort bij Vifhuizen (2018), Maraya Art Centre, Sharjah (2018), Ab/Anbar Gallery, Tehran (2017), AK Vienna (2016), and at the Lange, Berlin (2015, 2013 and 2010).
He lives and works in Berlin.

Mahmoud Sabri was an Iraqi artist born in July 1927 in Baghdad, who died in 2012 in England. He was considered one of the pioneers of Iraqi modern art and of the pillars of its modernism. He studied social sciences at Loughborough University in England in the late 1940s, where he developed a keen interest in painting and attended evening classes to learn. After a successful career in banking, he became a full-time painter.
In the 1950s his work was primarily focussed on social and political issues. Later he studied art formally at the Surikov Institute for Art in Moscow (1961–1963), after which he moved to Prague. In the late 1960s, he began to link art and science, from which his Quantum Realism manifesto and works emerged. In the 1950s he was actively involved in Iraq's arts community through his membership of various art groups. He was a founding member of the Avant Garde group which derived its inspirations from Mesopotamian art and Iraqi folklore. His 1971 *Manifesto of the New Art of Quantum Realism – An Application of scientific method in the field of art* addressed the graphic representation of the atomic level of reality using building blocks based on the atomic light spectra of elements in nature. His works are held in prominent collections, including the Barjeel Foundation, and he has been shown in a number of group and solo exhibitions both in the Middle East and internationally, including the Venice Biennale of 2011.

Samir Sayegh was born in Lebanon in 1945. He studied Fine Arts in Paris. He is a Master calligrapher, art critic, historian, poet, writer and researcher. Sayegh is the author of several studies and articles on contemporary and Islamic art. He was a lecturer at the Architecture and Graphic Design Department of the American University of Beirut from 1993 to 2007. Sayegh has exhibited extensively across the Arab World and in Europe, and has also created works for buildings and mosques. He is considered as one of the most avant-garde Arab master calligraphers and was recently honoured during the first biennial of Sharjah for Arabic calligraphy.
Samir Sayegh takes Arabic letters beyond the formal aesthetic of Arabic calligraphy into the geometric realm. He presents them as universal forms and stylised signs in which meaning emerges from the relationship between lines. Sayegh has held solo exhibitions in Bahrain, Kuwait, Beirut and Beittedine, and participated in group shows in Jeddah, Sharjah and Damascus. His work is held in a number of collections and at the Atassi Foundation.
He continues to live and work in Beirut.

Philip Taaffe was born in Elizabeth, NJ in 1955, and studied at the Cooper Union in New York. His first solo exhibition was in New York in 1982. He has travelled widely in the Middle East, India, South America, and Morocco, where he collaborated with Mohammed Mrabet on the book *Chocolate Creams and Dollars*, translated by Paul Bowles (Inanout Press, New York 1993). Taaffe lived and worked in Naples from 1988 to 1991. He has been included in numerous museum exhibitions, including the Carnegie International, two Sydney Biennials, and three Whitney Biennials. In 1990 his work was the subject of an extensive critical study in Parkett no. 26 (Zurich and New York). His work is in numerous public collections, including the Museum of Modern Art, New York; the Philadelphia Museum of Art; the Whitney Museum of American Art; and the Reina Sofia, Madrid. In the year 2000, the IVAM museum in Valencia organised a retrospective survey of his work, with contributions by Enrique Juncosa, Robert Rosenblum, and Robert Creeley. In 2001 an extensive survey of his work was presented by the Galleria Civica of Trento, Italy (with texts by Vittoria Coen and Francesco Pellizzi). In 2004 the Galleria d'Arte Moderna in San Marino presented a survey of paintings and drawings based on the artist's explorations with floating pigments and the paper marbling process, accompanied by the Skira publication, *Carte annuvolate* (Cloud Papers). In 2008 the Kunstmuseum Wolfsburg organised a retrospective survey, *The Life of Forms in Art: Paintings 1980-2008*, with a publication by Hatje Cantz, featuring contributions by Markus Brüderlin, Holger Broeker, Kay Heymer, and Brooks Adams. Recent museum surveys have included The Irish Museum of Modern Art in Dublin (2011), and the Neues Museum in Nürnberg (2013–2014). In 2018 a career-spanning retrospective monograph written by John Yau was published by Lund Humphries, London, in their Contemporary Painters Series. Philip Taaffe presently works and lives in New York City, and West Cornwall, Connecticut.

Gebran Tarazi was born in Damascus in 1944 (d. May 2010) in a family of craftsmen. He grew up in Morocco where his family relocated, but was ultimately known as a Lebanese artist. In 1958, he returned to Beirut, and after completing a bachelor degree in law in 1966, worked as a colourist in the family workshop. He has been known as an 'artisan turned artist turned artisan', deeply committed to bringing his Islamic heritage into modernity – with an approach not dissimilar to Bauhaus. He also took an interest in becoming an author while looking for abstraction in literature. In 1997 he published a 'nouveau roman' called *Le Pressoir à Olives* at l'Harmattan. Abstraction became a question of identity for Tarazi. In 1987 he pursued research on geometrical abstraction by producing 300 paintings. He had two exhibitions: *L'Amateur* in 1993, and *50x70* in 1997, and was also shown internationally. Subsequently his paintings were held in a single collection. In 2007 he published *Variations Géometriques* at Fine Art Lebanon detailing his procedures as well as a manifesto entitled *Eastern Yearning*. A major retrospective of the artist was held at Villa Audi in Beirut in 2012.

Roxane Zand was educated at Harvard and Oxford and began her career at the Tehran Museum of Contemporary Art, moving in 1980 to the UK, where she pursued her interest in the arts. In Iran she was art critic at leading newspaper *Kayhan International*, as well as head of art publications at the Niavaran Cultural Centre. Following freelance work at the British Museum and the V&A, as well as Asia House, she joined Sotheby's in 2006 where she is now Deputy Chairman for the Middle East. She has been appointed as a Deputy Lieutenant for Greater London for her services to Middle Eastern art, and is an avid blogger on the topic of art and culture from the Middle East, as well as being an arts editor for the *Encyclopaedia Islamica*. Her publications include *The Avesta* (transl.), 1978, *A Persian Requiem* (transl.), 1993; *Reza Derakshani* (Cramer, 2008).

Dr. Sussan Babaie teaches History of Islamic Art and Architecture at The Courtauld Institute of Art, University of London. She is the author, co-author and editor of several books and articles including, most recently, *Honar: The Afkhami Collection of Modern and Contemporary Iranian Art* (2017), *The Mercantile Effect: On Art and Exchange in the Islamicate World During the 17th and 18th Centuries* (2017), *Persian Kingship and Architecture: Strategies of Power in Iran from the Achaemenids to the Pahlavis* (2014), and *Shirin Neshat* (2013).